MW01232052

Lost and Found

Lost and Found

A John Muir Trail Thru-Hike

Happy Hiking!

Michelle

"Brownie"

Michelle "Brownie" Pugh

This work is a memoir. Events and conversations contained within are conveyed using the author's recollections. Some conversations and event details have been compressed, rearranged, or in some cases, expanded, in order to best convey the overall context of what occurred, while attempting to remain true to the original meanings. Any misrepresentation of events is accidental. All attempts have been made to portray people and places with the highest degree of accuracy.

My hiking partners and I made our best efforts to practice environmental responsibility and promote sustainability. Where possible we supported local stores and businesses. Despite my best efforts, I am confident my practices were not perfect. I apologize for any mistakes on my part, and commit to continually strive to learn the best behaviors to protect the natural world and all the beings that live in it.

Text Edits and Layout: Anna Ottosen
Photo Edits: M. Gregory Ballard
Additional Photo Credits: Sarah Jones Decker

ISBN-13:
978-1535211284

ISBN-10:
1535211288

To Dad, for teaching me to collect and celebrate days that prove my worth

PROLOGUE

My hiking partner was on fire.

I had been kneeling in front of a crumbling stone fire circle attempting to get a fire started. We were ten miles into an unfamiliar and unforgiving forest, and I was wondering why in the world we had picked *this* particular route for a hike. Suddenly behind me there was a suspicious WHOOSH.

I spun around on the heels of my Crocs and saw my father's abnormally large and horrified eyes through a wall of bright orange flames. I dropped my gaze from his seemingly-on-fire face to the flaming fuel canister and camp stove in his left hand.

"Shit, Dad! Drop it!"

In the split second it took me to leap to my feet, my mind raced through its knowledge of burn care from my job as an EMT (emergency medical technician). *How severely is he burned? What percentage of his skin is affected? Is his airway impeded? Will we need a burn center?* And then the two most dire questions hit me: *Do we even have cell service? Will I be able to get him to an ambulance from the middle of nowhere?*

Still staring at me, he tossed the blazing stove to the ground in front of him. With a crackling sound, the dry leaves and brush underfoot immediately caught fire.

I risked a glance at Dad's face, terrified. I was shocked to see pale cheeks, a gaping mouth, and his huge blue eyes staring back at me.

"Are you OK?" I asked, eyeing the smoldering leaves at his feet.

He stood rooted to the same spot and brought his hand to his face. "I'm fine." He examined his face with his fingertips. "I don't know what happened."

Realizing he wasn't hurt, I snapped my attention back to the stove ablaze at my feet. Using a couple of sticks from the pile I had collected, I stood the stove upright. I kneeled in front of it and, keeping my fingers as far from the flames as possible, finagled one stick into the triangular valve that controls the fuel. Twisting it counterclockwise, I cut off the fuel source. Then I grabbed the nearby pot of water for our supper and started sprinkling handfuls on the spreading fire. Dad was still standing awkwardly in the same spot.

"Grab our water bag," I instructed him. I covered the small flames with dirt and water, massaging them into a soupy mess with my bare hands until I was confident the fire was out. Finally I sat back on my heels, mentally and physically exhausted. The fire I had been building in the fire circle was dead too. I rolled my head around to stretch out my neck and went back to arranging kindling. I had to dry out my wet clothes or else I was going to revisit hypothermia.

In only two hours of a practice hike we had already experienced two falls—one resulting in a knee injury, and the other in the loss of two pieces of gear into a frigid river—and now we had almost started a forest fire.

And we were planning to hike the 220-mile John Muir Trail together. Perfect.

1

CHOOSING A GOAL

September 10, 2013

I should train for a marathon.

I settled my head on my flannel-covered pillow and imagined pinning a numbered paper bib to my shirt. I heard the blast indicating the start of the marathon and saw my sneakers hitting the pavement alongside waves of other runners. I could practically hear the crowd cheering and taste the Gatorade in little paper cups that volunteers would hand me at the hydration stations. Proudly, I envisioned crossing the finish line drenched in hard-earned sweat, grinning madly with adorably pink cheeks. I pictured the "I Survived the Fill-in-the-Blank Marathon" t-shirt I would live in following the race. The back of my car would proudly display an oval "26.2" decal.

Training for a marathon would be serious business, so I would buy a color-coordinated running outfit that fit me perfectly. My running shoes and fancy, cushioned socks would come from an actual running store. Maybe I would even get a reflective windbreaker or vest to help me stay safe during all my practice runs. I would download an app on my iPhone to help me train and load my iTunes playlist with upbeat songs. *This will be fun.*

I lay in bed letting my thoughts go wild, too excited about my plan to sleep. My body would be in exquisite shape after training for a marathon. Besides, all that running would give me a lot of time to think and solve the problems of the world—or at least the problems of my personal world. Since my calendar was pretty open the following day, I decided I would go shopping for the outfit and shoes in the morning. No sense in wasting time.

Still wide awake, I brought myself back to reality and reflected on my most recent three-mile run. After delaying from the moment I awoke until the last possible hour of sunlight, I got decked out in my running tights and my beloved-but-gently-used bright pink running shoes and hit the road. For the first two-tenths of a mile I ran awkwardly, feeling like my legs were at least an inch or so uneven in length. I worried about rolling an ankle and made a mental note to call my chiropractor. At last my legs seemed to equalize and I settled into a slow but steady stride. For the rest of the first mile I was enthusiastic and happy, enjoying the sound of my pink-clad feet pounding on the asphalt.

At mile one I noticed that one of my earbuds was making a strange whistling noise. Not wanting to trip, I slowed to adjust it. After a few attempts I got the noise fixed, but ten steps later the volume was noticeably too loud. Being mindful, I slowed down again to adjust. A mile and a half in, my run began to feel comfortable. I started analyzing my form so that I would be able to increase my distance. *Am I running too flatfooted? Are my strides long enough? Am I swinging my arms correctly? Is my breathing right?* Thinking about my breathing made me feel out of breath, so I slowed down a little. Around that time I noticed a wrinkle in my sock that seemed to have become the size of a grapefruit. I had to fix it right then—I didn't want to get a blister.

On mile two my sports bra felt too loose, my shoes were tied too tightly, and my running tights were bunching in a funny way at my waist. I was debating whether I should cut the run short. *Do I really need to run a 5K? Maybe two miles is enough. How much extra caloric burn or muscle tone could I gain by running one measly extra mile?* Begrudgingly I pushed on, though, because I had to get home one way or another. After two and a half miles I was struggling for breath and unnaturally red in the face. I had to force myself to keep placing one foot in front of the other. Just before the third mile it became clear to me that the reason my run hadn't been successful was the dreadful choice of music. *Who could possibly run effectively to this music?*

By mile three I was questioning my sanity in deciding to run, promising myself I would find alternative exercise options, and blaming my ridiculous pink shoes and also my choice of breakfast foods eleven hours ago for my discomfort. I blindly pushed through at the speed of an elephant in quicksand. When the program on my iPhone announced that I had finished the final tenth of a mile, I stopped immediately and doubled over on the sidewalk. *Who needs a cool-down?* Thirty minutes of running (OK, thirty-three minutes if I'm being honest) was plenty. I stood with my hands on my knees while my lungs struggled for air. *I will never run again. Ever.* Once I could breathe, I walked slowly toward my driveway and noticed how beautiful the setting sun was, how fresh the grass smelled, and how purifying it felt to sweat. *Tomorrow I'll run even farther. Or not.*

And all of this drama had occurred over a mere three miles. Maaaaybe twenty-six miles wasn't a realistic goal. I rearranged my pillows, folded my arms behind my head, and stared at the shadows on my ceiling. A conversation from earlier in the day replayed in my head.

"Are you writing a novel over there?" I teased from the second computer at the EMS station, where I was finishing a patient care report.

Mark Weber, my partner for the day, smiled while typing at lightning fast speed. "I'm writing a blog entry, actually."

This was the first day we had worked on the ambulance together, and I had known him for approximately five hours. Other than the fact that he wore a paramedic patch on his sleeve and had been very kind to our first three patients, I knew nothing about him.

"What's your blog about?" I asked.

"This entry is about waking up at four thirty in the morning to swim laps before work. I'm training for an Ironman and thought it would be cool to write a blog so people could follow along."

As the conversation continued, Mark shared that he had initially begun running marathons in memory of his dad, and then a coworker had suggested training for an Ironman triathlon.

In between emergency calls on a busy workday, Mark and I continued to discuss marathons, training schedules, caloric intake, and other topics related to endurance training. A contagious smile spread across his face as he shared the details of his strict training routine and preparations.

I came home from work feeling antsy. This wasn't a new feeling. For the past few months I had experienced a nagging feeling that something was missing from my life. I had been having trouble placing the source of this feeling because my life was so extraordinarily blessed. While trying to work through my restlessness, I had spent a fair amount of time reviewing my good fortune. *I have a job I enjoy that makes a difference in the lives of others. I own a beautiful home. I'm healthy. I have great friends from many parts of my life. My family lives nearby and we have strong relationships. I have many fulfilling hobbies.*

Despite repeated attempts, I had not been able to label my feeling of discomfort. Using a dry-erase marker on my bathroom mirror, each day for a month I had written three things for which I was grateful. This overwhelming list had helped me realize how phenomenally lucky I was. But still, the feeling of something missing had lingered.

I've kept a bucket list for as long as I can remember. I'm an obsessive list maker, and someone once told me that people who write down goals are more likely to achieve them. As I continued staring at the shadows on my ceiling, I mentally reviewed the major items I had checked off my bucket list in the span of thirty years:

- ✓ *Earning my Girl Scout Gold Award*
- ✓ *Graduating college*
- ✓ *Hiking the Appalachian Trail*
- ✓ *Buying a house*
- ✓ *Publishing a book*

Then I acknowledged the smaller goals I had recently achieved:

- ✓ *Becoming a public speaker for a non-profit organization*
- ✓ *Completing a mud run*
- ✓ *Traveling outside the country*
- ✓ *Taking a class for fun*
- ✓ *Trying yoga*
- ✓ *Starting a garden*
- ✓ *Learning to quilt*

I had ticked off a number of items from my substantial and ever-growing list. *So, what's missing—other than the traditional husband and 2.5 kids?*

I had been lying awake for hours (the joys of intermittent insomnia) when the conversation with Mark began replaying in my head. Thinking of his excitement and enthusiasm for working toward his goals, I finally recognized the nagging feeling: jealousy. I wanted a goal to work toward— something to be equally excited about.

It was at that moment I decided to run a marathon. Thirty seconds later, that plan was dead in the water (or on the asphalt).

Over the next couple of days, I thought continuously about my new realization that I needed to be working toward a substantial goal. I became confident that it was time to plan an adventure. *Maybe I'll take a road trip. Or I could visit another country.* While both of those would be fun adventures, I knew that neither was the type of trip I had been craving. I've always felt happiest and most at home in the mountains. My time on the Appalachian Trail stands out as one of my proudest accomplishments and best life memories. Suddenly it was obvious that I needed to set my sights on a much larger horizon: it was time to plan another long-distance hike.

This time around I would be much more limited. I was no longer a recent college graduate without definitive responsibilities. I was a full-fledged adult with a full-time job and the financial obligations of a mortgage, homeowner's insurance, car insurance, and other assorted monthly bills. I couldn't just quit my job to climb mountains. After a thorough look at my current allotment of paid leave, I figured I could plan a trip slightly longer than three weeks. Immediately I zoomed in on one particular item on my bucket list: the John Muir Trail.

A quick Google search confirmed that the John Muir Trail would take about three weeks. *Perfect.* Next I needed a hiking partner. Technically I had started the Appalachian Trail without a partner, but the John Muir Trail is much more remote and getting to the trailhead more complicated. I wouldn't feel comfortable going across the country and into an unfamiliar and secluded wilderness alone.

Picking a hiking partner was different from picking a vacation partner, though. We weren't going to be sipping daiquiris by a pool or eating in swanky restaurants. We wouldn't be flipping quarters to see who got the bed by the window or who would pick the radio station in the car. We would be climbing mountains, carrying large amounts of weight, eating from Ziploc bags, sleeping on the ground, and going without showers for days. The wrong partner could make an already physically and mentally demanding trip completely unbearable.

First, this person needed to be physically fit and willing to train. That one qualification narrowed my list to about five people. Second, it had to be someone with whom I could enjoy spending twenty-four (sometimes stressful and intense) hours a day, for a period of more than three weeks. My list dwindled to about three. Third, it had to be someone with both the available time and resources to make the trip.

The choice was obvious.

2

THE INVITATION

September 18, 2013

Armed with research, I nervously settled myself on my parents' massive stone hearth. I took a deep breath and then took the plunge.

"So, remember how when I was hiking the Appalachian Trail you were going to hike with me for a week?"

"Yes." My dad lowered his Kindle Fire.

I nodded, remembering the stories my amused mom had told me about his training on the treadmill wearing a backpack loaded with weights. I plowed on. "And you know how you're enjoying traveling in your retirement?"

"Yeeees…" He set down the Kindle on the round wooden table by his recliner and raised his eyebrows curiously.

"And you know how we had talked about hiking Kilimanjaro together but then Mom put the kibosh on that?"

"Hey!" Mom interjected. "Don't blame me." "You did say no," I reminded her.

By now Mom had lowered her magazine and was paying full attention. "Africa is not exactly a politically stable continent right now."

"Well, anyway, Dad," I continued settling my gaze on him, "Would you want to come on a different trip with me?"

He cleared his throat. "How far do you want me to walk?" His tone was lighthearted, but he tilted his head down and looked at me straight through the middle of his wire-rimmed transitional glasses, pinning me to the cold, hard hearth.

Easy here, make it casual. "Two hundred and twenty miles. Give or take."

There was a nerve-wracking moment of silence, during which I was confident he would turn me down before the conversation had really begun. I stared at the mountains through the giant window behind his chair while I waited.

"In what timeframe?"

He's going to say no. I swallowed forcefully. "Three weeks."

He steepled his fingertips together in his classic "I'm thinking" pose. "So that's about ten miles a day."

"Right." The heat from the fire felt hot against my back, and I began shifting uncomfortably. *Tough it out. If you move you might cut the conversation short.*

"That sounds doable." He adjusted his glasses. "Where? Is this the trail out west? The Pacific something?"

Mom's eyes were volleying back and forth between the two of us like she was watching a tennis match.

"It's called the John Muir Trail and it's in the High Sierras in California. Part of it is contiguous with the Pacific Crest Trail, which is the one that goes from Mexico to Canada and—"

"I'm not walking from Mexico to Canada," he interrupted.

I gave a nervous laugh. "I don't think we could do that in three weeks."

He re-crossed his legs and ran one hand across his barely noticeable five o'clock shadow. "What's the elevation like?"

"High. We would climb the highest mountain in the continental United States."

"And how high is that?"

"I don't know exactly," I told him honestly, and then added with a grin, "It's smaller than Everest."

"Good." The corners of his lips turned up, belying his amusement. "I don't want to carry oxygen."

"Me neither." *My winter-weight pack is plenty heavy.*

"It's not the distance I'm worried about. I could practice like I did when I was training to hike with you on the AT."

I nodded encouragement.

"We could hike in the mountains around here to practice the distance. I can train to walk ten miles a day. That's not going to be a problem. And even though I haven't really carried a pack before, I can prepare for that too."

"True. You're already in great shape."

He held up a finger as he finished. "But the elevation and how my body will handle it are out of my control."

"True." I tapped the screen of my iPhone a few times and held it up. "According to Wikipedia, Mount Whitney is 14,505 feet. But that's the tallest point on the trail and we summit it on the last day. We would build up to it. That's part of the reason for going north to south."

Mom cleared her throat. "We both had a little trouble with the elevation in Colorado last month on our Bryce Canyon tour, and we weren't even hiking," she reminded Dad. "Remember, we both had headaches and got dizzy?"

"Well, I've never hiked at elevation either," I quickly interjected. I didn't want Dad rejecting this proposal before he even had time to consider it. "In fact, I've never even been anywhere at a high altitude. I've done some research and there's a prescription medicine that helps with the symptoms of altitude sickness. It works by beefing up your red blood cells or something. I was planning to ask my doctor about it because I don't know how my body will react to altitude either." I already got migraines often and was worried they might intensify with the elevation. "We wouldn't be very high right away, though. And during the first part of the trip our bodies would acclimate to the altitude."

"OK." He nodded. "We can look into that more. I should probably run it by my doctor too."

Mom bobbed her head up and down in an exaggerated nod.

"Definitely. I'll need to do the same thing."

"What about food? Do we carry food for three weeks?"

"No. Food is heavy. Each person needs one or two pounds per day for backpacking. I'm planning to dehydrate food ahead of time and mail it. We would stop at a few points along the way to pick up mail drops and refill our bear canisters."

"Bears," Mom mumbled. "Great."

"Do we hang the canisters?" he asked.

My cheeks flushed slightly as I admitted, "I don't know. I don't think so. I've never used one. They aren't required on the AT yet—although I hear parts of Georgia and the Smoky Mountains are starting to consider it. I honestly don't know much about them, except that they're heavy, awkward, and expensive."

Note to self: research more about bear canisters.

Dad asked more questions about gear, food, travel arrangements, and potential trip dates. I answered the ones I could and assured him we would research the rest.

"Let me do some reading and some thinking. When do you need an answer?"

"No specific day. I just need to request time off at work. And of course I need to start training. Oh, and we would have to apply for permits, prepare mail drops—"

"Permits?"

"Yes. We have to apply for permits to hike this trail. They can be hard to get."

"When would we need to apply?"

"Six months to the day from the date we want to start hiking."

"So we still have some time."

"Absolutely," I assured him.

"OK. I'll think on it."

"I consider it a positive that you didn't say no right away," I told him as I walked into the kitchen and grabbed a brownie from a plate on the counter.

"I still have time," he said with a chuckle.

As I started down the stairs I heard him call out, "Hey, I have one more question. Where do we rent the Sherpa?"

September 21, 2013

A few days later I was back visiting my parents' house for the night. We were all sitting in their newly appointed study, reading. Dad looked up from his Kindle.

"According to Wikipedia the JMT is 'America's most famous trail,'" he told me.

So he's over there reading about the JMT. That's encouraging!

I nodded. "It's more famous than some of the other long-distance trails, but fewer people hike on it every year."

"It says here"—he tapped his Kindle screen—"that 1,500 people attempt a thru-hike each year. But that includes people hiking something called the PCT."

"That's the Pacific Crest Trail. It goes from Mexico to Canada through California, Oregon, and Washington. The JMT and the PCT are contiguous for about one hundred and sixty miles."

"I'm glad you aren't asking me to do the PCT."

I pumped my eyebrows up and down dramatically. "Not yet."

"Don't even start," Mom chimed in.

"According to this, the trail is officially 210.4 miles," Dad continued. "*Definitely* can't forget that last 0.4."

I laughed. "Yeah. And of course the JMT ends on top of Mount Whitney, so we would have to hike the ten miles back down to the trailhead at Whitney Portal too. So at least two hundred and twenty"—I paused and smiled at him—"*point four* miles. But of course we would have some additional miles for resupply. I'd want to consider the side trail to Half Dome too."

"You're going to add *extra* miles?" Mom asked. "Just thinking about it makes my feet hurt."

"We can get into that later," Dad answered. "It looks like the trail goes through three national parks: Yosemite, Kings Canyon, and Sequoia."

"Yes. And also through the John Muir Wilderness, Inyo and Sierra National Forests, and Ansel Adams Wilderness." I ticked them off on my fingers. "Oh, and Devils Postpile National Monument."

"Would I have to have a trail name for this trip?"

"You don't *have* to, but it would be fun. Trail names are part of the long-distance hiking experience."

"I don't know about that," he hedged.

"You could just use your real name. It's unique enough," Mom teased. "Everyone will think 'Burv' is some strange trail moniker."

I laughed. Dad's name is definitely uncommon. While I wasn't going to push the issue, I secretly hoped he would develop an actual trail name on our trip. For me, using a trail name had been a fun part of my AT experience. Somehow being called by an alternative name made the whole trip seem more adventuresome and magical. I was already looking forward to slipping back into my trail persona and being called "Brownie" again. *Will Dad call me Brownie?*

"Hey, I have a stipulation, by the way." Dad adjusted his glasses and looked at me.

"OK?"

"If you write something about this trip—a novella or something, it's only three weeks—I get to proofread it before you publish anything."

"That's fair. I was afraid you were going to say you didn't want to be a character in my next book."

He laughed and told me, "I still reserve that right."

"Well, he sure would be a character," Mom joked.

"Does this mean you're going to hike with me?" I asked.

He picked up his Kindle and flipped the case open, pausing dramatically before saying, "I don't know yet."

3

IS THIS MY HIKING PARTNER?

September 26, 2013

I set off for REI, telling myself I was *only* buying a bear canister. An hour and a half later, I headed for the parking lot toting DEET, an SPF 15 ChapStick, a fleece-lined down vest, a trowel, and the bear canister I had actually intended to buy. *This cannot be how each trip to the outfitter goes.*

When I got home I spread my new purchases out on the hearth and sat on my leather ottoman facing them. I stared at the giant blue plastic bear canister while I ate a Chipotle burrito the size of my head. *How am I going to fit that monstrosity into my pack?* I pondered as I continued eating the delicious mess of beans, chicken, and cheese smothered in hot sauce and sour cream. *I wonder if I could just dehydrate this to eat on the trail? At least then I wouldn't feel guilty about the calories.*

When I had devoured half of the burrito, I went out to the garage and brought the large Rubbermaid plastic tote with my camping gear inside. I plopped it on the carpet and started pulling items out—tent, sleeping bag, stuff sacks, rope, rain gear, stove, fuel. The smell of heavily used backpacking gear wafted up around me—a perfume of campfire smoke, sweat, and dirt. I smiled nostalgically and breathed in deeply. *Wait, was that the equivalent of men smelling their own dirty socks?* I stuck my face in my sleeping bag, closed my eyes, and breathed in again. *Nah. This smells like backpacking.*

I ran my thumb across the "2,000 Miler" rocker below the Appalachian Trail patch on my pack, and then set the pack aside. I began sorting. I wanted to try packing my backpack with all of my normal gear plus the new bear canister to see how it would fit. To get an accurate picture I would need to simulate my actual trail gear.

I hadn't been backpacking in an embarrassingly long time, so I had to collect clothes, toiletries, water bottles, a water bladder, my pocketknife, and bandanas from around the house. Fifteen minutes later, all of the gear was lined up on the carpet. After a few failed attempts, I shoved everything into my well-worn Mountain Hardwear Exodus pack. The bear canister took up so much space that I was forced to arrange things differently than the way I was used to. The top hat of the pack was almost fully extended, with lumps and bumps poking out haphazardly, and the seams were struggling to hold. Everything fit inside, but barely. I attempted to shoulder the pack anyway. It felt awkward and listed to the left uncomfortably.

I rearranged items a number of times and settled on my best (but still inadequate) effort. Then I unpacked the whole pack and filled the bear canister with my estimate of four days of food, filled the water bottle and water bladder, and repacked everything. When I shouldered the bag this time, I staggered under the clumsily distributed weight. *You'd think I had never packed a backpack.*

I tossed the lumpy pack in my car to bring to work the next day. My work partner that month, Janice, was an avid backpacker. I hoped she could help me make it all fit.

Janice was a true gift to me while planning this trip. We were scheduled to work together most months, which suited us just fine. She had been my field training officer when I first started working for the county and we had quickly discovered a shared passion for the outdoors. Janice had taught me to dehydrate my own food and to make an insulated cozy for rehydrating my meals.

Looking at Janice you would probably never guess she was such an experienced outdoorswoman. She is sixty-four years old and stands about five feet tall if she stretches. Janice runs a local outdoors group and regularly leads hiking, backpacking, and kayaking trips all over the East Coast. She was formerly a Boy Scout troop leader and a military wife, and she raised two sons. Janice likes to say she doesn't hike fast, but she always gets there.

My favorite characteristic of Janice's, though, is her continuous optimism. We had worked twelve-hour shifts together on a regular basis—shifts during which we saw horrible things, interacted with people who weren't always nice to us, drove at breakneck speeds, and did massive amounts of paperwork. Working on an ambulance brings younger providers to their knees some days, but her calm and pleasant demeanor rarely cracked.

I was counting on Janice's outdoor skills and positive outlook to find a solution to my unpackable pack. Together we spent the better part of the afternoon—in between medical calls—packing and unpacking my gear. We knelt on the filthy carpet reorganizing, restuffing, and even lashing gear to the outside of my pack, but we never made any real improvements. After at least a half dozen attempts, Janice stood up and flashed me her contagious smile.

"Michelle, it just doesn't fit," she told me. "I hope I never have to use a bear canister."

October 1, 2013

I was doing chores around the house when my phone rang.

"Is this my hiking partner?" Dad asked.

Grinning, I tried to temper the hope in my voice. "I don't know. Are you *my* hiking partner?"

"I think I'm in. I still have questions. I need to keep doing research about the trail, and I need to talk to my doctor, but I want to start seriously thinking about it. I think we should start doing some hiking."

"Really?" I could barely contain my excitement.

"Really. I'm going to need some gear to get started. Are you busy right now?"

I pushed aside the laundry I had been folding. "No. Why?"

"Want to meet me at REI? I thought we could look at some gear."

Glancing down at the rumpled pajamas I was still wearing, I asked, "What time?"

I found Dad standing in the shoe section at REI.

"Hey, Partner!" He greeted me with a high five.

I smiled at his greeting. Dad also called me "Partner" on the tennis court, and it warmed my heart each time.

"Hey, Partner," I replied. Have you found shoes yet?"

"I just started looking. Do you have any advice?"

"Well," I said, "every hiker has a different opinion on footwear. Personally I like trail runners better than boots. Boots are heavy. People will tell you that a pound on your feet is five on your back, so lightweight shoes reduce the strain on your body. They still have to be durable, though, and they need to cup your heel firmly. I like Vibram soles."

"Point me in the right direction."

We selected several different brands of trail runners and I recommended that he get a half-size bigger than normal since his feet would swell on the trail and the weight of the pack would flatten his feet. He diligently tried each pair. Dad and I have the same annoyingly skinny heels, which make shoe shopping a pain. When he found a comfortable pair I took him over to the steeply angled ramp.

"Try walking up and down."

"Are you sure?" he asked, eyeing the ramp skeptically.

"That's what it's for—to see if your toes slide forward and hit the front of the shoe going downhill."

"I've seen these in shoe stores before, but I never knew what they were for."

"I didn't know either until I started buying hiking shoes," I reassured him. "I've rejected shoes based on this test alone. I'll teach you a different way to tie your laces later to help anchor your heel and prevent blisters on the tips of your toes. For now just make sure your toes don't feel too squished facing down the ramp."

"Is 'squished' a technical term?"

"Yes."

He walked up and down the ramp with a comically serious expression on his face. After a minute he stared down at the Vasques. "These are the ones."

"I think you'll like them. I did most of the AT in Vasques."

With the shoes still on, Dad told me, "Today I just want to get the things I need for us to start with some day hikes. We can look at overnight gear another day if we get to that point."

"Sounds like a plan."

He closed the empty shoebox and picked it up. "Next I want to find zip-off pants."

I shook my head and glanced down at his feet. "Umm…Do you want to take those shoes off first?"

"Nope." He grinned. "I want to walk around the store in them and make sure I like them."

"Can you do that?"

"Sure. Watch." He headed toward the men's clothing. Dad has always made his own rules.

After three pairs of pants he settled on a pair he liked. I was jealous that he could find zip-off pants so quickly. Since I'm short, I usually struggle to find pairs that are the right length and have zippers that hit in the right place on my thigh. Still wearing the pants, he began browsing through shirts, debating the pros and cons of different types before settling on one he deemed worthy of the trail.

"Let's look at backpacks," he said. "I don't think I'll buy one today, but I want to see what they have."

I led the way to the backpack section. He followed me with tags flapping all over his body—now dressed in the not-yet-purchased zip-off pants, hiking shoes, and a button-down shirt.

An exceedingly patient sales associate helped Dad try on multiple backpacks. We talked about cubic inches, versatility of pockets, sizing, and weight capacity. At some point I saw Dad's eyes start to glaze over. He had absorbed as much gear information as he was going to for one day.

"Do you see how long I've spent in this store?" Dad asked in a stage whisper at one point. "This has to be a record for me. Usually I just go in for the kill. I know what I want, I walk in the store, and BAM"—he clapped his hands to emphasize—"I buy it."

"Hiking gear is a little different."

"I see that." He studied his reflection in the mirror. "I want to get trekking poles, but then I'm done for today. Like, really done."

By the time we made our way to the register, Dad had shoes, pants, a shirt, and poles. He did take them off to pay.

October 3, 2013

When my phone rang a couple of days later, I was just pulling into the garage after work.

"Hey, Partner. I've been thinking about all of the tasks we need to get done before our trip. Maybe we should make a Gantt chart."

"A what?" I hit the button to close the garage door.

"It's a tool we used when I was working. It helps keep track of all the upcoming deadlines to make sure everything gets accomplished on time."

"That sounds like a great idea," I agreed. I loved that my dad and I were equally organized. This was one of the many reasons I knew we would make great hiking partners. "What's the chart called again?"

"A Gantt chart. It's an acronym."

"What does it stand for?"

There was a long pause. "I can't remember. I'm retired. Google it."

I laughed. "Did *you* just use 'Google' as a verb?" Dad is notoriously technology challenged.

"I did. It's officially in the Merriam-Webster dictionary now. I saw a news article about it."

"Right. Should we plan a time to make a Gantt chart?" I asked.

"Are we planning to plan?" he asked with a chuckle.

"I think so."

"This is like being back at work!"

October 15, 2013

Dad and I met up again for our second round of gear purchasing. This time we were at Appalachian Outfitters. I had shopped there before and had been impressed with their expertise and customer service. I wanted to make sure we had someone knowledgeable helping us because the top priority this time was buying a pack for Dad.

A pack is a monumentally important piece of gear. Attached to you for the better part of each day, it becomes an extra appendage. It needs to be comfortable but supportive, easy to organize but not too complicated, and sturdy but easy to care for. Your pack has to hold every single item you will possess for the duration of your hike. If the bag lets you down, the trip is a disaster.

"Can I help you?" a young salesman with a nametag reading "David" asked as soon as we walked in.

"I need a backpack," Dad told him.

"No problem. I'd be glad to help you. Do you have any idea what size you need?"

Dad looked at me and then back at David. "Nope. I've never owned one before."

"Well, we can help you figure it out. Do you need a daypack? An overnight pack?"

"A backpacking pack."

"Do you know how many cubic inches you want?"

Dad looked at me.

"He needs a decent-sized pack. Not a lightweight pack because it has to carry winter-weight gear."

"OK. How many days are we talking?"

"Typically four to five days between resupply points. Except one time where we may have to go seven days or more." I let my eyes wander over the packs hanging on the wall. "Oh, and it has to be able to hold a bear canister."

"A bear canister? Are you going out west?" David suddenly seemed more interested.

"Yes," Dad told him proudly. "We're hiking the John Muir Trail."

I noticed another employee listening at this point. He casually inched closer. "The John Muir Trail? That's awesome, man. I want to do that someday." He was wearing shorts and Chacos despite the cool weather outside.

"We're going in August."

He nodded and grinned. "That is so totally awesome. I'm Scott, by the way."

"That really is great," David agreed after we had all introduced ourselves. "So do you have any idea what brand of backpack you want?" He glanced between Dad and me.

"Not really. I'm a few years behind on gear knowledge," I admitted. "I've owned an internal frame Gregory and an external frame Mountain Hardwear. Personally I like packs with a lot of pockets because I'm a tad OCD with my organization."

The corners of Dad's mouth tugged upwards as he asked, "Where could you have gotten that tendency?"

David began scanning the carpet-to-ceiling wall of colorful backpacks. While he mentally catalogued options, I tried to guess how much money was hanging on that one wall of the store.

"I have an idea of some packs we can start with," he said.

Dad tried on a couple of packs. Then David called over Jonathan, the store owner. Upon hearing our plans to hike the JMT, Jonathan recommended the Gregory Baltoro, a bag he and David each owned. Jonathan strapped Dad into the pack and stepped back.

"How does it feel?"

"I don't know." Dad shrugged his shoulders and swung his arms. "I don't know how it's supposed to feel. I've never worn a backpack. I haven't even hiked much, honestly."

Jonathan and Scott exchanged a wide-eyed look.

Dad must have picked up on their skepticism too because he quickly told them, "My daughter's the hiker. She's done the AT. I'm just a beginner."

"You've done the AT?" Scott broke into an instant grin.

"She wrote a book about it," Dad added, with what I hoped was a note of pride in his voice.

"Wait, are you Brownie?" Scott asked with a look of recognition.

I nodded, surprised.

"You wrote that book…," he trailed off and snapped his fingers.

"*Love at First Hike*," I supplied. "Don't worry, I can never remember book names either," I added honestly.

"Yes," Scott said, rubbing his palms together. "Yes! I've read it." He turned to Dad. "You'll be in good hands."

I shoved my hands into my back pockets as I felt my cheeks go pink. "I can handle the planning and the hiking, but I'm a little rusty on equipment. I haven't bought new gear since the AT. A lot has changed in"—I did some quick math—"nine years."

"We'll get you two outfitted," Jonathan promised. "Try walking around the store with that pack on," he advised Dad. "See how it feels."

Jonathan, Scott, David, and I talked about the AT, trail books, and gear while Dad strutted around the small store in the Gregory pack, looking a bit out of place in his dress khakis, button-down shirt, and Sperrys. He came back a few minutes later.

"This pack feels great just like this," Dad told Jonathan. "If she"—he thumbed his finger at me—"can just carry everything else, I think I'll be fine."

"I think we should base who carries what on a formula," I told him with a laugh. "A percentage of each of our body weights."

"No," he said. "I think it should be an algorithm factoring in age."

"The older you are, the more you carry?" I suggested.

I bet these guys think our odds of completing the trail are near zero.

"Why don't we try putting some weight in that pack just in case Michelle decides not to carry all of the gear?" Jonathan suggested good-naturedly.

As he added the weights to the pack, Dad flipped the price tag over so he could see it. He put his hand to his chest and pretended to stagger backward a step.

"This bag is on sale, by the way," Jonathan told him. "It's thirty percent off."

"I'm saving money already! I knew I liked you, Jonathan," Dad declared.

While Dad walked around with a weighted pack, I tried on a Gregory backpack too, just for kicks. I wasn't completely sure I wanted to spend the money on a new pack, but I hadn't yet found a way to fit the humongous bear canister into my old pack. Besides, they were on sale.

"We need to look at sleeping pads and tents," I told the small crowd of store employees who were eagerly helping us. "I just bought a Big Agnes Fly Creek online. I was thinking Dad might like the same one. I used a Big Agnes for the second half of the AT and loved it."

"What size Fly Creek did you get?" Scott asked.

"The one-person. They were running a crazy deal online last week and the reviews were good, so I snagged one."

"I saw that deal; that's probably perfect for you," he agreed. "You're small, but"—he turned to Dad—"I'd recommend the two-person for you, Burv. It only weighs a few ounces more. For me, the one-person is too confining. Let me see if I have a two-person I can show you."

Jonathan came back a minute later holding a tent. "This one has been sold, and we don't have any more in stock, but I can set it up to show you. If you like it, we can order one and have it in a few days."

While Jonathan set up the tent, Scott walked us back toward the sleeping pads. As I glanced at the selection, I was embarrassed to realize that the Therm-a-Rest I had raved about to Dad was outdated. The technology had completely changed in nine years.

"We'll trust your opinion," I told Scott.

This was a completely different approach from my Appalachian Trail hike, where I had researched every single gear choice meticulously. I had read trail journals, blogs, and every review I could get my hands on. I had tested out different options, carefully considering prices and weight. This time around I was trusting the people who had more knowledge without needing to understand each nuance myself. I felt that I had learned enough by this point to balance professional suggestions and product reviews with personal preference. It also helped that I wasn't quite as hung up on exactly how many ounces each item weighed because I knew I had survived the AT without going lightweight. I imagined it was like going from being a worried, slightly paranoid new parent to a parent of two who realizes the world will still turn if the kid eats dirt or you don't follow a guideline from a parenting book.

Scott recommended the Therm-a-Rest NeoAir and began inflating one with an air pump.

"How much does that weigh?" Dad asked.

"The sleeping pad?" Scott asked, still pumping in air.

"No. The pump. It seems big."

Scott managed to keep a straight face as he explained, "In the woods you don't use this. This is just for the store, to speed things up."

"How do I inflate it in the woods?" Dad asked, completely serious.

"You blow it up," I told him. "With your mouth."

He blinked at the partially inflated mattress for a few moments. "Every night? That's a lot of hot air." Dad turned to me. "Would you carry the pump for me instead?"

I just shook my head at him.

Dad took his shoes off at Scott's request and knelt in front of the tent. Watching him crawl into the tent on his hands and knees was comical. Once in, he spun around awkwardly and lay down on the mattress with his hands folded on his chest.

"It's comfortable," he commented after a few seconds.

"Good. How does the tent seem?"

"Good, I think. There's a lot of room in here."

"Great. Now get back out so you can see how to roll the mattress up and take the tent down," I told him.

Dad crawled out and watched as Scott began deflating the pad. He pointed at it and asked, "When you're breaking camp, do you take the sheets and comforter off before you roll it up?"

After a beat of silence I told him, "Dad, I don't think these guys always know when you're joking."

He gave me a sideways look. "Who says I'm joking?"

After Dad watched Scott deflate and roll the NeoAir and Jonathan take the tent down, he stared at the two small stuff sacks that now held the gear. "I have to do this every night?"

"Oh, that's not half of it, Dad. There are all kinds of chores once you get to camp. You have to filter water, cook dinner, dry out gear—"

"Plus tend to blisters and body ailments and repair gear," Scott added. "A lot of hikers who end up quitting trails do it because the chores become so overwhelming and monotonous. It's never-ending."

Dad spun his wedding ring on his finger. "This isn't encouraging, guys. I'm about to spend a *lot* of money on gear."

"Speaking of money, he's picked out a pack, a tent, and a sleeping pad. But we both need sleeping bags," I told them.

"More decisions?" Dad groaned.

"I know exactly which one," Scott said. "I just got a Mountain Hardwear Phantom and I love it. It's lightweight and warm. Let me show it to you."

Scott brought out a sample bag.

"What colors does it come in?" I asked, touching the fabric.

"You don't pick backpacking gear based on color," Jonathan told me.

"Maybe *you* don't…" I responded as Dad laughed. I knew functionality came first, but I also wanted gear I enjoyed looking at. I was pleased to find out that the women's fifteen-degree bag came in a pretty bluish-purple color.

"Should we pick out a water filter too?" Dad asked me. My MIOX had stopped working and we were going to have to get a new system.

Scott and Jonathan started to tell us about popular water filters but quickly their words began to blend together. I wasn't familiar with any of the brands they were mentioning, and I was feeling woefully ignorant about gear after looking at the newest in packs, tents, sleeping pads, and sleeping bags.

I held up my hands in surrender. "I don't think I can make any more decisions today. Let's save that for next time."

"Did *you* get tired of shopping before *me*?" Dad asked in awe as we headed toward the checkout counter.

Dad purchased a Gregory Baltoro 75 backpack, a Big Agnes Fly Creek 2 tent and footprint, a Therm-a-Rest NeoAir sleeping pad, and a Mountain Hardwear Phantom 32 sleeping bag. The backpack and sleeping pad were in stock, so he was able to take those purchases home that day. I bought a Gregory Deva 60 backpack, a Fly Creek 1 footprint, and a Mountain Hardwear Phantasia 15 sleeping bag. I was able to take my backpack home that day too.

We both spent a considerable amount of money, but we were excited and confident in our selections. The blow was cushioned some because the packs were reduced by thirty percent and Jonathan gave us a ten-percent discount on the rest of the gear because I'm a member of a local hiking group from Meetup.com. For at least the hundredth time in my adult life, I was thankful that my parents had taught me good money-management skills so that I had the ability to spend almost a thousand unplanned dollars that would be paid off the same month.

Meanwhile, I had a number of promotional events scheduled in October for my Appalachian Trail book, *Love at First Hike*. At these events I visited with old friends, met new characters, and renewed my love of the trail community. I came home invigorated and ready to tackle planning with enthusiasm. When I wasn't doing training hikes, reading JMT trail journals online, or researching dehydrated food and gear, I was daydreaming about the trail.

I had attended a festival called The Gathering in Shippensburg, Pennsylvania, with my best friend and former college roommate, Lark. One conversation from the festival reverberated in my head. A middle-aged man dressed in hiking clothes had approached me at my booth and revealed that he had read—and enjoyed—my book. He bought a second copy to give as a gift and we chatted for a few minutes. As hikers are apt to do, we discussed our recent adventures and hopes for upcoming trips. When I told him I was planning to tackle the JMT the following August, he challenged me, "Try to find a bad view—just one. You won't be able to do it. On the Appalachian Trail, you sometimes trek days at a time without a notable view. Often you struggle your way up a huge climb and there's no view from the top. The JMT is the opposite. There are beautiful views everywhere you look. Seriously, I challenge you to find a single bad one."

As I planned, I wondered if he could be right. Unlike many other hikers I've met and read about, I had never been bothered by the perceived monotony of certain parts of the AT. *If I was content for days on end without spectacular lookout points, will I overflow with joy at an endless array of beauty?*

Dad seemed to have caught the planning bug too. For weeks we spoke on the phone almost daily. We met for lunch and made what we were calling our "Gantt chart." Google had taught me that a Gantt chart (which, in fact, is not an acronym) is a bar chart illustrating a project schedule. What we actually created was just a calendar. We scheduled our hiking and backpacking dates months in advance and labeled each trip with our planned mileage and difficulty level.

Our "Gantt chart" also mapped out which day we would need to apply for permits, when we would prepare and package our mail drops, when we would mail them, and when we needed to book hotels and other final details for the journey. Our thorough plan was synced into both of our iPhone calendars. I was thankful that Dad and I shared a love of order and preparedness. The Boy Scouts had nothing on us with their "Be Prepared" motto.

October 23, 2013

"What are you doing the rest of the day?" Dad asked as we walked out of Appalachian Outfitters with two giant shopping bags. We'd just picked up our previously ordered gear and had also gotten a Sawyer Mini water filter and a few other small items.

"I don't have any plans. Why?"

"I was thinking I might go downstairs when I get home, drink some wine, and practice setting up all of my new gear. I figure it will take a few practice runs to get a system worked out. Do you want to come over?"

"Sure. That should be a show. Let me go home and get the rest of my gear so I can work on packing my pack too."

Later that evening, with the World Series playing in the background and two large glasses of red wine sitting on the table, I watched Dad meticulously cut the labels off each new piece of gear.

"Make sure to keep those labels and any manuals or instructions," I told him. "You might need them to know how to clean or store gear."

"Got it," he said, making an exaggerated show of placing a tag in a pile beside him. "I already have an envelope of these in the garage."

Clearly I'm not the only one in this family with a touch of OCD.

After Dad had carefully unpackaged all of his gear, he laid it out on the carpet and started moving the ottoman and chairs out of the way to clear a spot in front of the couch.

"I'm going to try setting up my tent. I don't want any help. I have to figure out how to do this on my own."

Mom hid a smirk behind her magazine.

I took a sip of wine. "OK."

I focused on packing my gear into my new Gregory Deva pack. The pack had plenty of cubic inches, but no matter how I arranged the gear the bear canister was bending the frame of the pack so that it poked uncomfortably into my lower back.

I glanced up occasionally to see Dad's progress with assembling his tent. Mom cringed and squeezed her eyes shut when he swung a pole through the air, coming precariously close to the piano. Since Dad's tent wasn't free-standing, he had to simulate staking it by holding the guy lines down with heavy pieces of furniture. When he had it set up, he crawled inside with his little Havanese dog, Hershey, and lay on his back, staring up.

"This isn't bad. I have plenty of room in here. Now I'm going to try it with the pad and sleeping bag."

"OK."

He crawled back out and sat on the couch to blow up his sleeping pad.

"This takes a long time," he complained.

"Yeah. And it feels even longer at the end of a hiking day when you're tired and just want to get camp set up so you can relax."

He blew a long breath into the valve. "That air pump is sounding better and better. How much did it weigh?"

I shook my head at him.

Dad shoved the sleeping pad and sleeping bag into the tent and crawled back in himself. I heard a lot of wiggling around and asked, "What are you doing in there?"

"I'm trying to get into the sleeping bag."

A shocking amount of rustling continued inside the tent. "How do I get it zipped when I'm inside it?"

Mom widened her eyes at me over her magazine.

I pressed my lips together to hold in laughter. "There's a zipper pull on the inside."

He wiggled around some more, and then it got quiet. "Can you come zip me in?"

I leaned into the tent and zipped his bag. "I'm not zipping you in every night on the trail."

"I'll have plenty of time to figure it out." He squirmed around on top of his sleeping pad like a worm. "This might take some getting used to."

Mom looked at me over the tent and then glanced pointedly at her watch. "You're going to have to get to the campsite at noon for him to set up his tent and sleeping gear in time for bed."

"I'll practice," he grumbled good-naturedly. Dad stayed in the tent for a few more minutes. When he crawled out, he asked, "How do I fold the sleeping bag to get it back in the pouch?"

"You don't. You stuff it."

Mom piped up from the couch, "Hence why it's called a stuff sack."

As Dad continued wrestling with his sleeping bag, he announced, "This is like feeding a horse to a boa constrictor!"

4

DEATH BY BURRITO

November 2–3, 2013

Dad had gear, and it was time to test it out. This wouldn't just be his first backpacking trip with me; it would be his first backpacking trip *ever*. Prior to this, his most recent overnight experience in nature had been platform tent camping at dad-and-daughter Girl Scout campouts fifteen years ago.

I arrived at my parents' house the night before our trip so that Dad and I could finish packing together. We ate dinner with Mom, and then Dad poured us each a second glass of wine before disappearing into the garage. When he reappeared he wore his fully loaded backpack and a proud smile.

"I went ahead and packed everything," he told me. "I know I still have to add the food, but I wanted to see how it all fit. It went pretty well."

"Great. Did you pack all the items from the list?" Since this was his first trip, I had emailed him a preliminary packing list the week before.

"Weeellll," he hedged, waggling his hand back and forth.

I set my own pack on the floor next to his. "What did you leave out?" My dad is an experienced and efficient packer thanks to years of cross-country travel for business trips. However, he is also a notoriously light packer. I suspected he had found my detailed list excessive.

"Just the rain gear," he confessed. "I checked the forecast and it isn't supposed to rain."

"Rain gear isn't just for rain, though," I explained. "It's also safety gear. If you fall and break an ankle and need to trap as much body heat as possible to prevent hypothermia until you're rescued, that can be an important layer. On every trip you have to carry pieces of gear you may never use. It stinks because of the extra weight, but it's just part of it."

"I'll pack it."

"Good."

"Hey, isn't that your old pack?" he asked, pointing at my Mountain Hardwear pack.

"Yep. The Gregory just didn't work with the bear canister, so I returned it. I'm having a lot of trouble finding a small women's pack that fits a bear canister. I'm still looking."

"Bummer."

We began sorting food on the kitchen island. Dad slipped a bottle of wine and a salted dark chocolate bar into the pile.

"For the weight," he quipped with a contagious grin. "If I practice with a heavier pack, I'll be in great shape with a lighter pack next summer."

In the morning I came upstairs to find Dad making omelets in his hiking clothes. I brewed coffee and sat down at the kitchen table to review the trail map. Dad set a plate in front of me and seated himself at the breakfast bar across the kitchen.

"Why don't you come join me?" I asked him.

"Because I want to sit here and read the paper. I'll be spending the next two days with you," he said, looking at me over his glasses.

"Afraid you'll get tired of me?"

He took a sip of his coffee. "I don't want to overdo it."

"We need to have a conversation before we head out. It might be easier if we sit together."

With an exaggerated sigh that was negated by his smile, he moved to the seat beside me.

"We need to talk about hiking safety."

"Rules?" He made a petulant face. "Is this a rules talk?"

I nodded.

"Who's the parent here?"

I took a bite of my omelet. "It's a nice role reversal, isn't it?"

He scrunched up his face. "Let's hear the rules."

"First, to make sure we don't get split up, we never go past a trail split, road crossing, or major point of interest without each other. Ever."

"That sounds easy."

"Second, if you're hiking in front of me but we're out of sight of one another, and you step off the trail for any reason, leave an identifiable piece of your gear on the trail so that I know when I've caught up to you. We don't want to pass each other without realizing it. We need to know who's in front."

"Why would I get off the trail without you?"

"If you needed to use the bathroom. Or maybe to get water. Or even to check out a campsite or a viewpoint. "

"Give me an example of a piece of gear I would leave."

"You could tie your bandana to a tree limb, or stick your poles in the ground."

He nodded and ate the last bite of his breakfast. "I've got those two rules. No problem." He pushed his plate back and crossed his legs. "What else?"

"Third, we always bring emergency gear."

"Like rain gear." He wrinkled his nose. "Got it. Is that it?"

"I think so." I took my plate to the sink. "Actually, there's one more thing. We'll leave our itinerary with someone each time, just in case."

"That's me," Mom announced, walking in from their bedroom as she flipped up the collar on her pink fleece robe and nestled into it.

I handed her a computer printout with information about the trail we were planning to hike, where we would be parking the car, and when we expected to return. "All of this information will also be on the registration card we leave in the box at the trailhead for the ranger," I reassured her.

When we arrived at Jones Gap State Park, only twenty minutes from my parents' house in upstate South Carolina, we confirmed our camping reservation at the ranger station. The ranger had us read over a list of rules and emphasized that all food must be hung. "We've had a decent amount of bear activity recently."

I nodded. "We have bear canisters."

He looked at me levelly under his tan ranger's hat. "You still have to hang them."

I returned his gaze evenly. "OK."

We had barely made it to the doorway before Dad said, "I thought we read that you don't hang canisters. We don't even have rope with us, do we?"

I widened my eyes at him but didn't respond. We *didn't* have rope, but I wasn't going to confirm that in front of the ranger.

We filled out a registration card at the trailhead and stepped onto the trail by eleven o'clock. A few feet ahead we saw a large wooden sign for the park that said, among other things, "No alcohol allowed."

Dad paused in front of the sign. "We're on a roll. We haven't even started hiking yet and we've already broken two park rules."

We hiked quickly on the Jones Gap Trail, following the Middle Saluda River to the trail split for Rainbow Falls Trail. This was a trail we had day-hiked together before, and I hoped that our previous hike would serve as a comparison for how different it is to hike with a full pack. We walked at a steady pace. Just before we made it to the falls, Dad slipped and scraped his shin trying to climb over a fallen log. The log had fallen at an angle, and Dad faced his body toward the lower end of the log as he stepped across, which caused his pack to scrape the log behind him and knock him over.

"Lesson learned," he stated when he was back on his feet. "When you're wearing a big pack you have to face the upward-angled part of the log to step over it." He wasn't badly hurt, but he did bleed through his new zip-off pants.

After a lazy lunch, we were crossing back over the water at the base of the falls when we met a group of hikers coming down the side of the waterfall.

"Hey, have you seen two guys and a girl?" they called to us.

"No. We haven't seen anyone," Dad answered.

"No one? How long have you been here? Our friends were behind us and we got split up about an hour ago. We haven't seen them since. We thought maybe they stopped here and didn't keep going up the side of the falls."

I looked up the path they had scurried down and considered telling them that it wasn't an official trail.

Dad beat me to answering. "We've probably been sitting here for forty-five minutes, and we haven't seen anyone."

The group exchanged nervous glances.

"Do you think they veered off onto the Rainbow Falls Trail like we did?" one of them asked. "We were still on the Jones Gap Trail when we lost them, right?"

"I think so," his friend answered, "but I don't really remember."

After wishing them luck and agreeing to pass along a message if we saw their friends, we continued back down the trail.

"That reinforces rule number one, doesn't it?" Dad asked me. "They don't even know if they're on the same trail as their group."

We continued walking and made admirable time. By mid-afternoon we had arrived at our campsite. I shook the contents out of my tent bag. I had practiced setting up my new tent once but had not yet used it with the footprint. Once the tent was set up, I stood beside it with my hands on my hips, staring at the tent and footprint in confusion. The plastic buckles for attaching the two didn't match up.

"It's crazy how often hiking gear doesn't come with instructions," I observed.

Dad looked up from where he was using a rock to pound stakes into the ground. "I think it's like a metaphor for life: the important things you have to figure out on your own."

I fiddled futilely with the plastic buckles. "When I pay this much money for a piece of equipment, I still want it to come with instructions."

I ended up getting the male end of one buckle stuck inside the female end of another, and gave up on the other three. I staked the tent over the unsecured footprint and hoped it wouldn't rain.

"I'm going to have to go to Appalachian Outfitters and get someone there to explain what I'm doing wrong. This is absurd. How can I have spent so many nights in a tent and not be able to set this one up correctly?"

"I don't know," Dad agreed. "I don't have the experience, but I'm struggling with mine too. I'd definitely like for them to show me what I'm doing wrong. I can't get the darn thing straight."

Dad's tent was amusingly cock-eyed. I tilted my head to the right. "If you look at it like this, it isn't so bad."

We fussed with his tent, staking and re-staking guy lines until we got it passably set up. The bottom floor of the tent was still more wrinkled than it should have been, and the archway for the door wasn't centered.

"I just don't know, Dad. I've always had stand-alone tents, so I'm not very familiar with tents like yours." I cocked my head to the side again. "But it seems like we should at least be able to make it look symmetrical. Let's make it a priority to go back to the outfitter."

Once we had our tents set up and our gear stowed, Dad remarked, "It took us about an hour to set up. That's not bad for a first try."

"It'll only get faster."

"True. But you know, if we could just find one good Sherpa to get to camp before us, heat up dinner, maybe greet us with a bottle of wine…" he trailed off. "I haven't seen one thing about Sherpas in my JMT research."

I shook my head. "We can get a Sherpa when we hike Kilimanjaro someday. But since we don't have one on this trip, let's go get ourselves some water."

When the short trail to the river dead-ended, Dad said, "Let me try the water filter, OK?"

I handed him the green drawstring bag containing our new Sawyer Mini. Dad dumped the contents onto the bank and picked up the small collapsible plastic bladder that came with the filter. We had tried it out once at home, so he was familiar with the pieces.

The river bank was entirely covered in large rocks. Dad hopped up onto one and reached down toward the water. His arm wasn't quite long enough to touch it. I watched him scout around and find a place where he could step across and straddle a small section of the river. The second rock wobbled precariously, but he maintained his balance. He leaned down and attempted to fill the container by submerging it. No luck.

I yelled over the rushing river, "Try holding it under flowing water." I pointed at a spot where the water cascaded over a small rock outcropping.

Dad nodded and leaned in that direction. Despite repeated efforts, the malleable container kept collapsing and would not fill more than halfway. Each time Dad had filled it as much as he could, he would screw on the filter and step back toward me. I held a CamelBak reservoir underneath while he squeezed the cold bladder to force the water through the filter. This required much more effort than we had expected, and it took an eternity to fill both containers. Dad's hands were bright red from prolonged contact with the cold water, but he wouldn't switch positions with me.

"This isn't supposed to be so difficult," I told him.

"Let's add this to our list of things to ask about at the outfitter. This is ridiculous. I don't want to fight with this thing every night."

"We'd better write it down." I was beginning to feel like we had issues with most of our gear. *Am I just getting pickier as I get older? Or am I making worse selections?*

Dad attempted to fill the collapsible bladder again and came away with only a few ounces of water. "This sucks. If there isn't an easier way to do this, I want to return the whole damn thing and get a different type of filter."

When we decided we had enough water, Dad tossed me the bladder. I missed, and it floated a few feet downstream before getting snagged on a stick. While reaching for the bladder, I dropped the whole filter into the water too.

"So much for keeping it sanitary," I said wryly.

Dad started to step back onto the bank, but the rock under his foot wobbled and he stepped straight into the water instead.

"Crap, that's cold," he complained, his leg submerged up to the knee. He recovered quickly and climbed onto the bank. He had a gash on his shin, wet pants, and a wet shoe but was otherwise fine. "I guess that's why we wear quick-dry pants," he observed.

We built a fire and ate dinner. As Dad was opening the bottle of wine, he said, "How appropriate. I brought Ricochet wine. I've been ricocheting off the ground all day."

I laughed as I held out my coffee mug.

Dad studied it. "We can't call these coffee cups if we're going to use them for wine too. Let's call them goblets."

"Goblets. I like it." I raised my goblet. "What are we toasting to?"

"Tonight I'm going to tie my lifelong record for nights spent in a tent on the ground. In my sixty-three years, I'll be at two total nights after tonight!"

"I hope this night is more successful than your last."

Although Dad had gamely attended those dad-and-daughter campouts, he'd only camped in an actual tent on the ground once before. When I was about ten, our family spent exactly one night in a large family-sized tent at a campground. The trip was somewhat disastrous, ending with my mom and sister in tears after Dad and I played a poorly thought-out trick and scared them in the middle of the night.

While we finished the wine and Dad smoked a cigar, our conversations spiraled deeper. We discussed absolute versus relative morality, abortion, and welfare. This was only our first night together in the woods and already we were tackling some serious topics.

When we decided to head to bed, we stashed our smell-able items in our bear canisters. In the dim light of our headlamps I could see Dad fumbling awkwardly with his lid.

"I can see how this would be confusing to bears," he observed. "It's not intuitive to me."

"See, who needs rope to stump the bears?"

In the morning we studied our route options on the map. We decided to continue slightly north on the Jones Gap Trail and then loop back around to the Rim of the Gap Trail. This would spit us back out near the trailhead where we had started the day before. I knew that this trail was rated as a difficult one, but since the mileage was relatively low, I didn't think it would be a big deal.

I was wrong. The seven-plus miles took us seven hours to hike. We used cables to climb slick rocks, navigated over and around downed trees, straddled crevices, climbed ladders, and slogged through standing water. While some of the obstacles might have been fun to tackle on my own—without a full backpacking pack—they lost their charm when wearing almost forty pounds and feeling responsible for Dad's safety and enjoyment level.

Our initially cheery conversations tapered off as we both became increasingly frustrated with the trail.

"Michelle?" he asked at one point.

"Yes?"

"This isn't fun."

"I know." *He's going to want to disown me. At the very least, he'll never hike again.* "I'm sorry. I remember this trail being so different," I told him. It had been years since I had hiked it.

"You know, there's an old saying that there's no harm in what you don't know. It's only what you think you know that isn't so."

I was relieved to hear a hint of humor in his voice. "Touché."

The rest of our hike was largely silent. When we finally reached the trailhead where we had started our adventure the day before, I called out, "Dad, we have to take one more picture. This is the 'We survived' photo."

He put his arm around me and smiled. "We smelled a lot better when we stood by this sign yesterday."

When we reached my car, Dad turned to me. "You were wrong," he chided. "Get the camera out. *This* is the last photo."

I snapped a picture as he kissed the car.

When we pulled back into my parents' driveway, Mom met us at the door.

"You're still smiling," she observed.

"She was out of the family for a while," Dad said, shutting the car door. "But we're friends again. And"—he clapped me on the back—"I may even hike again."

November 16–17, 2013

I was pleasantly surprised to find that Dad was ready for another overnight trip only two weeks later. We went to Paris Mountain State Park, another park in Upstate South Carolina, to put in a few miles and troubleshoot the tent and water filter using the tips we had acquired during our trip to the outfitter.

When we had almost arrived at North Lake, a couple headed the opposite direction without packs stepped to the side to let us pass.

"You guys look like you plan to be out here a while!" the man observed with a smile, eyeing our packs.

"We're camping overnight by the lake," Dad told them.

"That's wonderful," the lady professed. "I would love to start backpacking, but I have no idea where to start. I don't own any of that gear."

"She's experienced," Dad told her, pointing his trekking pole at me, "but I'm just learning. We did an overnight—one night—a couple weeks ago and I tied my lifelong record." He paused to let that sink in, and then told them with a grin, "I've now spent two nights on the ground in my sixty-three years."

"Maybe there *is* hope for us," the lady said to her husband.

"We're training for a big hike, actually," Dad told them. "In August we're going out to California to hike the John Muir Trail."

"How long will you be hiking?" the man asked us.

"Three weeks," I told them.

"It's about 220 miles," Dad added, with a tinge of pride in his voice.

I smiled at Dad's excitement to share our plans.

Dad and I continued around to the back side of the lake and came to the wooden sign for campsite number two. Down a barely distinguishable trail, we found a primitive stone fire circle with a bench made from a fallen tree facing the lake.

We located two flat areas nearby and made quick work of setting up our tents. The tips from the outfitter helped, and this time Dad's tent was much more symmetrical. I had learned that the issue with my tent was that I had ordered the wrong footprint. With a few tweaks the footprint was useable. I'd also ordered a new pack, but since it hadn't arrived yet I was making do with my over-stuffed Mountain Hardwear.

Even filtering water went more smoothly with the new Platypus GravityWorks system we had bought to accompany our Sawyer Mini filter. The GravityWorks is made up of two clear plastic four-liter water reservoirs and two hoses. Water is scooped directly from the source into the bag-like reservoir labeled "dirty." That bag has a zip-open top and handles, so collection is easy and instantaneous. Using the handles, the "dirty" reservoir is hung from a high spot (typically a tree branch). Water flows from that bag through a short hose into the Sawyer Mini, and then down another short hose into the "clean" reservoir. When working properly, this system can filter four liters of water in under three minutes, a huge improvement over our meager and painstakingly hand-squeezed ounces on the last trip.

Following a game of Yahtzee and a visit with some bizarre campers from a nearby campsite, we cooked dinner. This was our first homemade dehydrated meal, so I was anxious to see Dad's reaction. I'd selected burritos in a bag since we both love Mexican food.

I walked Dad through the process of boiling water in the camping pot and pouring it into the Ziploc bag containing the dehydrated food. We put the Ziplocs into insulated aluminum pouches that Janice had helped me make at work the previous week. Ten minutes later our dinner was ready. Dad gave dinner a good review and said that the recipe was definitely a keeper, but that he wanted more beans and less rice in his bag.

"I can do that. What meal should we try on our next hike?"

"What about chili mac? I liked that from Summit Home on our Jones Gap trip."

"You mean Mountain House." Dad has an amazing ability to butcher the names of places and products and yet an impeccable memory of people's names.

"Whatever."

"You do know the name of the trail we're going to hike, right?"

He held my gaze over the campfire. "The Justin Moore Trail."

In the morning we sat on a log by the lake and drank our coffee.

"My goal is to learn something on each one of these practice trips," Dad informed me.

I nodded and unwrapped my Clif Bar.

"Last time I learned the correct way to climb over a fallen log. This time I had a revelation. It was at about three o'clock this morning. At 3:07, to be precise."

I blew on my scalding coffee. "That's very specific. I guess that means you didn't sleep any better than last time."

"Actually I did, but here's my revelation: Some people remember trips like this by writing in a journal. Other people take pictures. But I'm here to tell you, a burrito toot in a tent at three o'clock in the morning is something you'll never forget!"

I snorted coffee as I laughed.

"No, really," Dad elaborated between belly laughs. "It was awful. I almost gassed myself out of the tent!" He slapped his knees and blinked as tears leaked from his eyes. "I was afraid you might find me dead this morning. I thought I had asphyxiated myself."

With Dad before the inaugural backpacking trip

Dad on the Rim of the Gap Trail

5

TRAIL ANGELS

Preparing for an extended-duration hike is largely about balance. We had to get Dad comfortable with his gear, we had to take hikes of increasing durations and difficulties both with and without full packs, and we had to expose him to back-to-back days of trail life. Plus, I needed to re-accustom my own legs to the rigors of hiking. *No problem. We can just squeeze all that in after Dad's golf tournament and before my tennis match.* Between my work schedule, Dad's active retiree social life, and both of our additional responsibilities, free time was limited.

Adhering to our excessively detailed calendar, Dad and I had done a number of day hikes throughout the fall and winter. We had tackled ten easy miles on the Cat Gap Loop Trail in Pisgah National Forest without full packs. On that trip I had chastised myself for putting us in the position of hiking without a map and decent directions, but I was proud of the joint decision-making skills that had gotten us safely back to our car. As I had predicted, our Type A personalities were working to our advantage. We had also gotten some practice hiking in below-freezing temperatures.

January 12, 2014

Since our first ten-mile hike had been so successful, we moved right along in our training plan to a difficult eleven-mile hike with day packs. We headed to nearby Table Rock State Park and approached Table Rock from Sassafras Mountain. The ascent was steep. We maintained our normal thirty-minute-per-mile pace and, as usual, our conversation was as consistent as our strides.

Around mile four, I realized I no longer heard Dad's voice or footsteps behind me. I turned around to check. He was stopped, leaning forward on his Leki poles.

I took a swig of water and watched. When he didn't start moving after a moment, I headed back toward him. As I got closer, I could hear a high-pitched beeping noise.

I stopped a few feet in front of him. "You OK?"

"I think so."

"What's the beeping?"

"My heart rate monitor." He looked down at his watch.

Dad exercises regularly. He often wears a watch that syncs with a band he straps around his chest to monitor his heart rate during exercise. The monitor ensures that his exercises are challenging enough to keep his heart rate in the target zone for maximum aerobic benefit. I'd seen him glance at the numbers before on the tennis court.

"Why is it beeping?"

"It means my heart rate is above the targeted zone."

I scrutinized his face. "How high?"

"It beeps above 140."

His skin is pink. He's speaking normally. He isn't sweating more than usual. My EMT training kicked in. "How do you feel?"

He shifted his weight off his poles and stood normally. "I feel fine."

"Do you have any dizziness or tingling? Are you light-headed or short of breath? Are you hurting?"

He shot me an amused look. "I'm fine. Really." He glanced at his watch again. "It's coming down already."

The beeping stopped.

"See. It's down to 125."

We sat down for a break anyway.

"Did you drink much water on the golf course yesterday? Dehydration can affect your heart rate." Dad and I are both notorious for forgetting to stay hydrated.

"That could be it." He looked at me pointedly and took a swig from his CamelBak. "You should drink some water too."

"I will. Do you want to turn around?"

"Nope. We're probably about halfway there anyway, right? I'll just keep an eye on it and take it slow. I feel fine." He angled the watch so I could see it. "My heart rate is almost back to normal."

We continued hiking and I made sure to stay close. Dad was joking and talking as he hiked, so I soon put the concern out of my mind.

Within minutes we crossed paths with a couple in their twenties from Columbia, South Carolina.

"Hey. Pretty day today, isn't it? Where are you guys headed?" I asked.

"To Table Rock," the man answered.

I glanced behind him. "Not in the direction you're going."

"What do you mean?"

Is he joking? I assessed him for a second. He seemed serious. "Table Rock is behind you. That's where my dad and I are going."

"I feel like we would have noticed changing trails," the guy mused with a bewildered expression.

"Well, we're headed to Table Rock and we're going to keep hiking in the direction you just came from. I've hiked the trail you started on a number of times. I'm positive Table Rock is behind you."

After pleasant goodbyes, Dad and I continued on. We noticed that the couple had turned around and was following along a distance behind us. In about ten minutes we reached a trail split. There was a giant wooden sign with arrows clearly affirming the direction of Table Rock.

Dad leaned on his poles and stared at the sign. "How could they have missed this? It's at least six feet wide."

"I have no idea."

When the couple joined us a minute later Dad inquired, "Do you guys have a camera?"

They did.

"Let me see it," he requested. "You're going to want a picture of the two of you with this *giant*"—he gestured at it—"*I* mean *giant*, sign."

We hiked the rest of the ascent and the entire descent without incident. Before we made it to the car we were already discussing our next outing.

February 7–9, 2014

Nine years after I had first extended an invitation, Dad and I finally made it to the Appalachian Trail together. Dad's heart rate issue hadn't repeated itself during any of his regular workouts or on an additional day hike we took in Pisgah National Forest. He had theorized that a bad night of sleep and dehydration might have contributed to his issue at Table Rock. We agreed to be careful but decided to proceed with our training plan.

We joined Janice's hiking group for a three-day trip near Standing Indian Mountain. This would be our first two-night trip and also our first trip with other people. Since I knew we would spend time with other hikers on the JMT, I wanted Dad to experience the camaraderie on a training hike. Plus, Janice and her friends are Dad's age, and I thought it might be nice for him to hike with people in his same season of life. We started on Kinsey Creek Trail and hiked 4.1 miles until we intersected the Appalachian Trail. Then we hiked 2.4 miles to Standing Indian Mountain. The entire day was uphill, but Dad and I felt strong and we easily stayed at the front of the group.

Janice and I had spent a lot of time together as partners on an ambulance, but this was our first time hiking together. It was fun for me to watch Janice and my dad interact since they had heard so many stories about each other.

"So, Janice," Dad said as he was adjusting his hipbelt straps, "I have a question for you, as the leader of this trip."

"Sure."

"Do we make reservations for the showers with you? I'm afraid we may run out of hot water tonight, so I want to get my time slot early."

Without missing a beat, Janice responded, "Do you want to sign up for your hot tub time now too?"

It turns out that a hot shower *and* a hot tub would have been nice that night. The wind was strong on top of Standing Indian, and despite being dressed in every piece of clothing I had packed, I was chilly as we set up camp and cooked dinner. We all went to bed early because we were unable to get a fire going—the result of the hiker version of "too many cooks in the kitchen." While I'm normally a night owl at home, I relish the extra sleep I get in the woods, so I happily retired to my tent. I braced myself for a few minutes of discomfort as I peeled off all but my bottom layer of clothing and slithered into my new mummy bag. I knew that, contrary to what seems logical, sleeping bags work best when you wear little to no clothing. I cinched the bag down so that only my nose stuck out of the opening and tossed my fleece over my face.

When I emerged from my cocoon in the morning, I found Dad bundled in winter clothing and stomping his feet outside his tent. He had caught his sleeping bag zipper on the baffling and spent the below-freezing night mostly unzipped and cold. His fingers, so nimble when picking the guitar, had never quite mastered sleeping bag zippers.

Although Dad and I packed up hastily, one of the group members was moving slowly, and we ended up standing around shivering for almost an hour. It stayed cold all day and we barely removed any layers as we hiked the ten miles to Betty Creek Gap. The last four miles were downhill. I had realized by now that Dad shared my love of downhills, and we breezed through the final miles to arrive at camp first and in great spirits.

We found the perfect spot for our tents on what appeared to be an old logging road underneath an arch of big-armed coniferous trees. Dad did his best job to date of setting up his tent. He had just told me that he was looking forward to a cigar and pulling out our new flasks when we heard a commotion.

I discreetly stepped closer to the group and I overheard that Pat, one of Janice's friends, was missing her tent. It had apparently fallen off the outside of her pack while she was hiking. *How do you drop a tent and not notice?*

As I listened from afar, Pat began crying. She explained that she was on a fixed income and couldn't afford to replace the tent. If the tent wasn't recovered, she wouldn't be able to backpack anymore.

They were able to confirm with a passing AT thru-hiker that the tent was on the trail about eight miles back. He even had a picture of it on his phone. Janice started brainstorming. "We're going to have to split up and finish the hike in opposite directions. We can't all hike the mileage back to the tent and still make it to the cars tomorrow night."

This was true. At least half of the group wasn't physically capable of that much added mileage on challenging terrain.

"OK, we could send…" I listened as Janice proposed ideas. I knew that no matter what the solution was, it would involve me. Despite the fact that Janice hikes more often than I do, I was the youngest in the group and had the most experience with long-mileage days.

I pulled my fleece hat further down on my forehead and walked slowly back toward our perfect tenting spot.

"Hey, Dad?"

He was puttering around outside his tent in his Crocs. "Yep?"

"I know you were looking forward to smoking a cigar and breaking out our flasks"—I paused, not wanting to have this conversation—"but I think I'm going to have to ask you to change plans."

"What's going on?" Dad asked.

I explained the situation. "You and I are the strongest combination of hikers. I think we need to offer to get the tent."

His shoulders visibly sagged. "You're kidding me."

"I'm not." I glanced at my watch and then the sky. "It's four miles back to that shelter and—"

"Uphill. It's four miles *uphill*."

"Yes." There was no point in trying to sugarcoat it. I was asking him to hike four miles *uphill* in the freezing cold at the end of a long day of hiking, with darkness fast approaching. "I'm thinking if we leave in fifteen minutes, we can make it back to that shelter before dark. I'll help you break your tent down and I'll carry it. I'm going to leave mine here for Pat to sleep in. We can sleep in the shelter so we don't have to mess with a tent. I think we can make the shelter, maybe even before dark, but if we don't we can both sleep in your tent somewhere else."

He jammed his gloved hands in the pockets of his down coat. "That's a fourteen-mile day."

"Yep," I continued. "And then tomorrow we'll retrace the other six miles we did today, plus the six and a half from yesterday. So it will be almost a thirteen-mile day tomorrow. Somewhere along the way we'll find that tent. I'll tell Janice and the others to go ahead and leave without us tomorrow because they'll only have a six-mile day and they'll beat us to the cars. Pat can carry my tent out and leave it with Janice, and I'll swap her tent for mine at work on Monday."

Dad looked up at the sky and sighed loudly. "This sucks."

"Yep. Consider it forced training. Remember how I said a hike never goes as planned?"

Dad began pulling his gear out of his tent. As I reached down to unclip his fly, I heard him mumble, "How do you lose a damn tent?"

In fifteen minutes we were hiking again. I was unsettled by Dad's silence.

"Are you sore?" I asked, bracing for an understandably grumpy response.

"I actually feel fine," he replied. "It's just that I had told my body I was done for the night. I was in relaxing mode, and now I have to get back into hiking mode. Just go at your pace. Don't worry about me." His voice wasn't angry or annoyed.

We hiked steadily but without talking. About a mile in we passed an AT thru-hiker and I stopped to chat, but Dad kept going, telling me to "catch" him.

I talked with the AT hiker for about five minutes and then followed in Dad's footsteps. I tucked my head down, leaned into my poles, and hurried as quickly as my short legs would propel me. Forty-five minutes later I still had not caught him. I began to wonder if somehow I had passed him. *He knows the rules*, I reminded myself. I pushed at lightning speed until I had to stop to catch my breath fifteen minutes later.

"Dammit, Dad," I mumbled under my breath as I rested my hands on my knees. It was just about dark and I was getting worried. *Where the hell can he be?*

"Hey, Partner."

I looked up, surprised. Dad was seated on a rock just around the corner. I swallowed my frustration. "Did someone light a fire under your tail?"

He laughed. "I guess so. I just got in a groove and I didn't want to stop. I figured you'd catch up."

"I've been trying. You were moving really fast."

"I've been sitting here about five minutes. I realized it had been a long time and you hadn't caught me. I started thinking that even though that guy was an AT hiker and he was probably OK, we didn't know him and maybe I'd left you with an axe murderer. I was going to give it five more minutes and then go find you."

"So, just to be clear, you thought maybe I was with an axe murderer and you were going to *wait* five minutes?"

He chuckled. "I didn't say it was the *best* plan."

Together we resumed hiking, the sunlight fading fast. I was debating digging out my headlamp when we saw the roof of the shelter through the trees. We had time to filter water and start a fire before darkness fell completely.

Inside the drafty shelter, we set up our sleeping gear and settled in for the night. A chilling wind whistled through the cracked walls and rattled the shingles on top of the shelter. There is no possible way to be quiet when changing positions on an inflatable mattress from inside a nylon sleeping bag. Based on the unmistakable rustling and squeaking noises, I knew Dad was awake much of the night like I was.

"Are you cold?" I whispered at one point.

"A little," he answered in a normal voice—Dad has never been able to whisper. "How do I close the bag around my head?"

"You don't have your hood cinched?"

"Nope. I've never used it."

"Here. Let me help." I unzipped my bag enough to snake my arm out and cinched his bag down until only his mouth and nose stuck out. "You should be a lot warmer now."

We were up and hiking at daybreak because we knew walking would warm and energize us. Despite intermittent sleep and chilled bodies, we were both in high spirits. We carried on effortless conversation as we hiked. Dad and I had always talked easily, but I often teased him because on the phone he reached an obvious point where he was *done*. I loved that on the trail he was a captive participant. We let our conversations segue naturally into others.

Six miles and at least a dozen topics later, we found the missing tent. Someone had set it on top of a fallen tree that stretched across the trail. The stuff sack was huge, easily more than twice the size of the sack for my own tent.

"How is it possible that she dropped this and didn't realize it?" I wondered aloud as I awkwardly strapped it to the outside of my pack. Hefting my pack onto my shoulders with the tent attached was like trying to lift a small house. (When I weighed the tent at home, I found out that it had added nearly six and a half pounds.) I staggered for a couple of steps as I regained my balance.

"Hey, let me get a picture of you with that strapped to your pack," Dad requested. "This is evidence."

I pointed at the stuff sack as I posed.

"Does this make us trail angels?" he asked.

Even with the extra weight and unplanned mileage, we hiked consistently at a thirty-minute-per-mile pace. When we reached the car at three thirty in the afternoon, we found a note from the other hikers. They had made it out at three o'clock. Dad and I had hiked 12.6 miles to their seven, in addition to four extra miles the day before, but still, they had only beat us by thirty minutes. We were pretty darn proud of ourselves— exhausted, but proud.

With Dad on Table Rock

With Dad on Standing Indian Mountain

With the recovered tent strapped to the bottom of my pack

6

WHAT CAN I SAY TO
MAKE YOUR DAY BETTER?

February 16, 2014

I was halfway through a double shift on the ambulance when my cell phone rang.

"Hey, Dad."

"Hey there, Partner," Dad greeted me. "Has your shift gotten any better?" He and I had texted earlier in the day, so he knew Janice and I had been busy.

"Sadly, no. We've been running our tails off—two wrecks, a cardiac arrest, a chest pain, and an 'I've fallen and I can't get up' just since lunch. I'm exhausted."

"That's not good with half the shift to go."

"I know. We may never catch up on paperwork."

"Well, what can I say to make your day better?"

"You could tell me we have JMT permits." There was a long enough pause that I became aware of the clock ticking beside me.

Obtaining permits to hike the John Muir Trail is notoriously difficult and becomes harder each year as the trail increases in popularity. The rules for the lottery were so complicated that at times I felt I needed a master's degree to interpret the requirements. Permit requests could only be submitted a certain number of days in advance and for a specific number of hikers, and only a set number of alternative trip dates could be requested. They had to be submitted by fax—and the fax line was often busy because so many people were attempting to transmit at once. After jumping through all these hoops, permit recipients were accepted by random lottery rather than by order of submission. It sometimes seemed like it might be easier to book a reservation on the next shuttle to the moon.

"We got the email from Yosemite," Dad finally answered. "We don't have permits"—he paused long enough to put me on edge—"but we have reservations!"

"Eeeeee!" I screamed and jumped up from the couch. "No way. No WAY!" My voice had risen two octaves in excitement.

Janice turned from the computer where she was about to clock out from her shift. "Permits?" she stage whispered.

I nodded emphatically and flashed her a face-splitting smile and a thumbs-up. The width of her smile almost equaled mine. I mouthed "Talk tomorrow" and turned my attention back to the phone.

"You're serious, Dad? We have permits? Seriously?"

"I wouldn't joke about this," he said. "The wording is very specific, though: this isn't a *permit*; it's a *reservation*. We pick up the actual permit in Yosemite right before we start hiking—which is on August second, by the way. Also, we got reservations for Half Dome permits—"

"Wait. Really?" I interrupted. "We got Half Dome too?"

Towering at 5,000 feet over Yosemite Valley and more than 8,000 feet above sea level, the granite monolith dome is a hiking icon. Half Dome is not on the John Muir Trail and requires a separate permit, but many JMT thru-hikers visit this popular mountain as a side trip. I had decided that since I was already traveling across the country to hike in Yosemite, I should experience Half Dome too. Although Dad hadn't been totally convinced he wanted to add *more* mileage to a trail of two-hundred-plus miles, he had agreed to apply for the permits so that we would have the option.

"We did," he confirmed. "And it's all thanks to your mom. We owe her big time. You're on speakerphone, so thank her. She faxed the application in the middle of the night, and that has to be why it went through."

I heard Mom singsong in the background, "That's riiight. It's all thanks to me, so you're welcome."

"Thanks, Mom!" I offered eagerly. "I just can't believe this." I paced in excited circles on the well-worn carpet of the station. "I was seriously starting to worry we wouldn't get permits at all." I had spent time that same morning researching alternative trails in case we didn't get permits. "Do you think there's any way this could be a mistake?"

"I don't think so," Dad reassured. "I've called the Yosemite office so many times that I'm practically on a first-name basis with the rangers. Today the ranger assured me that this email is official and all we have to do is show up in person to collect the permit. I've already printed the email with the confirmation number. I tell you, though, until I saw this email today, I was beginning to think we might not get permits. It was starting to seem hopeless."

"Ahhhem," Mom cleared her throat. "You're welcome. But now if one of you gets hurt out there, or something bad happens, it's all *my* fault because *I* signed you up for this."

"I don't know about that," I said. "But we definitely have you to thank for being able to go. We sent in four applications with three date requests on each one. So it took us twelve tries to get our permit—I mean reservation—and the one you submitted is the one that was successful."

"Actually," Dad edited, "this was our *fifth* application. So that makes fifteen tries total. But what matters is that we got it. We'd better get serious with preparing."

Having a definitive start date for our trip kicked our planning into high gear. Dad and I divided trail preparation tasks and we each diligently conquered our assignments.

Dad called Yosemite for clarification on some issues regarding our permits, booked our flight to Mammoth Lakes, California, and reserved a hotel for the night we would arrive. I bought five-gallon buckets from Lowe's for our mail drops and continued working on our itinerary.

In mid-March we updated our "Gantt chart" to include the final preparations for our hike. It was hard to believe we had only four months left before flying to California. Our calendar soon included days for our last training hikes and days to shop for food and supplies to put in our resupply buckets. There were days to finish dehydrating our food, days to pack the buckets, and a day to label and mail them. We each made notes to visit our doctors the month prior to our departure to obtain prescriptions for emergency antibiotics and altitude sickness prevention. Our trip was becoming more real every day.

7

THANKS AGAIN FOR INVITING ME

March 21–22, 2014

With our preparation time dwindling, Dad and I had a limited number of training hikes left. Janice helped me pick a three-day, thirty-mile route in Pisgah National Forest. Neither Janice nor I had hiked this trail before, but she had heard many positive reviews.

The sky was a clear, beautiful blue as we drove, and I was excited for our first training hike in warmer weather and without so many layers of clothing. The hike started out wonderfully. The trail was relatively flat and well marked, and the forest was starting to come alive with every shade of green and a few brightly colored wildflowers. It was a welcome sight following our largely monochromatic winter hikes.

During the first four miles Dad and I came across a number of other hikers and campers. It seemed that many of us were eager to enjoy the warmer weather. We crossed a stream over a couple of well-maintained swinging bridges and then once more, balance-beam style, on a log that had been split in half lengthwise. Repeatedly we commented to each other how beautiful the trail was.

We stopped for lunch at the edge of a small field that housed a tall stone chimney, which used to be part of a lodge for rangers in the old Biltmore Forest. Dad tried peanut butter and honey on a tortilla for the first time and immediately said it should go into our regular rotation of trail meals. This was a relief because Dad hadn't been eating well on our practice hikes, and I was constantly striving to find trail meals and snacks he would actually eat.

After lunch we continued hiking. The blazes indicated that our trail took a left turn at a junction. We followed the split and kept on trucking. About half a mile later, without warning, the trail dead-ended at a river. I looked up and down the embankment and couldn't see a bridge.

"Dad, did I miss a trail split?"

He came to a stop beside me. "No," he answered with confidence. "Why?"

"I don't see a bridge. Sometimes there are separate crossings for horses and humans. I thought maybe I had missed a junction to a bridge."

"I'm almost positive there was no trail, but let's double check."

We backtracked and confirmed.

"I guess we ford the river, "I concluded. "We knew there would be fords on this trail."

"What's this *we* business?" Dad asked. "*You* may have known there were fords. *I* didn't."

"Oops." I kicked at a rock and grinned. "*I* knew." Janice had told me there would be fords on one section. I studied the river. "You can check off one more skill for JMT preparation."

We took off our packs, shed our socks and shoes, and put on our Crocs. I showed Dad how to attach his boots to his pack, and then we re-shouldered our packs and stood tentatively at the edge of the river. I delayed stepping in for a long time. Not that many weeks ago the river had been frozen; the water was going to be frigid. With dread, I braced myself and plunged my right foot into the water. It was even worse than I had expected. Gritting my teeth, I forced my second foot to follow. I cussed out loud, hissed air through my teeth, and held my entire body rigid as I worked my way across the river.

Dad followed behind me, and we both reached the other bank without a problem. I pasted a smile on my face and slapped his hand in a high five. Carefully we dried our frozen feet, wiping off the water and dirt with bandanas, and replaced our socks and shoes.

We continued down the trail. To our astonishment we reached another river crossing about a quarter of a mile later. Our feet had barely thawed from the prior crossing. We looked in vain for a trail to a bridge. Surrendering to the inevitable, we repeated the process of removing our shoes and socks and easing across the glacial water. As we put them back on, we laughed at the absurdity of two fords being so close together.

We hadn't even gone half a mile when we once again found ourselves standing at the edge of the river with no bridge in sight. We trudged up and down the shore for long distances in both directions.

"This is nuts," Dad said, taking his hat off and running his hand through his sweaty hair. "Who would build a trail like this? Three river crossings this close together?"

He's never going to backpack with me again. How do we keep ending up on these ridiculous hikes? "Maybe the water level is usually lower," I suggested while removing my pack again. "We'll be really practiced at river crossings." I was just barely maintaining a sense of optimism.

We crossed the same river for the third time in less than an hour, pulled our socks and shoes back onto our numb, bluish feet, and started back down the trail. There was another crossing barely around the corner. We could actually turn back and see the spot where we had just crossed. My optimism vanished. I stared at the river.

"Why would Janice suggest this trail?" Dad asked in disbelief.

"To be fair, she's never hiked it."

"Clearly. If she had done this trail and then suggested it to others, I would question her sanity."

After this fourth crossing we decided to forgo putting our shoes back on. The way this trail was going, another crossing would show up in less than half a mile. We carefully picked our way down the trail with our feet making slurping noises in our Crocs. I worried about one of us twisting an ankle in the unsteady shoes, but I was also tired of changing my footwear.

When we had gone about half a mile, I decided we shouldn't tempt fate any longer. We stopped and put our boots back on. A few minutes down the trail Dad pointed out, "I think this is the longest we've gone without a crossing." He was walking in front of me. Not three minutes after making that observation, he stopped dead in his tracks. "You have to be kidding me!"

I didn't even have to look beyond him to know we were once again at the river.

He flung his pack on the ground. "This isn't funny anymore."

Without further conversation we crossed for the fifth time. This time the river was wider and the current was swift. I gave Dad a quick lesson in safe river-crossing methods to combat the current. We made it across safely and once again put our shoes back on. I watched in horrified fascination as the skin on my feet and lower legs turned from bright red to white as I pressed on it.

"My feet may never be warm again," I griped. I watched in horrified fascination as the skin on my feet and lower legs turned from bright red to white as I pressed on it.

To our dismay, the sixth crossing couldn't have been another half a mile further.

I leaned over to tie my laces. "I'm tired of putting my boots on," I complained.

"Yep." He consulted his watch. "How far do you think we've hiked since that split after lunch?"

"I have no idea. We've stopped so much to cross this river that it's hard to have any concept of distance."

"I hope we're almost to camp."

"Me too. So far I haven't even seen a place we could camp if we wanted to stop."

"Me neither." He strapped his pack back on. "Let's go."

I hiked down the trail, hoping we were done with the river. Normally I was grateful to have a ready water source while I hiked, but I was tired of being intimately acquainted with this particular river. Dad and I weren't talking much—probably because we were both wallowing in frustration. I turned around to make sure he was behind me and saw him lying on the ground in the mud.

"Dad?" I called.

He didn't answer.

I hastened back toward him, watching to see if he moved. "Dad? Dad! Are you OK?" I was having flashbacks to a fall he had taken on a day hike while I was training for the Appalachian Trail. On that fall he had slipped on the ice and split his head open, requiring five staples in his head.

He lifted his head up.

He's conscious, at least. I reached him and knelt down. "What happened? Are you OK?"

"I stepped in a hole that was covered up with leaves. My knee went one way and I went the other."

"Uh-oh. How's the knee now?"

"Not good."

Dad got up after a bit and wanted to keep hiking. His knee was sore, and he was walking with a definite limp, but he was afraid it would tighten up if he sat still for too long. I slowed my pace to reduce the strain on his knee. We slowly made it about another half mile before I saw water ahead of me.

When I came to a stop, Dad knew immediately.

"Dammit." He tossed his poles on the ground.

I looked out at the water. This was the widest, swiftest crossing yet. "We can take a break for a bit. We don't have to cross now."

He sat awkwardly on a rock and pulled at his shoelace. "I don't want to put it off. I'm going to have to cross it. Let's just get it over with."

"Maybe the cold water will be good for your knee?" I suggested hopefully as I stared out at the river trying to identify the best route across.

The water was still unbelievably cold, and by the halfway point I felt like my legs and feet were being stabbed with needles. I was slightly dizzy from holding my breath against the cold. Twice I had to stop and find another route because the water got too deep. Even with my reroutes, the icy water had soaked me to mid-thigh.

My hand was almost on the opposite shore when suddenly I started falling backwards. I was plunged into the river up to my armpits. My legs scrambled for purchase on the slippery rocks. One of my Crocs came off and my bare foot scraped across the pebbles and rocks. My arms reached toward the shore, and as I splashed around hunting for something to pull myself up, I felt my pole strap come loose. My mind was racing as I tried to think of how to regain my balance, wondered what gear was getting wet in my partially submerged pack, and worried about hypothermia.

When I got my feet underneath me and regained my balance, I glanced back to make sure Dad was OK and his face was scrunched in concentration. He was halfway across the river. I flung my pack onto the shore before even stepping out of the water. I pulled the soaked camera out of my hipbelt pocket and took out the batteries and memory card. Quickly I unbuckled my pack and started throwing gear on the riverbank. I was terrified that my sleeping bag would be wet. To my amazement, nothing inside my pack had even gotten damp.

I climbed onto the bank beside my scattered gear and stood there dripping water and shivering. I looked down forlornly at my one Croc.

Dad stepped carefully onto the shore beside me. "Are you all right?" he asked, flicking his eyes from my head to my toes.

"I think so. I'm soaked, but somehow my gear all seems to be dry."

He stared down the river where we could see my pole caught on a fallen tree. Further down, my Croc swirled in the current at the edge of a rock outcropping. Against our better judgment, Dad went back in after my gear. We weren't sure how I would successfully make any upcoming river crossings without my shoe or pole. His rescue mission was successful.

Dad plopped down on a rock beside me and reached for his boots. "I'm done with river crossings for today. Once was a new experience. Twice was practice. Seven times is ridiculous. We keep crossing the same damn river. If we get to another ford, I'm camping right there."

"I'm OK with that." A cold chill ran down my back and I stomped my boot-clad feet. "Let's go find a camping spot."

Dad followed me down the trail, limping on his swollen knee. We walked in silence for about a quarter mile. I was thinking through my plan for when we found a spot to camp. I needed to dry my clothes, eat some hot food, and, of course, set up my tent. Getting dry and warm quickly was imperative. Depending on how far we walked before camping, my clothes might already be partially dry.

Completely lost in thought, it took me a minute to recognize that the trail had once again dead-ended at the river. I flung my pack on the ground, fully prepared to camp right there.

"No." Dad leaned around me to stare. "You're kidding me."

"An eighth river crossing isn't something to joke about."

Dad pressed his lips together and was silent for a minute. Then he propped his foot up on a rock and began untying his laces.

"What happened to, 'I'm done'?" I asked, watching in surprise.

"I changed my mind. I either have to cross it now or dread crossing it first thing in the morning. I'd rather get it over with."

On the other side, Dad found a hidden trail to a perfect campsite. There were benches made from stacked flat stones, a rock fire circle, and plenty of level spaces to sleep. We made quick work of setting up our tents and I immediately began building a fire to brighten our moods and dry our clothes. That was when Dad tried to light the camp stove and nearly set his face—and the surrounding woods—on fire. It had been a long, exhausting, frustrating day.

"You're sure you're OK?" I asked.

"Yeah." He ran a hand across his face and shook his head. "I don't know what I did wrong."

"It might not have been you. Something might have been wrong with the stove. If you want, I'll cook dinner after I build us a fire."

He nodded and tossed some sticks into the fire circle.

We were both quiet as I reassembled the stove and lit it. While the water boiled I told him, "I have something for you."

"What is it?"

"You know those aluminum bags we were using to insulate our food while it rehydrated?"

"Yep."

"I got frustrated with the way they kept tearing in our packs, so I have a new option to try." I handed him a rectangular blue nylon bag that zipped across the top. "It's a Brownie Bag."

He turned it over in his hands. "Did you make this?"

"I did. It's quilted using four different layers of insulation. I have one too. They should keep our food nice and hot. The zipper-pulls are glow-in-the-dark so they're easy to find at night. And they also double as water-proof sit-upons." I demonstrated by sliding mine underneath me on the rock.

"These are neat," Dad said. "I like the name too. Let's try them out."

Our dinner cooked successfully, but Dad wouldn't eat more than a few bites. I got mad and we had our first hiking-partner fight. I worried that if he didn't learn to eat on our practice trips we would never make it on the JMT. Appropriate caloric intake is vital to the success of a long-distance hike. When we retired to our separate tents earlier than usual, I was still annoyed, but I slept soundly after all the events of the day.

Dad was gun-shy about using the stove in the morning, following the incident from the previous night, so he waited on coffee until I stirred from my tent. I set water on the stove to boil and poured instant coffee and powdered creamer into our goblets.

"Do you want grits or oatmeal?" Dad asked.

"Oatmeal, please."

He set two Ziplocs of oatmeal on the rock beside our goblets.

I guess he's going to eat.

Minutes later I poured the boiling water into the goblets and Ziplocs. While we waited for our oatmeal to hydrate, I scalded my tongue on my first sip of delicious coffee. *Only in the woods could instant coffee taste as good as Starbucks.*

Dad ate a hearty breakfast and we had a productive conversation about what we could change to encourage him to eat more consistently on the trail. I felt much better when he acknowledged that something had to change. Once we had cleared the air, he confessed concern over his still-swollen knee. He wanted to get back to the car that night if possible in case it got even worse the following day. We studied the trail map and decided on a shorter route back to the car. We had no way of knowing what river crossings lay in front of us, but we doubted it could be any worse than retracing our steps from the day before.

We hadn't gone far when we came to another bridge-less river crossing—our tenth. As we were lacing our boots back up on the opposite bank, Dad said sarcastically, "Hey, Michelle, thanks again for inviting me."

Why do I keep choosing disastrous trails?

We walked a few more minutes in silence before he spoke again.

"Do you have Janice's email address?"

"Yes. Why?"

"I'd like to send her a detailed review of this trail."

Dad fording a river in Pisgah National Forest

8

UPHEAVAL

Dad and I took another trip in early April on the Foothills Trail in South Carolina. We spent a long weekend backpacking approximately thirty miles with Gary, a friend of Dad's. Our three-day trip from Laurel Valley to Bad Creek Access was a success except for Dad's continued lack of appetite. Gary told me that although he had hiked with many groups, this was the first time he had ever seen a backpacker without a desire to eat. Dad and I strategized about food again and I remained hopeful that he would develop an appetite after a few days on the trail that summer. I just hoped he wouldn't accumulate enough of a calorie deficit to feel weak before his appetite kicked in.

About a month later, Dad went on his first backpacking trip without me. He and his friend Lamar were planning to tackle the entire seventy-seven-mile Foothills Trail. Dad excitedly gathered his gear and food for the trip. He even discussed in detail his plans to prevent his previous habit of skipping meals on the trail. I felt proud of his preparations and encouraged by his attention to food selections. We didn't have many more practice trips left, and I wanted to be confident about his food consumption before we left for California. I spoke to Dad the night before he left on his Foothills trip, and he sounded like a kid waiting for Santa on Christmas Eve. I suspected he wouldn't sleep a wink.

When Dad had decided to learn how to backpack, Mom had insisted that he buy a GPS tracking device. I didn't love the idea, because for me the woods are largely about escaping technology. I didn't want to have to think about turning it on each morning, sending messages regularly, or worrying whether the batteries were working. Also, on principle I believe you shouldn't be out in the remote wilderness if you need a GPS to feel safe. But I wanted Dad to backpack with me, and that meant Mom had to be comfortable with our safety. I agreed to learn to use the device if they purchased it. Dad did the research and we settled on a DeLorme InReach. For a monthly fee, the DeLorme transmits the user's exact GPS location at set durations. These points are transmitted to a website where authorized viewers can follow the hiker on a map. This meant Mom could track us almost in real time. By looking at the timestamps on the transmission points, she could even gauge our speed.

An additional bonus feature of the DeLorme is that it can send and receive messages using satellite technology. The user preprograms three messages that can be sent directly from the device with the push of a button. Ours were programmed to send, "Hi ho, hi ho, it's off to hike we go," "Still going strong!" and, "Another day completed. Setting up camp." We also had the ability to use the DeLorme in conjunction with our cell phones to type and receive personalized messages. Lastly, and most reassuringly for Mom, the DeLorme has an SOS button in the event that a hiker needs to be rescued.

We agreed with Mom we would send a message at the start and end of each day at a minimum, and we would check for messages from her once a day. However, we also agreed that she wouldn't contact the authorities with concerns about our safety unless she hadn't seen movement on the GPS tracker or heard from us in more than forty-eight hours. Since technology can have glitches for any number of reasons, we didn't want one or two missed contacts to be a reason for immediate concern.

Dad and I had practiced with the DeLorme on day hikes, and he took it on his trip with his friend Lamar. His messages the first night were enthusiastic. He and Lamar had enjoyed a successful first day and found an ideal camping spot. Unfortunately, the trip didn't continue so perfectly.

The next morning Dad again experienced heart rate struggles. Despite many breaks, staying well hydrated, and taking the mileage slowly, he just couldn't seem to keep his heart rate down. By late afternoon he had developed an intense headache and was experiencing general malaise.

When Dad's symptoms didn't abate overnight, he made the wise decision to leave the trail. Thankfully, they had camped near a park service road. Mom and Lamar's wife came to collect them after receiving a message Dad had sent on the DeLorme. When I spoke to him later that day he was disappointed and embarrassed, but safe. Dad followed up with his doctor and cardiologist, who didn't find anything concerning. Still, he and I were both worried. If this happened in California, we would be a helicopter ride away from help.

I was driving home from work the next day when Dad called.

"Hey. I want to talk to you about the JMT," he began.

"OK."

"I'm just going to be completely honest with you and lay it out there. We knew from the beginning that the plans were tentative and things could change. My doctors haven't found any specific cause for concern, but the reality is that we don't know if my heart rate is going to act up again.

"The way I see it, we have three options. One, we go out there and just hike less mileage, see some sights, have some fun. I would be OK with that, but I don't know if you would be disappointed if we didn't hike the entire trail. Two, we go out there and try for the whole thing, but we recognize that it just may not happen. Three, you find someone else to go with. And, if you choose option three, I won't be upset at all."

"I don't like any of those options," I told him honestly, my voice flat and dejected. I've never been able to hide my emotions well.

"I know, but it's the reality."

"I'm just not sure that going out there and doing less mileage would be any safer. We would still be in the middle of nowhere. We would still be at altitude. Plus, hiking fewer miles per day actually means carrying more weight because we would have longer distances between resupply destinations and would need to carry more food."

"I hadn't thought about the pack weight. Still, after what happened on the hike last week I just don't think we can realistically go ahead thinking we—*I*—can do the whole trail."

I took a deep breath through my nose and let it out slowly through my mouth. "I agree." I willed my voice to remain at a normal octave. "I'd also never forgive myself if something happened to you while we were out there."

"The bottom line is that if I go on this trip at all now, your mother's going to be worried the entire time. And you and I are both going to worry too. It'll always be in the back of our minds."

"I know," I agreed. *This is* not *how this was supposed to go.*

"I think you should look into finding a replacement partner. Do you know someone who would go with you?"

I swallowed hard to push down the tears I was fighting and tried to stop my voice from wobbling. "I might. But I wanted to do this with you."

"I did too. But this is *your* dream, not mine. I don't want you to give up on this just because I have to. We can still hike together. Just not the JMT."

I said a pleasant (and I hoped believably cheery) goodbye to Dad. When I got home, I curled up on the swing bed on my screened porch and cried. Although I knew Dad was making the right decision, I had set my heart on sharing this trip with him. We had worked hard on preparations together and I had had so much fun sharing the time with him. I cried over all the physical training he had done for a trip he wouldn't take. I cried over all the money he had spent on camping gear because of me. I cried over all the time he had spent on arrangements for hotels and permits.

But mostly I cried over the experience I thought we were going to share that we now wouldn't. One by one I erased the mental pictures I had created of us on our trip: an image of us arriving at the airport with our packs, an image of us on the bus to Yosemite, an image of us by the JMT terminus sign, and countless images of us grinning from mountaintops and posing beside our campsites.

Only three months remained before the start date, and I had no hiking partner.

The next day I called Sarah. I had met Sarah in 2013 at an Appalachian Trail festival called Trail Days in Damascus, Virginia. We had both been there as vendors. Sarah was selling her famous AT blaze poster and her trail photography, and I was selling my AT book.

It was my first festival as a vendor, and I was extremely nervous. Sarah had been the first person I met when I arrived in town, and we had become fast friends as I helped her set up her booth. Over the course of the weekend I had told her I was planning to hike the John Muir Trail the following August. She had joked that if I needed a backup partner, she was available. The JMT was on her bucket list too.

Since meeting, Sarah and I had seen each other at a couple of other festivals, including Trail Fest in Hot Springs, North Carolina. During that festival I stayed at Sarah's house and had the chance to meet her husband, Morgan.

On the phone Sarah and I talked about the 2014 Trail Days festival we'd be attending in a week. Then I asked her, "Were you serious when you said you would be my backup hiking partner this summer?"

"Totally!" she affirmed.

"Well, I happen to be in need of one."

"Wait, what happened to hiking with your dad?"

I proceeded to tell Sarah about Dad's heart rate episodes and our concerns about his hiking remotely and at altitude. As an experienced hiker and backcountry medical provider, Sarah understood and agreed with our concerns.

"I know this isn't much notice," I continued, "but the spot on the permit is yours if you want it."

"I want to talk to Morgan, of course, but, yes," she gushed. "I hate this for your dad, but ahhh! I'm so excited! The JMT has always been on my list, and I didn't know when it would be able to happen, you know? Morgan can't leave the farm in the summer because harvest is the busiest season for us."

"Right."

"We had talked about the JMT for our honeymoon, but once we bought the farm the timing didn't work out. I would hate to leave him during harvest time, but who knows when I'll have this opportunity again. I'm hoping I'll be pregnant by next summer, so it would have to wait awhile."

Sarah and I briefly discussed dates, equipment, and cost. We agreed to talk more at Trail Days the following weekend.

Within days Sarah had called back to confirm. I had a new hiking partner. Granted, she was a partner with whom I had never, ever hiked. A partner with whom I had never spent more than intermittent moments at crowded festivals. But, a partner who had willingly jumped in at the last moment. A partner I knew could do this because she had thru-hiked the AT, and a partner who had immediately become excited about this adventure.

We waited until we had Trail Days behind us, and then we planned in earnest. Sarah played an incredible game of catch-up since I had been preparing physically and mentally since the previous September. Thankfully, Sarah's lifestyle meant she was already largely ready for the trip before she ever knew she was going to take it: in addition to working outside doing manual labor on her farm, she was also a river guide and ski instructor, which meant she was in phenomenal physical shape. She already owned all of the gear except for the bear canister, which she borrowed from Dad. She was a pro at dehydrating food because she had dehydrated meals for her AT hike and for her honeymoon bike trip. And, since she had done the AT, she was intimately familiar with the realities of long-distance hiking.

Sarah booked her plane tickets, I called repeatedly to confirm our hotel reservation and airport shuttle, and we both dehydrated food like crazy. After some research on tent logistics, Sarah found out that freestanding tents were recommended on the JMT because staking can be difficult on the rocky areas of the trail. Since Sarah's tent was not freestanding and I owned a two-person freestanding tent, we agreed that we would share my tent and split the weight so that she didn't have to buy a new tent just for this trip. I was a little bummed about not being able to use my new one-person tent, but Sarah was certainly sacrificing a lot to plan this trip at the last minute. Changing tents seemed a small price to pay for having a hiking partner.

We met at my house for a planning session and Sarah reviewed the itinerary I had prepared. I knew we wouldn't stick to the itinerary, but we needed an outline so that we could estimate arrival dates and food quantities for mail-drop pickups.

The schedule for the first half of the trail was simple, but since the second half of the JMT is remote, there aren't many options for resupply. We arranged and rearranged the daily mileage plan for the last part of trail and couldn't find one we liked. Some hikers take a side trail leading to a road and hitchhike into Bishop, California, but we didn't want to add nearly twenty extra miles and spend an entire day resupplying, so we ruled out Bishop.

Other people carry about twelve days of food, but that's a lot of weight. I also suspect that you have to break the rules to do this since all smell-ables are required to be in a bear canister. I can't conceive of any way that twelve days of food would fit unless you ate only oatmeal.

Sarah and I spread out our meals and supplies on my floor and kitchen island and began dividing them into piles for each resupply. As we sorted and re-sorted, we discussed excitements and fears about the trail. We had both experienced and witnessed hiking partner drama before, and we agreed to communicate clearly if we were annoying one another and to take space when we needed it to avoid problems in such close quarters.

After a very late night, all of our resupply buckets were finally packed. A few days later, at the last minute, we decided to take the financial hit and book a pack mule service to bring out our final resupply. We would ship our final resupply bucket to an outfitter, and a cowboy leading pack mules would meet us at a predetermined destination to deliver our supplies. With no time to spare, I repackaged and labeled our last resupply.

The next morning I dressed in business attire and loaded the resupply buckets in my car. I had an unusual day ahead of me. A month before, I'd received an unexpected phone call offering me a job interview. I had been surprised because it had been a long time since I'd completed the detailed application process and I'd thought the opportunity had come and gone.

Originally I'd learned about this job from Mark DeJong, a friend I knew through a previous EMS job. Mark had changed jobs too—he was now working for a Fortune 500 company. His job entailed a combination of EMS, fire, safety, and security. He had said it paid really well and had excellent benefits—and they were hiring. I had agreed to think about it.

And I had thought about it. *Am I looking for a job? Am I happy?* The truth had been that I *was* happy. There were many rewarding things about my job in EMS—but the paycheck wasn't one of them. I wanted a job where I could earn more money, build a larger retirement fund, and set myself up for opportunities to advance. *I would be a fool to ignore an exceptional opportunity with a well-reputed company.* So I had applied.

After leaving my treasured mail drops with the post office, I drove to a three-part interview. It went well and I was optimistic, but I also knew that a number of people had been interviewed. I hoped for the best and turned my attention back to preparing for the JMT.

Two days later I received a phone call.

"I wanted to let you know that we were really impressed with your interview," the hiring manager said, "and it is unanimous that we want to offer you the position." He reviewed the salary and benefit information and told me they were hoping to fill the position by August 4.

My heart started hammering in my chest. *Oh, no.* My hike was starting on August 2. *Will I be forced to choose between a job and my hike?*

"Would that work for you?" he asked.

It was the moment of truth. I swallowed forcefully. "I'm extremely excited about this opportunity, and I'm almost positive it's the right fit for me," I began. "However, to be completely honest, I have a bit of a complication. I have a trip planned that interferes with the start date. You may remember from my interview that I'm a hiker, and I've been training for another long-distance hike for over a year—one of my bucket list items. The entire trip is booked, including cross-country flights and backcountry permits that are difficult to obtain. I have quite a bit of money and time invested in this experience, and it would be devastating to cancel. I don't want you to get the impression that I believe play comes before work—because it doesn't—but this is an extenuating circumstance."

The hiring manager expressed understanding and asked me when I planned to return from my trip. He told me that he would have to talk the situation over with the manager and would get back to me as soon as possible. In a mere hour, which felt like an eternity, he called me back. He told me that he'd talked with the manager and that she was more concerned with getting the right person in the position than with rushing a timeline. They generously offered to let me start on September 2 instead, saying that my adventurous spirit was something they had appreciated about me during my interview. Graciously, but nervously, I accepted.

I hung up and sat on my porch staring into the front yard, feeling nervous. This was the first time I would be leaving a job I loved for an opportunity about which I knew little. My life was about to change dramatically. But first, it was time to hike the John Muir Trail.

9

LEAVING ON A JETPLANE

July 30, 2014

"Hey, hiker girl!" Dad greeted me on the phone.

"Hey, Dad." *No more "Partner."*

"Are you ready for tomorrow?"

"I guess. I've been through my gear so many times I'm not even processing it anymore."

"Knowing you, you've probably been fully packed for weeks."

I glanced sheepishly at the filled bag at my feet. Packing and repacking is how I release excited energy before trips.

"I'll be at your house to pick you up at three this afternoon."

I was spending the final night before my flight at my parents' house so that I could see family members who were visiting from out of town.

"Sounds good. I'll need to make one stop on the way to your house."

"For what?"

"I need to buy a shirt."

"You want to *shop* the day before this trip?" Dad asked, his voice managing to convey both amazement and annoyance.

"Well…yes. I talked to Sarah last night and she had an email from a friend who has done the JMT. The one piece of advice her friend gave was to wear a long-sleeved, collared shirt for sun protection. As much as I don't want to wear that type of shirt, I've heard the same advice twice now. I don't want to end up sunburned and miserable—and we both know how easily I burn. So I guess I'll buy a shirt."

Typically concise, Dad just replied, "I'll see you at three."

When my dad arrived—a predictable fifteen minutes early—my cousin Ryan and his girlfriend Stephanie were with him. They were visiting from Florida with Ryan's parents, my Aunt Barbie and Uncle Dwight. Ryan and Stephanie had tagged along with Dad to see my house and spend a few extra minutes with me before I left.

At REI the four of us probably looked at every single women's button-down, long-sleeved, wicking shirt in stock. The irony of being back in the store where Dad and I had first bought gear together, and where he had bought a button-down shirt that *I* had questioned, was not lost on me.

With Stephanie's patient input, I settled on a maroon sun-protective shirt. It wouldn't win any fashion contests, but I hoped it would spare my startlingly pale skin from high-altitude sunburn. Eighty (painfully spent) dollars later, we were back on the road.

I hated that this family visit overlapped with the day I was preparing to leave town. I wanted to enjoy an evening of visiting with them, but in the recesses of my mind I worried over trip details. *Is there anything I could leave behind to lighten my pack weight? Could I have forgotten anything?*

With amusement, everyone watched as I emptied and repacked my backpack one final time. I laid hands on each piece of equipment to assure myself that all of my gear was accounted for. My relatives all took turns trying on my pack and marveling at the weight. Then they watched as I wrestled the pack into a nylon laundry bag and duct-taped it shut. I was worried about my pack straps getting torn on a conveyer belt at the airport.

When the extended family had retired for the night, I retreated to Dad's study where I settled lotus style on the thick carpet with my airplane bag in front of me. I pulled out my paperwork folder. Copies of my travel itinerary and Sarah's—*check*. Contact information for the hotel—*check*. Itinerary—*check*. JMT guidebook—*check*. Maps—*check*.

I'm not normally a nervous person, but preparing for long trips and plane rides turns me into an obsessive-compulsive triple- and quadruple-checker. I like to be in control and don't enjoy being at the mercy of air-traffic patterns and shuttle schedules. While I was quadruple-checking,

Mom appeared at the open French doors holding a Coke Zero. "You ready?" she asked.

I ran my hand across my face. "I guess."

"You're ready." She sat down on the chair across from me. "Have you looked at the wildfire updates recently?"

I snapped my head up. "The *what?*"

"You *do* know there's a wildfire in Yosemite, don't you?"

I blinked at her with my mouth hanging partially open.

"You haven't seen it on the news?"

"Mom, I haven't had cable in seven years."

"Let me grab my computer."

I stared at the flowered pattern on the carpet and took a few deep breaths while I waited for her to come back. *What are we going to do if the woods around the JMT are on fire?* She returned a minute later holding her MacBook. I heard the sound of keys tapping.

"OK," she said. "Let's see what the latest update is." I could hear her clicking on different links. "It looks like the fire is mostly under control now. Some of the access roads to Yosemite are closed, though."

"You're kidding."

She clicked some more. "Which entrance road are you using?"

"I have no idea, Mom. I'm taking a shuttle."

"Well, what direction is Mammoth Lakes from Yosemite?"

I stared at her blankly. "You know I have no concept of direction." For as much as I spend in the woods, I have an abominable sense of direction.

"Michelle!" she chided. "You don't know what side of the park you're entering?"

My face remained unchanged.

"I don't know how you made it to Maine," she mumbled under her breath. Then at a normal volume she continued, "Let's just look it up."

She determined that the Yosemite entrance road Sarah and I would take was unaffected by the fires. Parts of the park were closed, though, and we would need to monitor the conditions when our planes landed.

Great.

July 31, 2014

Both of my parents drove me to the airport. Dad had volunteered to go alone, but we both knew Mom would go too. She isn't a morning person, but the need to lay her eyes on me as I departed was stronger than her desire to stay in bed a few more minutes.

As Dad drove through fog and rain, Mom turned around from the passenger seat and handed me an envelope, a card, and a folded piece of computer paper.

"Here are your letters. One from me, one from Barbie, and one I printed from an email from your friend Carrie."

"Thanks." I tucked them carefully into my travel folder for safekeeping.

Dad made eye contact in the rearview mirror and told me, "I broke the rules—not that that should come as a surprise."

I noted the rebellious twinkle in his eyes. "OK?"

"Instead of giving you a letter to open on your hike, I have this." He handed me a pocket-sized spiral bound notebook. "Open it now and read the first page only."

"So you broke my rules, but I have to follow yours?"

"Exactly."

I opened to the first page:

Michelle,

I know you asked those close to you to write letters that you can read from time to time on the trail for encouragement. But I have chosen to do it a little differently (there's a surprise, right?!?).

Instead there is—after this little introduction—one page for each day of your hike, and my hope is that you'll read it sometime during the day. I've hiked with you enough to know how much you enjoy "debating and pondering," so I hope these little tidbits will provide content for some of that pondering.

I enjoyed training for this hike and look forward to getting out more after you finish it. While I will miss doing this trail with you, I know it was the right decision, and I'm at peace with it.

I'm proud of you, I love you, and I'll be your biggest cheerleader for the next 25 days!

Dad

"Thanks, Dad." I blinked back tears and tucked the tiny notebook into my growing folder. *He's supposed to be going on this trip, not handing me a motivational letter.*

My flight from Greenville, South Carolina, to Atlanta was uneventful and my layover in Atlanta was the perfect length of time. Sarah and I united at LAX. We had time to share garlic fries while we waited for our final flight to Mammoth Lakes, California.

The plane was tiny, so we were spared the roulette game of determining seatmates by swapping to sit together. One complimentary glass of wine beside a booger-smeared window later, we were landing in Mammoth Lakes. It had been a turbulent flight, so I was glad to be back on the ground.

We landed in what appeared to be a parking lot surrounded by a chain link fence. Abutting the fence were one small metal building and one plastic-looking white dome. We deplaned directly onto the asphalt. I could smell and taste smoke as soon as I stepped out the plane door. As I descended the rickety metal steps, I looked around in awe. Massive mountains loomed behind the plane. A large sign above a turnstile in the fence read "Mammoth Lakes 7,128 feet." *I haven't left the airport yet and this is officially the highest altitude I've ever experienced.*

As we were herded through a turnstile like cattle, I saw people pointing and waving at deplaning passengers from the other side of the chain link fence. I felt like a zoo exhibit. Glancing around in amazement, I spotted what had to be the luggage collection point.

"Sarah, look. You won't believe it."

In front of us was a wooden structure that almost resembled a three-sided trail shelter. It was basically a wooden shelf with a roof over it. One uniformed airport attendant was unloading luggage from a wheeled cart onto the shelf. The other Mammoth Lakes first-timers were evident from the amused expressions that mirrored our own. It was a relief to see my navy nylon bag on the shelf appearing relatively unscathed.

A single-lane road ran in front of the baggage claim shelter. I saw two shuttle buses and a couple of personal vehicles. There were no other cars in sight. Our hotel shuttle wasn't there, so we settled at an outdoor table to wait.

A group of three men with hiking backpacks stood nearby. One of them must have noticed the AT patch on Sarah's pack, and he approached us.

"You've hiked on the AT?" he asked her.

"Yeah," she replied.

"What part?"

"All of it, actually."

He wrinkled his nose skeptically. "Did you thru-hike?"

"I did." She gestured at me. "So did she. Over two thousand miles and all we got was a patch," she laughed.

I glanced up and smiled.

"Now we're going to thru-hike the JMT," Sarah added.

"Yeah, well, hiking out here is completely different." The man shouldered his dirt-free, scrape-free, incredibly large pack.

"We're looking forward to it," Sarah responded agreeably, ignoring his know-it-all tone. "Where are you guys hiking?"

"In Yosemite."

"Cool."

"Good luck with the JMT," he sneered. His patronizing tone made it clear he thought we needed luck to be successful. "Those girls are trying to do the JMT," he told his friends with a laugh as he boarded a shuttle.

"Did you hear that asshole?" Sarah asked me.

I glanced up from the folder where I was hunting for the hotel phone number. "Yeah."

"I hope we see him on the trail so he can be outdone by two women. Ugh." She plopped down in the chair beside me. "*Good luck with that,*" she mimicked. "*I'm just out here with my brand-new pack that I don't even know how to pack and my shiny new boots.*"

I shook my head.

"Asshole. Guaranteed we make it farther than him."

"I doubt we'll ever see them again," I told her. "I'm going to call the hotel to find out about our shuttle. I'm hungry and ready to be settled in for the night."

I moved around until I found a spot with one bar of cell service. The receptionist who answered at the hotel told me they didn't have an airport shuttle scheduled for that day.

I took a deep breath of smoky air and immediately started coughing. I closed my eyes and repeated to myself, *Honey not vinegar, honey not vinegar, honey not vinegar.* My mom has reminded me five hundred times that you catch more flies with honey than with vinegar. Attacking people with vinegar is often my natural inclination. After flying cross-country to find my thrice-confirmed shuttle absent, I was feeling particularly full of vinegar. With enough honey to attract Yogi Bear from the next county, I re-negotiated a shuttle.

The hotel lobby at the Sierra Nevada was charming. It was made of large exposed wooden beams and had warm lodge-like furniture. There was a grand piano, a huge 360-degree fireplace with padded seating all the way around, a well-stocked coffee station, and a bar. I felt myself relax.

By the time we resolved an issue with the reservation (again using honey when I felt like vinegar) and made it to our hotel room, I was worn out and could tell I was on the verge of becoming hangry (hungry angry). We opened the door to a hot, airless room. *Ugh!* I dumped my backpack on the floor and flopped down on one of the beds.

When I picked up the phone to call the reception desk to inquire about shuttles to Yosemite, the line was dead. *Seriously? Can one thing go smoothly?* Unamused and developing a throbbing headache, I walked barefoot to the front desk. The receptionist knew nothing about the shuttle and claimed to have no pamphlets or other references. Since the town of Mammoth Lakes survives on tourism, I was a little befuddled.

A few internet searches later Sarah and I had what we hoped was the correct information for the morning. A shuttle across the street would take us to a stop where we would catch the YARTS (Yosemite Area Regional Transportation System) bus twenty minutes later. YARTS would take us directly to Yosemite.

Public transportation is not something I deal with often, and it was making me nervous. *What if we miss the bus? What if we get on the wrong bus?* I recalled Lark's amazement that even though I would willingly go off into unknown woods alone, I would not ride the D.C. metro by myself to meet her at her office when I visited. This made complete sense to me. I wasn't nervous about hiking the John Muir Trail—I was nervous about *getting* to it.

Sarah and I left the hotel on foot. I noticed with trepidation that I was breathing much more heavily than normal even though I was on relatively flat ground without a pack. *Altitude? Smoke in the air? Nerves?* I pushed my worries aside and took in Mammoth Lakes. We backtracked to the entrance to town and took photos by a large sign with the beginning of a John Muir quote: "The mountains are calling...."

As we approached a pizza place, we spotted some rugged-looking people with backpacks sitting in a bus shelter. Sarah asked, "JMT?"

"Yeah, man! Finished today!" one hiker enthused, pumping his fist in the air.

"Woot, woot!" yelled another.

"You go!" Sarah cheered as we crossed the street and high-fived them.

We probably didn't appear very hiker-credible in our jeans and cotton t-shirts without packs. Sarah told them, "We start the day after tomorrow."

"You'll have good timing," the girl told us. "The wildflowers weren't quite blooming yet when we went through, but they should be perfect for you. We had a lot of snow still."

Interacting with hikers who were still grungy from days in the woods made the trip seem much more real. By the time our pizza was on the table, I was beginning to relax. *We're* in *Mammoth Lakes. This is really happening.* "Tomorrow we'll be in Yosemite," I announced.

Sarah grinned. "And the day after that we'll be on the John Muir Trail."

We high-fived across the table.

Back in our hotel room, we retired to our separate sides of the room. Sarah turned on the TV, but I had no desire to watch. Although I had sorted and organized my gear a hundred times, I needed to do it again to assure myself that everything was here with me in California. I unpacked each item from my pack and my airplane bag. I planned to make two piles—a big pile of things to pack in my backpack, and a small pile of things to leave in storage at the hotel. I wanted my backpack ready to go before I went to bed.

I dumped out my blue electronics dry bag. In front of me was a tangle of cords and devices: an iPhone, an iPhone cord, a Powerocks portable battery charger, a DeLorme GPS unit with spare batteries, a Kindle, and a camera with a charger. Famed hikers Grandma Gatewood and Gene Espy would probably be horrified at this technological mess. To be honest, *I* was a bit horrified. This was a huge change from having only a camera nine years ago on the AT.

Sorting the rest of my gear was easy. Town clothes stayed, trail clothes went. Town toiletries stayed, trail toiletries went. Town shoes stayed, Crocs and hiking shoes went. Everything else was trail gear. In five minutes I had my belongings completely sorted. I laid my hiking clothes out on a chair for the morning. Five more minutes was enough time to fully pack my backpack and stash it in the corner. I would add my abundant electronics in the morning and be ready to catch the shuttle.

While Sarah showered I settled on the bed to flip through brochures I'd snagged from the lobby. I learned that Mammoth Lakes is located in Mono County, California, about 32 miles south of Yosemite National Park, and is home to around 8,000 people. It is bordered by the Ansel Adams and John Muir Wilderness Areas and has views of the Sherwin Range and Mammoth Mountain. Situated at 7,880 feet, the town is a popular place for high-altitude athletic training. The Mammoth Mountain Ski Resort is a top ski destination in California and is integral to the town's economy. *Maybe I'll come back and ski here one day.*

I was exhausted from a full day of travel and anticipation for our hike. I read a few chapters on my Kindle and plugged it in for a final charge before turning out my light at ten thirty.

10

YOSEMITE

August 1, 2014

All night I felt like I was sucking air through cheesecloth while wearing a corset, thanks to the smoke-tinged air from the forest fire. *Is this what asthma feels like?* The back of my throat tickled and I had a dry cough that made me get up every hour or so for a sip of funny-tasting tap water. I tossed and turned uncomfortably on pillows that were too tall and firm, with cases that were too starched. After a miserable few hours, I was awake for good at three thirty in the morning.

Since Sarah was still asleep in the next bed, I pulled on jeans and slipped out of the room. I grabbed a coffee in the lobby and wandered outside to a red Adirondack chair at an empty fire circle behind the hotel. At that hour, I had the entire space to myself. The air was just as smoky outside, but the slight breeze made me feel like my lungs were marginally more functional. While I sipped my coffee, I stared at the mountains in the hazy darkness and visualized the upcoming weeks. Backpacking trips tend to make me pensive, and I wanted to identify what I was hoping to think through on this trip.

The mountains in front of me were the largest I had ever seen, and they weren't even particularly close yet. I couldn't imagine the views I would soon have while standing on top of and below these towering peaks. The sun peeped over the horizon too quickly, spreading oranges and purples above the mountaintops. I read a few more chapters in the pinkish early morning light while the last vestiges of purple and orange faded into morning blue.

Once Sarah was awake, we quickly readied ourselves to leave. I tried to relish my shower since I wasn't sure when I would take one again. Almost reverently I donned my uniform for the next three weeks—a khaki hiking skirt, the maroon long-sleeved button-down SPF shirt, and wool socks with a flower pattern around the cuffs. Taking a last look in the mirror, I looped my collarbone-length dark brown hair into a low ponytail.

Sarah had on her uniform too—coral running shorts, a pale green long-sleeved button-down SPF shirt, and wool socks. As she plaited her waist-length light brown hair into a braid, I put the finishing touches on my backpack. We stowed our plane bags in the hotel storage room to pick up at the end of our hike and paid our bill.

The YARTS bus was exactly on time, but we had arrived early enough to get coffee and breakfast at McDonald's across the street. We stored our packs underneath the bus and took seats near the front. I didn't like having my backpack out of sight in the storage bin, but I was grateful for a safe way to travel the four hours to the park. If it weren't for the shuttle, we would be hitchhiking.

Across the aisle was a family with a toddler and a baby. The mother nursed the younger child while the older child chatted enthusiastically with Sarah and me. The family had been out on a week-long backpacking trip and they all seemed relaxed and happy. I filed away this memory so that I would have no excuse to delay camping trips when I had young children one day.

The bus made a number of stops as it ventured away from Mammoth Lakes. At one of the early stops three women with backpacking packs boarded the bus. I noted with interest that each of the women had on three visible layers of socks. Sarah wandered down the bus aisle to speak with them and found out that they were also thru-hiking the JMT. She was not able to learn much else, though, because they were not particularly friendly. Since we never learned their names, we took to calling them the Three Sock Tribe. This was the beginning of a tradition where Sarah and I gave secret nicknames to many of the hikers we met.

From the bus window I stared out at towering mountains that were completely different from any I'd ever seen. I took picture after picture through the smeared glass. Even though I knew the pictures wouldn't be clear, and even though I knew I would soon see a thousand prettier views, I couldn't stop taking photos. Just as I was starting to feel the stirrings of motion sickness, the bus stopped at Yosemite. I plan to visit every national park in my lifetime, but Yosemite was the first I had been to on the West Coast, and I was thrilled to check it off my list.

When we had left Mammoth Lakes, the weather had been pleasant. As soon as I stepped off the bus in Yosemite, though, the heat was oppressive. The smoky air and high temperature made it difficult to breathe and my eyes watered from the assault of the smoke. *How do the wildland firefighters stand this?* Beads of sweat began rolling down my spine before I had even collected my pack from under the bus.

Our first order of business was to pick up our permit. I was still nervous that somehow we wouldn't get it, especially since the reservation was made in Dad's name. We followed signs pointing us toward the Valley Wilderness Center. By the time we left our packs on a bench next to a couple of others and stepped inside, I had already soaked my shirt with sweat. The thermometer keychain on my pack said it was close to a hundred degrees.

Inside I gave a young, shaggy-haired ranger Dad's name. I barely breathed while he scanned a sheet of paper. To my excessive relief, he pulled out our permit without delay. Before releasing the permit, the ranger reviewed every single bullet point on the back. He was exceedingly thorough and went so far as to underline each and every word as he emphasized the rules and regulations. The ranger beside him actually processed two groups with permits before our ranger finished with our one. Sarah and I had to avoid looking at each other to keep from laughing. He cautioned us that the permit had to be stored somewhere easily accessible at all times so that we would be able to show it to rangers at their request.

I paused on the front porch to safely store the permit and Yosemite map in a Ziploc bag in the top of my pack. Finally confident that our hard-earned permit was secure, I took my turn at the ritual of weighing my pack on the hook-scale hanging from the porch ceiling. I was a little sad to see it tip the scale at thirty-four pounds. *And that's without the five pounds of water I'll carry tomorrow.* Even though this was heavier than I would have liked, I knew I could carry the weight since I had started the AT with forty pounds.

Sarah and I shopped for souvenirs in the Yosemite Valley Visitor Center and mailed our findings home from the on-site post office. We were about to leave when we saw the sign for the Ansel Adams Gallery. Overwhelmed by the masses of people, Sarah was tempted to skip it and escape to a less-crowded area of the park. However, I knew that Ansel Adams was one of her role models as a professional photographer, so I encouraged her to at least take a peek while we were there.

We propped our packs on a bench and walked inside. The gallery contained work from Ansel Adams as well as contemporary photographers and artists. Outdoor enthusiasts appreciate Ansel Adams not only for the incredible scenes he caught on camera, but also for his environmental conservation efforts. After finding a few more mementos in the gallery, we had to make one more stop at the post office.

While Sarah mailed our package, I sat on a bench outside with our packs. A heavily bearded older man dressed in cargo pants and a worn wicking shirt approached me. "That's a big pack for someone your size," he observed condescendingly, gesturing at my backpack. "It won't be fun to carry that. You could probably really lighten that load."

Regardless of the size of the hiker, we all require the same gear. I resisted the urge to glare at him. "I'll be fine."

"Where are you planning to hike?" he asked, undeterred.

"We're doing the John Muir Trail."

"You're planning to do *all* of it?"

"Yes."

He shook his head. "I finished yesterday."

"Congratulations."

"It's not an easy hike. I hope you know what you're doing."

I intentionally kept my tone neutral. "I'm an experienced hiker."

He pointed at my AT patch. "On the AT?" He practically rolled his eyes. "This isn't like hiking on the East Coast. There's unpredictable weather, high altitudes, long sections without resupply—"

I took a deep breath and forced a smile. *Honey, not vinegar.* "Yes, I'm aware."

"You have a permit?"

This guy was really starting to tick me off. If I hadn't been sitting there watching Sarah's pack, I would have walked away and ended the conversation. I enunciated my answer with exaggerated politeness. "Yes, we have a permit."

"And a bear canister?"

I licked my lips and waited for a second before I answered. "Yes. We're fully prepared."

The conversation continued to deteriorate until eventually I stood up and turned my back toward him while pretending to look for something in my pack. He eventually took the hint and wandered off.

When Sarah came back I told her I had met another male backpacker who was skeptical about the possibility of two women from the East Coast completing the John Muir Trail.

"What an asshole."

"Yeah. He kept going on about how *hard* this trail is and how it's nothing like hiking on the *East* Coast."

"He sounds like more than an asshole—he's Captain Asshole. That should be his trail name."

I laughed.

"No, really. I wish I had been here," she responded. "I would have loved to say a few things to him. The negative attitudes about our hike are starting to piss me off. Point him out if you see him later."

To protect the park and prevent traffic problems, personal vehicles are not allowed in Yosemite. Since we still had daylight to burn, and since neither of us had any idea when we might have another opportunity to explore Yosemite, we hopped on the free transport bus. The route looped around Yosemite Valley and allowed us to see some of the views we would miss on the John Muir Trail. I had been getting a bit of a headache from the smoky air, so I was glad to sit back on the air-conditioned bus and enjoy the sights. I hadn't expected Yosemite Valley to be so hot.

From the bus windows we saw the location of Yosemite Falls, which was dry as it often is in August. We got off the bus at the stop for El Capitan and Cathedral Rocks. As we gazed up at the 3,593-foot summit of El Capitan, I reminded myself that we would camp more than a thousand feet above that the next night, and that we would not see a point that low again

until we had finished the JMT. It was hard to believe that the summit of
Mount Whitney was almost 11,000 feet above the top of this mountain
towering above me. We had some serious elevation to climb.

We finished the bus tour and made it back to the main area of
Yosemite. Backpackers are permitted to use a special campsite for one night
before and one night after their hikes. We were planning to stay at this site
and were ready to find it and get settled. The ranger had given us a rough
map of the location, but the directions were unclear.

According to a map we consulted, a different bus route would take us
to the backpackers' campground. The bus was packed, so we had to stand
in the aisle, awkwardly holding our packs. Many stops later, the bus dropped
us off beside a dirt road and a sign for a car-camping campground. The
information from the ranger told us to follow the signs from here to the
backpackers' campground. We walked down the dusty road and
encountered an unmanned information booth.

"So, I guess we won't be getting directions here," I observed drily. With
sweat dripping down my back and a scratchy throat, I was no longer amused
by the constant struggle to get anywhere on this trip.

"Maybe there's a map posted somewhere," Sarah suggested.

We saw signs warning of recent bear activity, signs explaining where to
wash dishes, signs with guidelines for generator usage, pictures of missing
hikers, and the schedule for horseback riding lessons. Finally, on a nearby
bulletin board, Sarah found a map. We took a picture for future reference
and started walking in what we hoped was the direction of the backpackers'
campground.

After a few wrong turns, we weaved our way around the horse stables,
past the bear-proofed dumpsters, through the car-camping area, around the
bathhouse, up a dirt path, over a bridge, and into the very full backpackers'
campground. There were people filling the small camping area as far as I
could see. I spotted at least thirty tents in small groups. We circled the area
trying to figure out where to set up camp. We ran into the Three Sock Tribe
and also saw Captain Asshole. Many hikers looked up as we passed, but no
one spoke to us or offered a spot. This was a stark contrast to the endlessly
welcoming community I was accustomed to encountering on hiking trips.

Sarah and I had paused to discuss the best place to set up among the crowds when we heard a voice.

"Hey, girls?"

A middle-aged couple was beckoning to us from a picnic table while the woman waved enthusiastically.

"There's a spot right here! We'd be glad to share our picnic table and the bear box. Come set up over here if you'd like."

"They seem a lot nicer than the Three Sock Tribe and Captain Asshole," Sarah observed as she unclipped her waist belt.

"Sold."

Frankly, I would have camped anywhere. I just wanted to put my pack down, eat some dinner, and go to sleep. The two preceding sleepless nights, exacerbated by the struggle to breathe in the smoke, were catching up to me.

We ate dinner with the couple, Allison and Tom, who were camping with their fourteen-year-old twin grandsons, Hezzie and David. After dinner Sarah went to take a few photos before the sunlight completely disappeared. While Allison and the boys played cards, Tom and I talked about previous travel adventures, philosophers, and books.

Sarah returned shortly and excitedly asked us to follow her. She had found a perfect view of Half Dome. About thirty yards later, as we stepped over fallen logs and into a small meadow, I was surprised to find myself out of breath. I pulled smoky air into my lungs and pushed it slowly back out as I looked up at the distant peak. It was hard to believe we would be standing on top of that peak in two days. I stared up at the mountain in the fading light until I caught my breath. From this perspective it was easy to see why people thought I was crazy to backpack. *What sane person chooses to walk up that carrying forty pounds?*

I decided to head back to the tent while Sarah wrapped up her photos. I was extremely tired and felt the throbbing beginnings of a headache behind my eyes as I zipped myself into the tent. I knew I desperately needed sleep, but I wanted to journal first.

In the tent I pulled out my clothes from their stuff sack. I had worried about being cold on this trip, and my "pajamas" were long underwear. It was clearly too hot for those. I tossed the whole bag to the bottom of the tent, took my socks off, and stretched out in my clothes. It was too hot to even consider getting in my fifteen-degree sleeping bag. *Will I be hot during this entire trip?*

I situated my belongings around my Therm-a-Rest and pulled out my journal for a brief entry. Only minutes after Sarah had joined me in the tent, I clicked off my headlamp and tried to get comfortable. It proved impossible. I was hot, excited, and having trouble breathing. The night seemed to last an eternity. I barely slept and had to get up multiple times to trek to the bathroom. I tried my hardest not to make noise, but it is impossible to get out of a tent quietly. I wondered how quickly Sarah would tire of my nighttime restlessness and worried I would keep her awake too. My chest felt heavy and my throat raw as I breathed in the smoky air and tossed and turned.

Tomorrow we start the John Muir Trail.

11

WHERE'S THE TRAIL?

Monday August 2, 2014

> Slept: Little Yosemite Valley Campground
> Miles: 5.0
> Weather: hot/sunny/smoky
> Dinner: walking hamburgers
> Mood: frustrated preparation didn't help more
> Letter: re-read Dad's intro
> Dad's quote of the day:

A JOURNEY OF A THOUSAND MILES BEGINS WITH A SINGLE STEP.
—LAO TZU

When the sun first peeked through the giant trees overhead and shone on our suffocatingly hot tent, my first emotion—despite a third sleepless night, the oppressive heat, and my seeming inability to breathe—was excitement.

Sarah and I had packed up and said goodbye to Tom and Allison early. With temperatures expected to exceed one hundred degrees in the valley, we wanted to start our day before the heat peaked. By the time we made it back to the (still unmanned) information kiosk by the car-camping area, my shirt was already soaked with sweat and my hair was plastered to my head. I felt like I was inside an oven.

We passed signs for stables, the bus around Yosemite, the trash bins, and a walking path, but there were none for the start of the JMT. After circling the dirt trails in frustration we decided to follow a worn walking path near the stables. We spotted the Three Sock Tribe ahead of us and took that as a positive sign that we were headed in the right direction. But after we had followed the path for a while and crossed the main road, we still hadn't seen any signs for the JMT.

"You'd think this would be more clear," I observed. "A lot of hikers must stay in the backpackers' campsite before starting the JMT since it's the only legal spot to sleep the night before."

"I know, right?"

I sucked in more smoky air. "Why aren't there signs?" When I had visualized the start of the trail I had imagined a beautiful, picturesque scene. I figured there would be a neatly sculpted stone archway or a giant, meticulously carved wooden sign. At this point I would've settled for a simple confirmation that we were moving in the right direction.

Finally we saw a sign on the road indicating that the JMT was ahead. Relief washed over us and we picked up our pace. But when we got to the area, it still didn't seem right. It wasn't the trail sign we had seen from the bus the day before.

A sign reading "Mist Trail" pointed toward the trail and indicated that Nevada Falls was ahead—nothing about the JMT. We wandered around the trailhead speaking with people, many of whom were headed up to Half Dome. Since that was our destination the next day, it seemed likely that we had found the correct trailhead.

We spent a good fifteen minutes debating and then started up the paved path, passing some hikers and being passed by others. The majority of the conversation snippets I overheard were in foreign languages. I reflected on how sad it was that few Americans seemed to be out seeing this beautiful part of our country. *I wonder what percentage of national park visitors are U.S. citizens?*

Sarah quickly got ahead of me, and I didn't try to catch up. The paved path was brutal underfoot and the air was still noticeably smoky. My pack seemed to have gone from forty pounds to four hundred. *What the hell did I pack?* I rounded a curve and found Sarah leaning against a rock wall.

"No one else has backpacking packs," she announced in greeting.

"I noticed."

"And where is the Three Sock Tribe? How could they get that far ahead of us?"

"Yeah, where did they go?" I tried to talk as though I weren't practically hyperventilating. "We haven't seen them since the path turnoff at the campsite."

Sarah adjusted her baseball cap. "This doesn't feel right."

"I know. But nothing else seemed right either."

"The sign at the beginning of this trail didn't say 'John Muir Trail.' It said 'Mist Trail.' Maybe this isn't even the JMT."

"The sign on the road said it, though. Maybe the trails are conjoined here or something." I fiddled with my pack strap quietly for a minute. "I just can't believe no one told us how difficult it would be to find the beginning of this trail."

Sarah tossed her braid over her shoulder. "How ridiculous is this? Two AT thru-hikers and we can't even find the beginning of the trail."

We shared an amused look and a forced laugh.

"What should we do?" I asked her, finally able to breathe almost normally. "Do you want to turn back?"

"I don't know. I want to know where the f—ing trail is."

"Me too. I don't know what to do. If we go back and find out this *is* the right trail, we'll have to re-hike it." I turned toward the steep paved path curving away behind us. "But if this *isn't* the trail, we're wasting mileage and daylight."

"Is it so much to ask to see a goddamn sign?" Sarah asked.

I sighed and wiped sweat off my forehead. "Apparently."

We decided to hike for another thirty minutes before making a decision. Even though we had fewer than five official trail miles to hike that day, we didn't want to end up needlessly walking many more if we were going to have to turn around.

As we kept going up the steep path, I noticed we were still the only hikers with backpacking packs. I envied the perky day hikers with their small packs containing nothing but water. As Sarah hiked on ahead of me, I focused on forcing air into my lungs and placing one foot in front of the other. Suddenly I heard voices and looked up to see a wooden bridge with more than a dozen people gathered taking photos and peering over the edge.

I didn't see Sarah at first, but I found her on the far side of the bridge. Nearby there was a sign for water that indicated it was the last potable water source before Half Dome.

"That seems positive." I pointed at the water sign with my pole. Our guidebook had mentioned a bathroom and water source. "And I see bathrooms over there."

"Let's get the map out again."

We studied our multiple maps and guidebooks intently but found nothing helpful. I tossed them onto the rock beside me. "I have no idea."

"I'm so pissed right now," Sarah seethed. "I want to hike the *whole* John Muir Trail. Not all of it except the beginning."

I nodded. "If we aren't on the trail, though, I vote it doesn't count against us. If anything, we're probably hiking extra mileage. We can't be held accountable when there weren't any signs."

"It's not just the mileage. What if at the real trailhead there was a huge sign? It could be an awesome photo opportunity."

I sighed. She was right. I wanted to hike the whole trail too—not just most of it. And, stupid as it may have been, I also wanted a photo by the giant sign if it existed. "Let's go to the bathroom and then make a decision."

When I came out of the bathroom, Sarah was talking with two attractive guys holding tools. I joined the conversation and learned that they worked for Yosemite and were doing maintenance on the privies. I felt a glimmer of hope. Surely if they worked for Yosemite they would know where the beginning of the John Muir Trail was.

At a break in the conversation I interjected, "So, I know this may sound dumb, but what trail are we on? There was a sign near the road pointing this way to the JMT, but then the sign at the beginning of the trail said Mist Trail."

"We get questions about this all the time. I don't know the name of the trail," one of the guys responded.

"Is this the trail that leads to Half Dome?" Sarah tried to confirm.

"Yeah." He leaned on the wooden handle of his shovel. "Most people hiking this trail are either going to Half Dome or to the waterfall right up ahead. They don't even know what the John Muir Trail is."

"OK, but is this also the John Muir Trail?" I asked.

He shrugged and picked at something on his flannel shirt. "I don't know. There's a sign about a quarter mile ahead that says John Muir Trail on it. I'm not sure if where you start matters."

Sarah jumped in. "So there are two ways to get to this point. Where we started didn't have any signs for the JMT. Does the other way? Did we miss anything important at the beginning? Is there a sign or information or anything? I don't want to miss a photo opportunity. I'm willing to go back."

He shrugged. "Nah. Nothing. So you guys are hiking the whole thing?"

"Yep," Sarah confirmed, her tone telling me she was annoyed that we still didn't have a definitive answer.

"If we ever find it," I added.

"That's totally awesome. We hike on the trails a lot for our job, but do you know that ninety-five percent of park visitors never even leave the valley?"

"We *want* to leave the valley. We just can't find the damn trail," Sarah half joked.

"People start both ways." He ran a dirt-smudged hand through his wavy, dark hair. "I don't know which way is official, but you haven't missed anything. You'll see the sign in a bit."

We thanked them and went back to the rock where we had left our packs. We ate a snack while fearless squirrels came right up to our hands looking for freebies. "I say we keep going," I declared. "Even if we aren't technically on the JMT, if we didn't miss anything at the beginning and we've hiked equivalent mileage, I see no point in backtracking."

"I just hope they're right. It's so f—ing ridiculous."

We had barely started hiking again when we ran into the sign pointing toward the JMT. Relieved that at least we were definitely headed the right way, we snapped pictures before heading on.

Soon we encountered a woman flipping through a thick stack of index cards as she walked. She told us she was studying for the MCAT exam and couldn't take the day off, but she had wanted to join some friends hiking Half Dome. I was astounded. I was struggling to simply breathe, and this woman was *studying* while she hiked. *It takes all kinds.*

Next we met three guys, David, Dennis, and Matt, who were hiking the JMT together. It was comforting to finally see other hikers with backpacking packs. We learned that they were longtime friends who had taken a trip together every year for many years. Matt was an engineer and brand-new dad, Dennis was a nurse, and David was a flight medic.

"I guess you guys are the group to be around if we get into any trouble," I teased.

They stopped at a large rock expanse with a waterfall to the right and a river to the left. We invited ourselves to join them on their lunch break. While they ate, we all dipped our feet in the frigid water. The conversation flowed easily. After having had several negative encounters with discouraging hikers over the past few days, I was relieved to find easy companionship with these three. We learned they were planning to finish the JMT the same day we were.

We resumed hiking together but had to part ways at the turnoff for Little Yosemite Valley Campground. Our permit required us to stop there for the first night, while they had to keep going. The rangers assign camping sites for the first night to reduce overcrowding and wear on the trail.

Sarah and I waved goodbye and stopped at the composting toilet at the edge of the campground. This was the first two-story privy I'd ever seen. As best I could tell, the downstairs level was for waste storage and maintenance access and the upstairs contained the stalls. Raising our eyebrows, Sarah and I dropped our packs and climbed the stairs. I took a deep breath before opening the wooden door to a stall. After my dozens of experiences with foul-smelling, toilet-paper-littered, overflowing privies, I was shocked to find a pristine stall with hardly a trace of odor.

We had to chase frisky squirrels away from our packs when we returned. As we wandered the campsite looking for a spot, we met Noah and Cory, two guys about twenty years old who were childhood friends. We learned that they were on a road trip because Noah had run a marathon earlier that week. He was still walking tenderly as he nursed a foot injury from the race. They had decided two months ago to hike the JMT and had arrived at Yosemite without permits. They revealed that they had shown up that morning and gotten walk-in permits. I stared at them speechlessly.

I had prepared for the better part of a year and had applied for permits fifteen times. And now here were these young guys with brand-new, never-used gear, no permits, and no itinerary. They hadn't done any research and had no plan for how to resupply food. Sarah and I told them about our multiple prepared mail drops.

"Oh man, that's probably a good idea," Cory said.

Who comes on a hike of over two hundred miles with no plan for getting food?

Sarah and I wandered down to the lake, and she swam while I watched from the shore. I was definitely hot enough to swim, but I was also too modest to strip down to my underwear in front of so many strangers. I hoped there would be other opportunities to swim because that was one thing I hadn't done on the AT.

As I sat on the sand watching Sarah and others in the water, I felt the dull pulsing of an impending headache. I squinted at the sunlight reflecting off the surface of the lake as I purified water to use for cooking dinner. My headache was intensifying and I was ready to set up camp, so I was glad when Sarah finished swimming and we went to pick a campsite.

We chose a spot not far from Noah and Cory. Across from us was a scattering of backpacks, but no people were in sight. A brave squirrel kept chewing on one pack.

"Those suckers have no fear!" Sarah observed, throwing a stone toward it.

"Everyone warned me about the marmots, but no one said a word about the squirrels," I added.

"They're evil, weird-looking things."

As we watched, the squirrel climbed right back onto the top pocket of the same pack. Sarah threw another rock. When the squirrel scampered away, she went over to investigate.

"There's food in there. I can see it. That cocky shit chewed a hole right through. We'd better not leave our packs unattended anywhere." She picked up the pack and set it next to ours. "We can watch it until the owner comes back. The hole is already through the pack's brain, though."

I glanced at the pack. "You call the top pocket of your pack a brain?"

She nodded. "What do you call it?"

"A top hat."

"Everyone called that a brain when I was on the AT," she explained.

"I guess they both make sense."

Sarah left to hang out with Cory and Noah, but I had no interest in socializing. My headache was growing worse by the minute, and I just wanted to finish the camp chores quickly. I unclipped my Crocs from my pack and bent over toward my shoelaces. Immediately my head pulsed with a hammering pain and my vision became fuzzy as my stomach somersaulted. I eased onto the ground with my back against a tree and rested my head on my bent knees. I couldn't remember the last time I'd had a headache like this. Trying to ease the pounding, I focused on breathing in and out deeply and slowly. When I was able to open my eyes again, I eased off my shoes and slid into my Crocs.

I moved awkwardly, reaching for the medicine container in the hipbelt of my pack while trying not to change the angle of my pounding head too much. I tapped the pills into a dirty palm and fished out two Excedrin Migraine caplets, which I immediately popped into my mouth. My head pulsed nauseatingly as I tilted it back to swallow. Trying to think ahead, I laid out two blue Advil PM to take before bed.

For fifteen minutes I sat against the tree with my eyes closed, willing the headache to recede. Knowing that dehydration contributes to headaches, I sipped from my CamelBak hose every few seconds. *Is this fatigue or altitude?* I've gotten headaches my whole life, but rarely have they been that bad. Lack of sleep is definitely a trigger for me—and I hadn't slept well the last three nights—but I also knew that altitude sickness could cause headaches. Since I'd never been at altitude before, I couldn't be sure why an entire percussion section had taken up residence in my head.

I gingerly set up my stove to boil water, using the bear box as a table. Yosemite provides bear boxes—large metal bins that look like sideways lockers—to store smell-ables at the campsite. I wasn't hungry, but I knew I needed to eat and hydrate to begin feeling better. While I waited for my "walking hamburgers" (hamburger gravel inside a tortilla with cheese, mustard, and ketchup) to rehydrate in my Brownie Bag, I pulled out my journal and settled against the tree to write about my first day on the trail.

I had promised myself I'd write every day on this trip, and I didn't want to make excuses on the first day, even with a crushing headache. Besides, despite my frustration over the lack of trail signs, the smoke in the air, and the miserably hot temperature, Yosemite was beautiful and I wanted to remember it in as much detail as possible. When my meal was ready, I leaned back against the giant tree and stared at the massive branches overhead as I ate. *Could this be a redwood?* The pounding in my head made chewing tedious. I had to fight waves of nausea to swallow each bite.

I was thankful I had intentionally made the first night's meal smaller. When I had cleaned up and put my cooking gear and food into the bear box, I sat on a giant fallen tree to blow up my Therm-a-Rest. This was my second time using Dad's Therm-a-Rest, but he had blown it up the first time. Normally I could inflate my own Therm-a-Rest in about a minute with medium effort. Dad's required much more air, though, and between my headache, the growing nausea, and the smoke in the air, the inflation process was painfully slow. *Did I make the right choice in bringing a mattress that was so much thicker? Will it take this long to blow it up every night? Will it become harder as we gain altitude?*

Sarah returned and we quickly set up the tent and threw in our gear. Someone started a fire in one of the communal rings and I wandered over to socialize. My head still hurt, but I wasn't quite ready to sleep and I didn't want to seem completely antisocial on the first night of the trail. I hoped the volume around the campfire might be low enough for me to tolerate briefly while I waited for the medicine to kick in.

I was impressed with Cory and Noah's food. They had a bunch of home-dehydrated vegetables that they had mixed together into a meal that smelled wonderful. Apparently they had been hiking together their whole lives. I mentally chastised myself for the negative and judgmental thoughts about their lack of preparation—if their outdoor cooking skills were any indication, they had a lot more experience than I realized.

My headache wasn't receding, so I didn't talk much, but I listened to the conversations around the fire. Many hikers said they had had their permits checked multiple times that day. *By whom? We didn't see a single ranger.* A young woman who was hiking alone told the group she had gotten a walk-in permit that day. I knew that Yosemite reserved a certain amount of permits for daily walk-ins, but I just couldn't imagine taking that risk. The obsessive planner in me was aghast. *What if I had flown across the country and not gotten a permit? Those people must not have strict timelines on when they need to be back home.*

I made my way back to our campsite and double-checked my pack for any smell-ables. I didn't want the daring squirrels rummaging through my things while I slept. Exhausted, I settled into the tent. I barely had time to marvel at how hot it still was before I fell sound asleep on my inflatable pillow.

12

ANTS AND ALTITUDE

Sunday August 3, 2014

Slept: between Sunrise Creek and Merced Lake Trail
Miles: 7.5 (Sarah), 5.5 (me)
Weather: overcast then rain; much cooler
Dinner: grits and sausage
Mood: worried, humbled, sad, nervous
Letter: Mom
Dad's quote of the day:

> THESE WOODS ARE LOVELY, DARK AND DEEP.
> BUT I HAVE PROMISES TO KEEP. AND MILES TO GO BEFORE I SLEEP.
> AND MILES TO GO BEFORE I SLEEP. —ROBERT FROST

I woke up with a wet spot under my face. For me, drooling is always an indication that I've slept soundly, so I was actually relieved to find myself with a slimy cheek. I moved my head from side to side experimentally and felt only the faintest hint of a headache across my forehead. Cautiously, I opened my eyes and was relieved when the pain didn't intensify. As I propped myself up on one elbow and dried my face on my shirt sleeve, I heard Sarah stirring beside me.

"Good morning." She stretched her hands over her head.

"Morning."

Sharing a tent with someone I barely knew had been one of my greatest fears for this trip. Having limited space with confined odors is challenging enough when you're in a tent by yourself. When you add another person to the mix—particularly someone you don't know well—it can become downright uncomfortable. After night two I was feeling more at ease.

Knowing we were about to climb Half Dome, Yosemite's icon, I was filled with nervous energy as I packed up camp. When I ventured over to the bear box to pull out food for breakfast, I was surprised to find two blue pills on top of the box. Apparently I had slept hard enough to drool without even taking my Advil PM.

Sarah and I were back on the trail quickly. The first mile and a half passed smoothly, with the DeLorme pinging away our location to our followers. The day was overcast and cooler than the previous two had been. I was enjoying the reduced humidity and heat. My headache was still present, but it had lessened to a dull buzz in the background, like elevator music. I was hopeful that, with the help of Ibuprofen and the prescription Diamox I was taking to prevent altitude sickness, it wouldn't get any worse.

When we reached the left-hand turnoff to the Half Dome trail, I was surprised. I'd thought it would take longer. We stopped to fish out only what we would need for the climb and ditched the rest of our packs behind a tree just off the trail. There were lots of other packs stashed around the small area. *We need pack cubbies—like the ones for kids' shoes at Chick-fil-A play areas.*

Supposedly, Half Dome would be one of the most amazing views of the hike. We chattered in anticipation as we started the ascent—about how long it might take us, what the granite stairs would look like, and how steep the fixed cables near the top would be. We wondered about the weather and discussed the people we had met so far. When I felt my headache begin to pulse behind my eyes, I forced some deep breaths, hoping the extra oxygen would temper it.

"Wasn't it crazy how many people last night said they had their permit checked multiple times?" I asked Sarah between deep breaths.

"Yeah. Where were all those rangers when we needed to find the f— ing trail?"

"No clue. It sounded like they were everywhere. We may be about the only people who didn't have our permit checked."

"Just about."

"Can you believe how many people said they didn't have permits ahead of time? I can't imagine just showing up in Yosemite without a permit. I would be a nervous wreck," I told her.

"I wouldn't do it," she declared. "I would never spend all that money to fly across the country without knowing I had a permit. And a lot of those people weren't from California or even the West Coast. It's insane."

"Yeah," I agreed. "Some of them didn't seem to know much about the trail."

"Did it kind of piss you off?" Sarah asked. "It took you what? Twelve times or something to get a permit?"

"Fifteen," I confirmed.

"OK. Fifteen. And these people just show up with no research and no applications and get a permit like that," she said, snapping her fingers.

I groaned and shook my head as I stepped around a huge boulder. "Don't remind me."

"Hey, speaking of, you do have our permit, right?" She glanced over her shoulder.

I stopped abruptly. "Shit."

"You're joking." She stopped and turned around to stare at me.

"No. When we ditched our packs I didn't even think about it. It's in the Ziploc with my journal."

She sat down on a log at the edge of the trail. "I'll wait for you here."

I stared at her for a minute and resisted the urge to make a snarky comment. *Thanks a lot.* Granted, the permit had been in *my* pack. But *we* didn't think about it. *We* had started up Half Dome without it. I couldn't believe that she was just going to sit there and make me hike back alone, especially since she knew I had a headache.

Exhaling forcefully, I turned around. *It's not worth a fight.* I walked back to my pack quickly, fueled partially by frustration. Getting mad hadn't helped my headache, but I felt pretty good other than that. I got the permit out of the Ziploc where it was safely stored with my journal and stuck it in my pocket. Trying hard to swallow my annoyance at Sarah for sending me back about half a mile alone, I restarted the climb.

It seemed like it was getting harder to breathe. *Is it the altitude? The smoke? Am I imagining it?* I consciously slowed and deepened my breathing. *Get more oxygen in. You're fine.* Even wearing sunglasses on a cloudy day, I was squinting as I hiked, trying to protect my throbbing eyes from the light.

When I made it back to the log where Sarah had stopped, she was lying down with her legs propped up. She saw me and bounded to her feet.

"You got it?" she asked.

"Yep." I was aware that I sounded snappy, but I couldn't stop myself.

"Good. That was close. Imagine if we had made it all the way up there without it."

You're welcome.

She started walking.

That's OK. I didn't want to take a break. I just hiked an extra mile with this headache. No problem. Since you're *rested, let's just keep going.*

As I hiked I reprimanded myself. *Drop it. You could have said something. You agreed not to be petty on this hike. Either say something to her or get over it.* I forced some deep breaths and let it go. *It doesn't matter. Extra calories burned, right?*

I squinted my eyes into slits behind my sunglasses and swallowed hard against the growing nausea. When I paused for a minute at a switchback, I noticed that my hands were tingling. *Weird.* I flexed my swollen fingers, shook my arms out, and told myself to climb to the next curve in the trail. I reached that curve and leaned against a rock. *Why are my hands tingling?* Sarah was getting farther and farther ahead of me.

Fifteen minutes later, I found Sarah sitting on a rock outcropping with a magnificent view. We took pictures and enjoyed the vista below.

"Can you believe that just about everything we'll see from today on will be higher than this?" Sarah asked.

I shook my head and immediately regretted the movement when I felt a surge of nausea. I swallowed hard and closed my eyes.

"You OK?" She lowered her sunglasses to look at me.

I could tell she was genuinely concerned, and I let the last of my annoyance dissipate. Fighting with a hiking partner is detrimental to both parties. We needed each other. "I don't feel great," I admitted.

"What's going on? Do you still have a headache?"

I rubbed my face with my hands. "Yeah." I wiggled my fingers. "My hands are tingling too. And I'm nauseated."

"How bad is it?"

"I'm pretty uncomfortable."

"Have you been taking that medicine you got to prevent altitude sickness?

"Diamox. Yeah. Since the day before we flew out to California." I shielded my eyes with my hands. "Are tingling extremities a sign of altitude sickness?"

"I don't know." She shrugged.

"Me neither. But it seems like they could be." Ironically, I later learned that tingling fingers and face are two odd side effects of Diamox.

"I've been at altitude a ton since I live in Utah in the off season. I've never had altitude sickness." She looked out at the mountains in front of us. "Sometimes, though, when I'm working ski school the parents come straight from the airport to the slopes without giving their kids time to adjust. Some of them actually start throwing up on the slopes."

"Geez."

"Yeah. I'm sorry you feel bad. Do you need to stop?" she asked.

"Not yet. But I need a minute."

"OK. Maybe drink some water."

I nodded and sipped from my CamelBak.

Stopped at the viewpoint with us were a group of siblings who were hiking Half Dome for one sister's fortieth birthday. They had done the same thing a few years before for another sibling's fortieth and were making it a tradition. I eyed the fit, smiling group and hoped I would have their energy in another decade. *What am I talking about? I'd love to have it now. They look a lot better than I feel.*

"Let's keep going," I said to Sarah. "I'm going to be slow, though."

A few more minutes up the trail I realized my hands were totally numb. *Maybe you're exaggerating. You're fine. You aren't even that high up yet. If you can't do this, how will you climb Whitney? Buck up.* I decided to test myself. I stuck my hand in my mouth and bit down—hard. I barely felt it. When I pulled my hand away there were deep teeth marks. I sucked in breaths and squeezed my eyes shut for a minute. *Hike to the next switchback,* I encouraged myself, peering up at the visible turn ahead on the trail. I made it about another quarter mile with this ridiculous combination of internal coaching and self-degradation.

I stopped and dry heaved on the side of the trail. *OK. This is real. I'm getting worse. I need to turn around.* I saw Sarah looking back at me from where she was leaning on her poles up ahead, and I slowly started toward her.

"Brownie, you OK?" she called down.

I shook my head slowly as I approached.

"Not feeling any better?"

"Worse." I swallowed hard. "If I keep hiking, I'm going to vomit." I steeled my chin and pushed back tears. "I have to turn around."

"Are you sure?"

Through misty eyes I stared off at the mountains in silence. Sarah put her arm around my shoulders and squeezed.

Hot tears rolled down my cheeks and in a wobbly voice I explained, "I don't want to turn around, but if I push too hard today I might not…I might not make the rest of the trail." I paused to sniffle and groaned as the pressure surged through my head. "I have to listen to my body. I've got clear symptoms of altitude sickness. I can't go any higher."

Sarah squeezed my shoulders tighter. "You might feel better if you get back lower."

I pursed my lips and ignored the tear that slid down my cheek.

She glanced up the trail. "Will you hate me if I keep going up?"

"No. Not at all." I sniffled and looked up the trail wistfully. "I want you to go on." And I was telling the truth. It killed me that I had to stop. I wasn't about to ruin it for her too.

"It's just…I might not get another chance."

"Go." I wiped a tear from my cheek and tried to force a smile. "Take pictures."

"You'll be OK?"

"Yep. There are plenty of people on this trail. I'll head back to our packs and rest." I pulled the permit out of my pocket and handed it to her.

She hugged me tightly.

"What if I can't do the rest of the trail?" I asked through choked sobs.

"It's just one mountain, girl," she reminded me. "It's not even on the JMT. It doesn't count."

I didn't know how confident she actually was, but her words gave me the strength to turn around and start walking down the trail. I kept my sunglasses on and tilted my head toward the ground to avoid eye contact with all the hikers coming up. Tears leaked from beneath my wrap-around lenses and splashed down my cheeks and onto my stupid long-sleeved button-down shirt. Despite the orchestra-sized percussion section thumping in my head and the elephants somersaulting in my stomach, I walked back to the trail split without stopping.

When I reached the small clearing at the turnoff to Half Dome, I was exhausted. I swallowed two more Vitamin-I (the hiker name for Ibuprofen) and sat shivering against my pack, wallowing in misery and willing my body to regain equilibrium. Keeping my eyes open was impossible. I put on my fleece hat and my down coat and lay down on the pine needles with my head on my bandana. Within minutes I realized how cold my legs were, but I didn't think I could bend over enough to put on pants. I settled for draping my rain coat across my legs. I pressed my pulsing head against the hard ground and curled into a ball with my pack spooned against my back.

Forty-five minutes later I woke up with drool caked on my mouth and pine needles stuck to my face. *This is the second time today I've woken up coated in drool.* I slit my eyes open and peered around. I had fallen asleep on top of pinecones in a fairly populated area. Experimentally, I lifted my head; the staccato drumming behind my temples had quieted some.

Physically I felt better, but emotionally I was wreck. *I came across the country to hike the John Muir Trail, and I didn't make it through the agenda for day two. What the hell am I doing? Will my body ever acclimate? How can I know? How long should I give it?* I squinted up at the sky through partially open eyes and let a few more tears slide down my cheeks. When I wiped the tears away, I felt sap, dirt, and something else caked to my face. *What is that?* I swiped at it and looked down to see ants on my hand. I sat up as quickly as my weakened body would allow and glanced up and down my limbs. There were black ants all over my skin. I brushed them off and was relieved not to see any bites.

I opened my pack and pulled out my journal and a snack. I never journal at home, but in the woods I write daily. I do so much thinking on trails that it seems important to capture a small amount of it on paper. I poured all of my frustration with my body into my purple Moleskine journal—the staggering headache, the nausea, the tinging hands, the sleepless nights, and my continued inability to breathe normally. Venting my complaints helped, as if writing them down on paper allowed me to let them go.

It seemed like it had been a long time since I had separated from Sarah, and I wondered if I should worry about her. I calculated the distance she'd had left to climb and the time she might have spent socializing, taking photos, and soaking in the view from the top of Half Dome. Then I turned on my iPhone to check the time. *She should be back any minute.* I figured my headache had altered my perception of time.

While I forced myself to eat small bites of trail mix, I randomly selected one of my letters to read. The whole purpose of the letters was to encourage me, and I sure needed some encouragement.

Dear Michelle,

It's hard to believe it was over nine years ago when you started your AT hike. It was so hard to watch you walk off into those woods with that 40-pound pack on your back! I had to fight the urge to chase after you and bring you back to the safety and comfort of your family circle. At that time, I knew relatively little about long-distance hiking or trail life or what lay ahead for you. Blissful backpacking ignorance—it was probably what saved me from maternal meltdown while you stomped around the woods all those months!

Today...I know more. Oh, so much more. (Remember? I read your book!) No, I'm still not a hiker myself, but I've listened and learned from you, and I am now a very knowledgeable "hiker's mom." And that, my dear daughter, is probably both my blessing and my curse as you head off to the JMT! I know that majestic wonders await you...as well as daunting challenges. I know that you will laugh and sing and be drunk with the joy of the outdoors...and I know that your feet will hurt, your tummy will rumble, and you will probably shed a few tears. I know that you have planned and prepared and that you are a cautious hiker...but I also know that unexpected things can happen out in the wilderness. And I know that the thrill of all those unknowns is part of what draws you back to the trails time and time again! Yes, I know you well. So even though I don't have the urge to hike hundreds of miles, or eat rehydrated food, or pee in the woods, or climb a 14,000-foot mountain...I understand why YOU do. And I love you for it.

The JMT will be so different from the AT. (Don't hikers ever spell out the whole trail name?? LOL!) The AT may be longer, but the JMT is so much higher. I'm guessing it will literally leave you breathless the first couple of days! And if heaven is "up," then you should feel really close to God on this trip. But then, how could you not, with all the awesomeness and beauty of nature that you will behold? (And just a motherly reminder, you'll also be a lot closer to the sun, so slather on that sunscreen!)

I will be your number one tracker, watching daily (quite possibly hourly!) those little hash marks appear across the map as you "ping" your way through the mountains. (Thank you, satellite technology!) And, no, I won't worry any less than I did the last time you decided to take a walk in the woods. But my worry will be tempered by the anticipation of hearing about this new adventure—another check mark on your bucket list! I am happy for you. I am proud of you. I am confident in you.

Go shout with joy from the mountaintops! Then come back home and tell us your story.

I love you—so very much!
Love, Mom

My barely dry eyes welled with tears all over again. Mom has always been good with words. She was the master editor for all my high school papers. While we don't love all the same things—including hiking—she has an amazing ability to support my aspirations and passions even when they don't align with hers. She had done a perfect job of summarizing why I love to backpack. *This is exactly the letter I needed right now.*

I folded the letter back and tucked it safely into my Ziploc. Some hikers burn papers once they've finished using them—letters they've read, map sections they've completed, or even sections of paperback books. I'm not a materialistic person generally, but I can be nostalgic—so I keep all of those items, extra ounces be damned.

As I sat massaging my temples, Sarah plopped down beside me a few minutes later. "Hey, friend," she greeted me. "You feeling any better?"

"Yeah. I made the right choice. I fell asleep pretty much immediately." I pointed at the ground underneath us, which was littered liberally with pinecones. "I woke up lying facedown on these, covered in ants."

"Geez."

"What did I miss? How was Half Dome?"

"It was cool, but I'm sure we'll see better views later. It wasn't worth making yourself sick."

I nodded. I suspected she was downplaying the experience, but I appreciated her not wanting to make me feel left out.

"I brought you something." She held out her closed fist and dropped a small rock into my hand. "This is from the top of Half Dome. It's not illegal, because we're borrowing it, not stealing it. You have to return it when you make it up to the top next time."

I squeezed my fingers around the rock and closed my eyes for a second. "Thank you."

After a few seconds of silence Sarah added, "A hiker up there told me something that might help you. He said he's had some real issues with altitude sickness before and that Benadryl and Dramamine really help. He's tried that Dia-whatever stuff you're taking, and he said it was useless for him."

"Really?"

"Yeah. And apparently you can buy Benadryl at Tuolumne." Tuolumne Meadows was a resupply point we would be approaching in a couple of days.

"I have Benadryl with me, actually. It makes me feel kind of gross. I only packed it in case of an allergic reaction, but I guess I already feel gross, so what's the difference? Did he say how much to take or how often?"

"No."

"All right. I'll take a normal dose now. Thanks."

"No problem."

For the first time that day I felt truly optimistic. I was still going to keep taking the Diamox, but at least I had two chances at feeling better now. Three chances if you included the passage of time.

"Did you eat lunch?" Sarah asked.

"No. I waited on you."

"Let's eat."

I was relieved that even though I had skipped Half Dome, I hadn't actually missed any JMT miles. This was the one day I could miss mileage and still be a thru-hiker. It felt good to get moving again after lunch. Sarah hiked ahead of me but stopped and waited occasionally to make sure I was all right.

About an hour later it started to rain.

"Are you f—ing kidding me?" Sarah asked. "California is in a drought. And it rains our first full day on the JMT?"

I laughed half-heartedly. The trail did seem to be trying to defeat me.

There hadn't been any easily identifiable landmarks since Half Dome, so it was hard to track our progress. I suspected I was hiking slower than my normal pace since I didn't feel great. When we stopped for the night, we knew we probably hadn't made our intended mileage.

It was misting at our camping spot, and as soon as I stopped hiking I began getting cold. I ducked behind a rock and stripped off my wet clothes in exchange for my long underwear and down coat. It was almost unbelievable that in Yosemite Valley it had been too hot to sleep with pants or socks on.

Sarah and I were both so accustomed to setting up and breaking camp that even without much history doing it together, we moved quickly without speaking much. We tossed our gear into the tent to keep it dry. It was still too early to eat dinner, so I climbed into my sleeping bag to write. I wanted to stay warm because I feared that shivering would bring back the crushing headache.

When I emerged from my cozy writing cocoon, I selected my least favorite dinner to cook—grits and sausage. I figured I needed to save the encouraging meals since things weren't likely to get easier right away. We ate quickly and retreated to the warmth and dryness of our tent.

Sarah and I journaled side-by-side in companionable silence. Just before switching off our headlamps, we spoke briefly about our mileage for the following day. I was grateful that she seemed to share an appreciation for quiet, reflective time in the evening since that's one of the parts of camping I treasure most.

13

SWIM HARD

August 4, 2014

Slept: Lower Cathedral Meadow
Miles: 9.3 + 0.5 to camp = 9.8
Weather: cold, overcast, sometimes drizzly
Dinner: cheesy taco mac
Mood: happy, relieved, quiet
Letter: Nicole
Dad's quote of the day:

> "DEAD LAST" IS BETTER THAN "DID NOT FINISH,"
> WHICH BEATS "DID NOT START." —UNKNOWN

It was the type of paralyzingly cold backpacking morning where I had to give myself a motivational speech to convince myself to emerge from the warm confines of my down sleeping bag. I was grateful that I felt much better: my hands weren't tingling, I wasn't nauseated, and my headache barely registered. Still, preferring to be safe instead of sorry, I chased my breakfast bars with Diamox, Benadryl, and Vitamin-I.

Two peaceful miles into our day we hopped across a small stream and saw a tent on the left side of the trail. When we got a few steps closer, we saw Noah and Cory lounging by a small campfire cooking breakfast. Even though we had only hiked a couple of miles, we stopped and had a snack with them.

Noah stretched awkwardly on a log as Cory bounced around the fire ring barefoot. I looked around the messy campsite and saw hand-knitted cotton socks in a puddle on a stump, a metal two-deck card tin, a gallon-sized plastic water jug, and a pair of rock climbing shoes. *How can stuff get this scattered in one night?* These were two very attractive, very fit guys, but their gear was appalling. I thought anyone attempting a long-distance hike would know not to wear cotton socks. Yet I was fairly confident that despite their unorthodox gear choices they would easily speed past me and would probably finish the entire trail. I had learned on the AT that having the right gear isn't a guarantee for success, and having the wrong gear isn't a guarantee for failure. Mental toughness and physical ability go a long way.

"Getting a late start today?" Sarah asked them.

"It was a long night," Noah told us. "I used my first aid kit as a pillow." He rubbed his neck.

"We've got some kinks to work out, man," Cory groaned from their tent, where he was collecting belongings into a colossal pile.

I glanced at Noah rubbing his neck. "I guess you mean that literally."

Noah shook his head. "It's been rough. What do you use as a pillow?" he asked in our direction.

"I put all the clothes I'm not wearing in a stuff sack," Sarah told him, pulling her braid out and re-doing it as we talked.

Noah turned his eyes in my direction.

I swallowed a mouthful of dried apples. "On this trip I actually brought an inflatable pillow. It weighs three ounces or something. But usually I do the same as Sarah."

Noah poked at the fire. They didn't seem to be in any hurry.

"What's in the metal tin?" I asked, pointing.

"Matches," he explained as he used a lighter to light a joint.

"That's a lot of matches. Especially considering you have a lighter."

"Five lighters, actually." He inhaled deeply and passed the joint to Cory, who had wandered back to the fire circle—apparently having given up on packing. "We wanted to have backup."

"Why are they in the tin?"

"We didn't want them to get wet."

"How about a Ziploc bag, man?" Sarah asked, sitting down beside Noah. "Seriously, would you guys like some help with your gear? We could do a shake-down with you. Between the two of us we have a lot of experience—thousands of miles."

"That would be sweet," Cory said, bobbing his head. When he sat down on the log next to me, I saw a blister on his filthy bare heel.

"Why are you walking around barefoot?" I asked.

"I don't have camp shoes. I didn't want to carry three pairs of shoes and I wanted to bring climbing shoes so I could boulder." He took a hit from the joint. "I thought it would be OK, you know, because my feet are pretty tough. But it hurts. And this blister is totally killing me."

So you'll carry weed, rolling papers, and six methods for lighting a joint, but not protection for your feet around camp. "Are those your cotton socks?" I inclined my head toward the soggy pile on the stump.

"Yeah. My mom made them. Why?"

He held the joint toward me, but I shook my head and said, "Homemade stuff is great. But typically wearing any type of cotton isn't a good idea when you're backpacking. Have you heard the phrase 'cotton kills'?"

"No." He wandered over to the stump and picked up the grubby socks. "They're soaked. I put them out here last night." He wrung water from them to demonstrate.

"You're better off drying them in your sleeping bag," I told him. "Well, actually, you're better off just not wearing cotton. Wool socks wick moisture away from your skin. The wet cotton is probably not helping that blister."

Sarah turned her attention to his foot. "That looks bad. You don't want it to get infected. Do you have blister stuff?"

"We have the first aid kit."

"Do you want me to teach you to pad it? I'm pretty much a pro at it."

Sarah helped Cory with his feet while I got us more water. According to our guidebook the trail might not have many water sources for a while. It was such a gamble. At 2.2 pounds per liter, extra water is too heavy to carry needlessly. But I also didn't want to run out—ever.

Cory and Noah weren't planning to hike very far that day because of Cory's blister and Noah's sore feet from the marathon. They were also meeting a friend in Tuolumne Meadows and were running ahead of schedule, so they needed to burn some time. They didn't seem to have a definite itinerary. Sarah and I had a schedule to keep, though.

"If we see you again up the trail, I'll be glad to help you guys do a shake-down," Sarah reminded them as we walked off.

After we had hiked about five minutes, I stopped and tried unsuccessfully to reach around to the back of my pack without taking it off. Giving up, I called ahead to Sarah. "Hey, can you help me real quick?"

She turned around. "What's up?"

"I think I forgot to turn the DeLorme back on. Can you see if the light is blinking?"

Sarah checked the light and we got the DeLorme activated again. "That thing would drive me nuts," she told me.

"Well, I don't love it, but it makes my mom feel better. She thinks it'll keep me from ending up dead on a hike."

"It seems more like dead weight to me."

"Deadweight. That's what we should call it."

With Deadweight now tracking appropriately, we pushed onward. According to our map we had a big climb coming up. I was nervous because uphills are always more challenging for me and my body hadn't exactly been cooperating so far. A couple of times as I ascended I felt my heart rate accelerate, and I slowed my pace so it could drop back down. I wasn't worried about my heart; I was worried that a drastic increase in heart rate or blood pressure might cue that unwelcome intracranial percussion section.

The route was so nicely graded that I only needed to slow down to moderate my heart rate a few times. Along the way we passed a horse train packing out trash from Sunrise High Sierra Camp. It fascinated me that we were somewhere that packing out trash by horses was still the preferred method. The wrangler guiding the horses wasn't much for conversation. Visually, though, he was an exact replica of a cowboy from a Western movie. He wore leather chaps over his jeans, a dusty black cowboy hat, and a bandana tied around his neck.

We were approaching Long Meadow and I was excited to see the area of protected alpine vegetation. Right before we got there, I saw my first pika. It was adorable, like a fat, tail-less, skittish gerbil. I'd been hearing their high-pitched squeaks and could finally put a face to the noise.

In Long Meadow I was careful to stay on the worn path. The meadow was so pretty that we wanted to stop for lunch, but we also didn't want to damage anything. We settled for perching on two rocks just off the path.

After lunch we continued on to Lower Cathedral Lakes. For the last mile or so we hiked with a guy named Stuart. He was a college student who was out for a summer adventure. Stuart's dad was picking him up in ten days. That meant he had to average twenty-one miles a day to finish the JMT in time. It was his first day—he had started at Yosemite Valley that morning—and he confided that he was going to fall shy of the necessary twenty-one miles.

That still means that just today he's hiked what I hiked today, yesterday, and *the day before combined.* When I was on the Appalachian Trail, twenty-mile days became the norm after a while. But the AT doesn't have the same elevation or smoky air, and I certainly didn't hike twenty miles on my first day. I was impressed by Stuart's feat but didn't envy him. I wanted to enjoy the JMT, not just complete it.

The three of us set up camp together in some trees near Lower Cathedral Lake. It was a beautiful area, full of deer and greenery. Once again I had to hurry into my warm, dry clothes as soon as we stopped. *How cold am I going to be when we're above 10,000 feet?*

Soon after we set up camp it began misting again. We hurried down to the lake to get water. There must have been a dozen deer on the path to the lake, and they weren't at all intimidated by us. Humans pose no threat to these animals because they live in a protected forest where hunting is not allowed. While Stuart pumped water and Sarah took pictures, I sat on a rock above the lake and gazed around at the serene setting. I was glad that my water collection process didn't require time-consuming effort.

We weaved our way through the deer-filled clearing back toward our campsite. By mutual agreement we gathered on a large slab of rock under the trees to cook dinner. It was still drizzling, but I was dry inside my rain clothes. I cooked cheesy taco mac. This was a meal I had traded Sarah for. I was excited because tacos are my favorite food ever and macaroni and cheese is one of my favorite trail meals. Combining the two was so genius that I was sad I hadn't thought of the combination on my own. When I opened my Brownie Bag, the smell that wafted out was intense. The meal did taste good, but it was surprisingly spicy.

The spice must have jolted my insides awake, because within minutes of finishing dinner I was hurrying for the trees with my trowel in hand. I had been constipated since we landed in California. Only a hiker who has been eating copious amounts of junk for days can understand the joy of functioning bowels.

Full and exhausted, I returned to our tent, snuggled into my sleeping bag, and thanked myself for my foresight in purchasing a fifteen-degree instead of thirty-degree bag. Most of the JMT information I had read during our preparations suggested that a thirty-degree bag would be plenty, but I've always been pretty cold-natured, and the older I get the less I seem to be able to maintain my body temperature.

Finally I was feeling almost normal. The headache, nausea, and numbness seemed to be gone. My legs weren't sore, and so far I had no bruises from my pack and no chafing. I was hopeful that my body might be getting the hang of this backpacking thing again.

After journaling, I pulled out my next letter.

Dear Michelle,

I imagine you reading this right now out in the wilderness, exhausted and with that pensive, business-like look you get sometimes. Your feet are probably aching and you've had several adventures already that need writing up in your new book (that I will edit!).

Let me just say that you are hiking for me as well. It truly inspires me for the "endurance runs" I have as a mom. If you can hike your mountain, then I can hike the metaphorical mountains in my own life—endless laundry, patience for fifteen hours with the kids, the disaster of whatever Benjamin and Jack just did, and the long days where I just have to put one foot in front of the other until we're there. You help a lot of people hike their own hills and you don't even know it. One foot in front of the other. I love that Grace has you to look up to.

So I'm super excited to hear about the hike when you get back. I'm sure you've had some crazy stuff go down, but you seem to always handle it gracefully and with confidence and competence. What I am most jealous of is the peace you will soak up just being outside, absorbing the quiet and shaking off the over-stimulating world of humans and our self-imposed stresses. But what I don't envy is the food. Drying out food and then re-hydrating it gives me flashbacks to Space Camp. Astronaut food. Pass.

OK, I love you, so be careful. I worry about you! And not to freak you out, but California is supposed to fall off into the ocean sometime, so I'm glad you're lifeguard certified. And, hold onto your shoes. You know what happened in the book Wild. Yep, that's all I got—don't throw a shoe down a mountain, and swim hard if the state falls into the Pacific. I'm sure you'll be fine.

Take it all in, have deep spiritual questions to think on, and put one foot in front of the other. So proud of you!

XOXO,
Nicole

I smiled at Nicole's worry and wit and clicked off my headlamp. As I zipped myself fully into my mummy bag, I tried to imagine what Nicole might be doing right then. Drinking hot tea and working on her dystopian novel? Reading bedtime stories to little boys dressed in superhero costumes? Folding mountains of laundry for her family of five? I smiled, picturing the loving chaos at her house.

I was at that discordant point in life where some of my friends were married with kids, while others were still dabbling on dating websites and meeting friends for cocktails and late-night dinners after work. Although the current state of our lives couldn't be more different, I treasure my friendship with Nicole. Her transparency and humor have been valued parts of our relationship since we met in college more than a decade ago. When I turn to her for advice, she has said on more than one occasion, "I'm going to tell you what you *need* to hear, not what you *want* to hear." Even if my feathers get ruffled or my feelings hurt, she's honest with me. And, annoyingly, she's usually right.

Nicole and I have a lot in common despite the fact that she was probably potty training a toddler or playing her eighth consecutive game of

Uno while I lay in a tent in the High Sierras. We both believe in the importance of manners, in honesty, and in the power of the written word. We both value education, friendship, and transparency. Despite our differently hectic lives, we regularly have lengthy phone conversations and schedule visits as often as possible. A phone call or text from Nicole never fails to brighten my day.

Often I envy Nicole's life. She has a doctor husband, three smart, cute kids, and a minivan. I had assumed I would have a similar life by age thirty-one. I knew there was still time, but it hadn't happened yet. As I looked up at the stars through the open tent door, I thought about the fact that the only reason I was able to be here was because I didn't have any of those constraints. *Not having one thing I want is allowing me to have another thing I want. The world works in mysterious ways.*

JMT view

14

THE LADY WITH A TAIL

August 5, 2014

Slept: Lyell Canyon
Miles: 13.5 (6.5 to Tuolumne Meadows, 7.0 to camp)
Weather: cold in the morning, warmed
Dinner: beef stroganoff (eh…)
Mood: happy
Letter: Janice
Dad's quote of the day:

PEOPLE OFTEN SAY THAT MOTIVATION DOESN'T LAST. WELL, NEITHER DOES
BATHING; THAT'S WHY IT'S RECOMMENDED DAILY. —ZIG ZEIGLER
(HOPE YOU'RE DOING BETTER ON THE MOTIVATION THAN THE BATHING!!)

I am not a fashionista. I like my clothes comfortable, easy to wash, and inexpensive. When something comes into style that I like, I latch onto it (hello, flannel shirts and vests!). On the trail my attire choices are even more questionable. When I woke in the morning to find it still uncomfortably cold, I had to re-think wearing just my skirt. Rain pants don't breathe, so it quickly gets sweaty and sticky inside them. I didn't want to suffer that, so I found an alternative.

I wore my white long underwear under my khaki skirt. Adding my burgundy shirt, red coat, grey hat, black gloves, and flowered gaiters, I was ready for the runway. Before I started hiking, I settled my teal Oakley sunglasses on my face. *Look out, Hollywood!*

The trail from Lower Cathedral Lake to Tuolumne Meadows was easy trekking. We traversed the six and a half miles quickly. I was relieved that my body seemed to be remembering how to do that "hiking thing." The John Muir Trail enjoyed throwing challenges our way, though, so even though the terrain was pleasant, we encountered obstacles.

Some trail intersections had no signs at all, and the signs for others had fallen down so that we couldn't tell which way the arrows were intended to point. The difficult navigation on the JMT was becoming an unwelcome—and endlessly frustrating—trend. Sarah and I can both read maps, but the maps didn't correlate with what we were seeing on the trails—there were turnoffs in real life that weren't marked on the maps, and turnoffs on the maps that didn't exist in real life. On the scant signs we did find the mileage wasn't accurate, and sometimes the arrows pointed in the wrong directions.

After guessing which way to turn for at least a handful of trail splits, we found ourselves standing on the side of a road—an actual, paved road. We looked around for the continuation of the trail for more than twenty minutes but found nothing. Not sure what else to do, we decided to follow the road into Tuolumne Meadows. I had no fathomable idea which way to go, but Sarah felt pretty confident. Thankfully, her sense of direction is better than mine and she was correct.

Tuolumne Meadows was to our left as we trudged down the road, and even in my frustrated and partially frozen state I couldn't help but notice its magnificence. The expansive subalpine meadow, situated at approximately 8,500 feet, is filled with wildflowers and bisected by the winding Tuolumne River. Pine and hemlock trees backed by impressive granite cliffs surround the meadow, emphasizing its majesty.

This popular site in Yosemite National Park was created by granite, glaciers, and magma. It is accessible to park visitors via the park's Tioga Road, which crosses the southern edge of the meadow. This road actually marks the northern end of the largest contiguous wilderness in the United States; no other road crosses the High Sierras until after Mount Whitney.

Tuolumne Meadows is sometimes partially flooded with water from the groundwater, snowmelt, and runoff flowing into it. This water eventually flows south to the Hetch Hetchy Reservoir and then becomes drinking water for the people in San Francisco. I looked out over the meadow and tried to imagine the water traversing the distance to the faraway city I'd never seen.

I don't know exactly what I expected the Tuolumne Meadows Store to look like, but it wasn't what I saw. A giant canvas tent atop a cement slab was sectioned into three parts. On the left was a small camp store, in the middle a counter with a sign reading "Post Office," and on the right an order-at-the-counter grill. Huddled underneath a stand of trees across the parking lot from the canvas tent was a group of backpackers who were as bundled as we were. Gear was strewn about the picnic tables in a colorful explosion as hikers worked to fit resupply items into their packs.

I left my pack on a picnic table and wandered toward the post office. A laminated sign told me that packages were handed out once an hour, on the hour, after a bell was rung. I looked at my iPhone and saw we had about twenty minutes. I ordered a cheeseburger, fries, and a salad and shivered on a bench in the cold while I ate them. Unfortunately, as usual, my eyes were bigger than my stomach.

Another hiker had been sitting on the picnic table next to me rearranging his pack. He had a long, grey braided ponytail and was wearing sunglasses even on this gloomy day. He sported a tank top and shorts despite the cold, windy weather and had a large knee brace on one leg. He was also thru-hiking the JMT and had introduced himself as Yogi Beers earlier.

"Hey, Yogi, do you want my fries?"

He immediately seated himself across from me and started eating. Normally I wouldn't offer a stranger my leftovers, but food is sacred in the hiking world and it would have been *more* rude to throw them away. Besides, his name was Yogi, which suggested he was used to getting free food.

A number of other hikers were hanging out at the picnic area. There was John, a forty-something Jewish guy from L.A. who was an amateur comedian. He wore a glow-in-the-dark orange shirt and had a dark, curly beard. He was thru-hiking too. There was also a father on a one-week hike with his young son. The father was carrying food for both of them and had two large-sized bear canisters, making his pack gargantuan. Other hikers took turns trying to pick up the dad's pack and staggered under the weight.

As the group ogled the bizarrely large pack, another hiker bragged about being an ultra-lighter. He was so ultralight that he didn't have enough layers and had to go to the store down the road to buy long underwear. The store didn't have any men's shirts in his size, so he came back with a women's scalloped-edge long underwear top. *I wonder if he'll go so ultralight next time?*

After we ate, Sarah and I collected our first resupply package. We were both visibly relieved that the package had arrived. We restocked our packs and Sarah had a small pile of extra belongings to mail home. Although my pack was still heavier than Sarah's, I had yet to find anything in it that I wasn't using. I was comfortable with my pack and opted to keep everything.

While she went to the post office counter, I called home. My parents were surprised to hear from me already. I gave them the abridged version of my brief encounter with altitude sickness and my failed attempt at climbing Half Dome. Mom said she had figured that was what was going on when she saw my tracker turn around partway up the mountain. I had intentionally not given them any details through the GPS messaging and hadn't realized they would be able to see that I'd turned around from the tracker.

Our original itinerary had us staying overnight at the campground in Tuolumne, but with the dreary weather we thought we would be warmer walking than sitting around all afternoon. We said goodbye to the other hikers and headed off toward the trail.

Not surprisingly, we had trouble relocating the JMT. Our map was confusing in this area, so it was of little help. We stopped to ask people for input and walked in circles for a while. Sarah and I were both getting snippy, and being cold wasn't helping the situation. Finally we stumbled upon a Pacific Crest Trail (PCT) sign. From this point we would be contiguous with the PCT for about the next 160 miles.

"Maybe since we're also on the PCT now, the signs will be better," I said to Sarah, trying to find a silver lining.

"They can't be worse."

She was right. The JMT had been abysmally marked so far.

"Maybe when I get home I'll start a Kickstarter campaign to raise money for signage for this trail," she said. "I'll come back and do the trail on horseback and put up signs at every single damn intersection."

"Good luck figuring out where to put them."

Soon after we found the JMT, we ran into John and Yogi. The four of us hiked together for the rest of the afternoon. No camping is allowed for four miles after Tuolumne, so we knew we had to go at least that far. The conversation flowed easily. John shared that he edited TV ads for a living and told us this was this third JMT hike. He also confessed that he wasn't having as much fun this time—partially due to not bringing the right gear for the unexpected rain and cold and partially because he had gained weight and was out of shape.

John also told us about his favorite trail, the West Coast Trail, which is in Canada and includes ladders, cable cars, and several Indian villages. As an added benefit, it can be hiked in only one week. *Heeeeey, Daaaaad!*

Yogi, whose real name is David, was probably in his mid-fifties. He casually made references to time in jail and his missing eyeball. He also talked about working as an electrician. He had hiked a good bit on both the JMT and PCT previously and was trying to piece together the entire PCT.

As we all talked about the different approaches to the JMT, Yogi said, "Hikers have all kinds o' plans. Just whatever works for them, ya know? Some people, they do it in six days. They're the ones what run on crank and coffee."

He highlighted just how differently some hikers operate when he told us that he doesn't cook at all on the trail. I thought this meant he ate things like granola bars and peanut butter, but I was later surprised to see him eating spaghetti he had rehydrated with cold water. Resupply points often have containers called hiker boxes where people can leave excess supplies for others to pick up. Etiquette states that you should take only what you need, but some hikers use these boxes more like personal resupply stores. Yogi had scavenged the spaghetti, along with most of the rest of his food, from a hiker box. According to him, the food tasted just the same cold. On some level I guess that's true, but I always looked forward to my hot meals and couldn't imagine eating only cold food for three weeks.

With all the conversation the time passed quickly, and before we knew it we had traversed about seven miles. The four of us set up camp together, and Yogi jumped into the river for a bath. Cleaning up sounded good, but it was way too cold for a wimp like me. I settled for changing into my dry camp clothes.

We picked a rocky area away from our tents as the "kitchen" and all sat together to cook and eat. Sarah and John were both making macaroni and cheese with broccoli, so we joked about having a blind taste test to determine who had the better recipe. This led to a whole conversation about an idea for a backcountry chef TV show.

John had run out of fuel for his stove, so I let him use mine. He was the first hiker I had met who left the fuel on the entire time he cooked. He never let the noodles soak and didn't use any kind of cozy. Since he used my fuel first, I had to wait a long time to cook. I became worried that I might run out.

As I waited my turn for the fuel, I listened to the conversation around me and marveled at how quickly friendships form in the hiking world. These were two people I would probably never encounter in my day-to-day life, but out on the trail our shared experience was enough to unite us for however long our paths crossed. I tuned in just as John was telling the group that he was drinking chocolate protein shakes during the day and only eating a solid meal at dinner each night.

"This is my belly-be-gone hike," he explained as he jiggled his generous belly with both hands. "Out here is the only time I feel superior to my skinny friends. I don't have to eat much because I have plenty to burn."

The conversation continued with everyone chiming in about what food they carried and what medicines they bring in a first aid kit.

"I should have a patch across my chest, like a NASCAR driver, that says 'Sponsored by Tylenol,'" John exclaimed in a TV announcer voice, waving his hand across his chest dramatically. "Tylenol is what keeps me going out here. I pop it like candy."

After I'd had my turn to cook and eat dinner, I headed down to the water source to take a sponge bath and collect water. I heard the cheery greetings of hikers introducing themselves back near our campsite. Glancing up, I saw an AT patch on one hiker's pack. While gravity was working its wonders on my water filter, I went over to introduce myself.

"Yo! What's up?" a man about my age called as I approached.

"Hey. I thought I'd come meet you guys."

"Awesome. Totally." He told me his trail name, which I promptly forgot.

"I'm Brownie."

"Hey, Brownie. Great to meet you. You're doing the JMT with those guys over there?"

"Well, no. Actually, I'm hiking with the other woman, Sarah—her trail name is Harvest. We just met those guys today at Tuolumne."

"Totally awesome. So you're going south. That's great. We're headed north. We just met two weeks ago," he said, inclining his head toward a figure setting up a tent in the dark. "She was hiking the JMT southbound and I'm doing the PCT northbound. We just totally hit it off the night we met, you know, so the next day she turned around and started going north with me."

On cue, a colorfully dressed woman with a short, spiky haircut bounced up beside him and draped her arm over his shoulder. "Heeeey!" she said to me. "I'm Jenniraffe, like Jennifer and giraffe, you know."

"I'm Brownie."

"So he was telling you our story. Yep, I guess it was love at first sight. We just knew it was right so I turned around and hiked with him. I'm so glad because the group I was with southbound was, like, totally toxic. They were ruining the whole vibe of the trip for me, you know? I was depressed and just not, like, enjoying it at all. Since I've turned around I'm having fun and actually, like, noticing how beautiful it is, you know? Everything is so much brighter when you're in love."

"I'm glad you're having fun." I squinted my eyes to look at her more closely in the fading light. "Are you...." I paused as I considered whether or not there was a polite way to ask. "Are you wearing a tail?"

She glanced at me as she leaned down to pick something up. "Oh, yeah. I always wear a tail." She said this matter-of-factly, as though she was telling me she always wears her hair up or wears sneakers every day.

What the hell? "Oh." I tried to keep quiet, but I just couldn't. "Why?"

"It started as a last-minute costume for Halloween one year. But then I realized I'm more comfortable wearing a tail. People always stare at me, but this way I can pretend it's because of the tail and not just, like, because they think I'm weird. It just kind of fits me, you know? I feel more natural."

No, I do not know. "So, you made it yourself?" This seemed like a safer way to take this conversation than debating the normalcy (or lack thereof) of wearing a tail.

"Yep. Look." She came closer and held the tail in her hand. It was made of brown and yellow yarn woven together. "This actually came from part of a purse that I upcycled."

"That's what she does for a living," her boyfriend chimed in proudly. "She works in trash." He turned to her. "Show her that cell phone case you made."

Jenniraffe hurried over to her pack and came back with a small pouch. When she handed it to me I could tell it was woven from multi-colored plastic shopping bags. It was uneven and awkwardly shaped. I'm a crafty person myself, but this I just didn't understand.

"That was just, like, a prototype."

I turned it over in my hands. "Neat."

"Yep. That's what she does full time. She goes to all these different places to get recycled supplies and turns them into art and sells it."

Jenniraffe picked up a hula-hoop that was leaning against a tree. "It can be hard to make a living, but I don't mind. It's, like, my passion."

After a few seconds of silence I asked, "So, you carry a hula hoop backpacking?"

"Everyone has an extra item, right? Some people carry books or a journal." She jerked her thumb at her hiking partner. "He carries speakers. And I carry a hula hoop." She spun it around on her arm. "It's collapsible, though."

Oh, in that case it makes perfect sense.

I wished them luck and said goodbye. In the tent I inspected my gear and found that one of my FITS socks had a hole in the toe. *Day three and I have a hole in my sock. So much for these being better than SmartWool brand.* I also had a small hole in the mesh kangaroo pocket on my pack and a stuck zipper on one compartment. *I wonder if Jenniraffe checks her tail and hula hoop?*

I turned my attention to my body. A thorough inspection of my feet by headlamp revealed that they were blister-free. My nausea and finger-tingling had dissipated, but the headache still lingered. My gear was good; my body was coping. I finished up my bedtime routine and rewarded myself with my next daily letter.

Hi Michelle,

Where and when you are reading this I hope all has gone well; however, knowing the way life works I am sure you have had frustrations, changes, and other problems crop up during your travels. Hopefully all of the problems have been worked out and you are charging ahead on the trail. Here's to sore legs, hungry and tired hikers, and hopefully blister-free feet. We set out to explore, to observe, to meditate, to enjoy nature, to test our strength and skills, and to enjoy the fellowship and fun times with other backpackers. There are miles when we wonder, "Why do I put myself through this?" and then we walk out on that bald or slide down the snow or look at the beautiful waterfall or wildlife and we know every pain is worth it.

I am not a fast hiker but I have found that when other faster hikers get tired they use me as an example. Little snail puts one foot in front of the other and keeps on going. So keep on going one foot at a time; stop, look, and listen; take lots of pictures; soak up the scenery; and most of all I sure hope you are having a fun time.

One other thing, please do not kill your bear canister until you get back to the hotel. It does have a purpose in life even if it is a pain. Enjoy the hot showers when you can get them and "real" food when you are around it; and have a safe trip home.

"Climb the mountains and get their good tidings. Nature's peace will flow into you as sunshine flows into trees, the wind will blow their own freshness into you, and the storms their energy, while care will drop off like Autumn leaves." – John Muir

Best of everything to you.
Janice

Looking fashionable near Tuolumne Meadows

Me, joyous at finding the JMT again

15

IS IT KOSHER?

August 6, 2014

Slept: Thousand Island Lake (9,844 feet)
Miles: 13.5
Weather: gorgeous, then AWFUL—sleet/rain/cold
Dinner: black beans and rice (good, but needed more spice)
Mood: ecstatic. Happy to be alive!
Letter: Erin
Dad's quote of the day:

AGE WRINKLES THE BODY. QUITTING WRINKLES THE SOUL.
—DOUGLAS MACARTHUR

Considering that California was in a drought, we'd been encountering a ton of rain. Waking to find the sun shining brightly through the mesh of our tent immediately put a smile on my face. While I packed up, I overheard a conversation between Sarah and Yogi.

"That'll keep you regular." Sarah looked with wide eyes at Yogi, who was drinking cold water with coffee grounds stirred in.

"Know what else keeps you regular?" he asked, swiping the back of his hand across his mouth after a giant swig. "Not filtering your water."

"You don't filter your water?"

"Nope. Never have."

I smirked at the ground. *I wouldn't want it cold, but I do wish I had a coffee.* Until I had started hiking with Dad, I had always eaten a cold breakfast on camping trips. Dad is a coffee drinker, though, and I thought he might take to backpacking better if I made sure he still got his daily coffee—even if it was of the instant variety. Since we were already boiling water for coffee, I typically made us a hot breakfast too. Quickly I found that I enjoyed a warm meal in the morning as much as he did.

I had initially planned to bring coffee on the JMT and cook breakfast. Sarah isn't a regular coffee drinker, though, and she eats a cold breakfast on the trail, so I opted to do the same. I didn't want to feel rushed or like I was holding her up. Truthfully, I'm not a morning person anyway, and the fewer tasks I had in front of me before hitting the trail, the better. I did miss the coffee, though.

Since we had traveled an extra seven miles the day before, Sarah and I arrived at our intended destination by ten thirty. We ate a leisurely snack, peered at the clear blue sky, and decided to go ahead and climb Donohue Pass.

Before researching the John Muir Trail, I honestly hadn't been sure what a pass was. I learned that a pass is a route through a mountain range or over a ridge. At first I mistakenly thought this was the same thing as a col. A col, however, is the lowest point between two connected peaks. A pass isn't necessarily the lowest point; it is merely a traversable route. The Sierras have so many formidable ranges that the mountaineers who laid out the JMT had trouble finding a crossable path to connect some of them.

Donahue was technically our second pass of the trip. There are ten named passes on the JMT: eight major ones and two minor ones. Cathedral Pass, our first, had been so minor that we wouldn't have even realized it was a pass if we hadn't seen it labeled as such in the guidebook.

At 11,056 feet, Donahue would be our highest elevation yet. It is the sixth-highest pass on the trail. Donahue would also mark our exit from Yosemite National Park and our entrance into the Ansel Adams Wilderness and Inyo National Forest.

Since the mountain was mostly slab, it was difficult to tell where the trail went. We encountered a number of false summits, but I was so busy marveling at the vast views of Lyell Canyon below me that I hardly cared. This was my first time hiking in an alpine environment and I couldn't get over the plant-less surroundings. I'd expected areas above the tree line to feel barren, but this was magnificent. The views were unending and the colors so crisp.

As I stopped to reapply sunscreen for the third time, a lady coming down the pass stopped me. "Your pack is so small!"

I resisted the urge to hug her. After all the negativity we had encountered from the men at the airport, Captain Asshole, the Three Sock Tribe, and others who hadn't even been worth mentioning, it was nice to hear someone praise my packing job. I had an extra spring in my step as I waved goodbye.

When I reached the bare pass—devoid of plants, trees, and even people (with the exception of Sarah, who was perched on a rock waiting for me)—it was still before noon. I looked around at the expansive rocks and naked landscape as I posed for pictures. Then Sarah and I descended slightly to get out of the wind. We found a sunny place to dry out our tent and gear while we ate lunch and journaled. Sarah took off her sock to inspect her heel and found a substantial blister. She resolutely set about making what she called a "house" of bandages to protect it. Though she didn't complain, I knew it had to hurt a lot.

After lunch we continued ascending and were surprised to realize we hadn't even arrived at the pass yet. A little more climbing and we reached the true pass, where there were signs signaling the southern barrier of Yosemite National Park. We took photos and noted the nearby signs prohibiting fires above 10,000 feet.

On long backpacking trips I'm typically too tired at night to care about making a fire. However, I had enjoyed our frequent campfires so far on this trip and was disappointed to realize we might not be able to have many more.

Before starting back down, I tilted my head up to the sun and closed my eyes. A few days before, I'd been scared I might not be able to finish the trail. Now I had ascended to an elevation above 10,000 feet and had gotten ahead of schedule. *Mount Whitney, here I come!*

The descent down the south side of Donahue Pass started gradually. As was becoming the trend, it started raining. Sarah and I ignored the raindrops for a few minutes. I think we were both hoping that if we didn't acknowledge them, they might go away. But soon the rain became too steady to disregard and we begrudgingly stopped to put on raingear.

"Do you think we should set up camp?" Sarah asked as she stared at the darkening sky.

"I don't know," I hedged, balancing awkwardly on one foot to shove the other muddy boot into my rain pants. "I don't love hiking in rain, but setting up camp in the rain is miserable too." A raindrop ran down my spine and I shivered. "Plus, we would have to just sit in the tent bundled in our sleeping bags. We'd be cold even if we were dry, so we might as well make mileage."

"Yeah. I agree." She tucked her braid inside her raincoat. "This really sucks."

Soon the rain picked up force and was pelting us with cold drops from all angles. The clouds were materializing en masse, and it was getting noticeably darker in every direction. My sweaty body got more and more chilled, and I found myself uncharacteristically hoping for an uphill climb to make me work harder and raise my body temperature.

After about an hour the rain stopped. I flipped my hood off my head gratefully and brushed the raindrops from my face.

"That was bad, but at least it was short," I said to Sarah.

"Definitely."

Not ten minutes later, the rain started again with gusto. It got darker immediately, like nighttime had come early.

After alternating between rain and hail a few more times, the storm let up. When the relentless wind had died down, the lightning and thunder had stopped, and the rain had subsided to a steady annoyance, we decided to continue over Island Pass. We reasoned that moving would warm us up, and we could always turn around if the weather worsened again. Besides, there was nowhere to camp nearby.

I hunched my shoulders inside my raincoat and moved my legs in a metronomic rhythm. Soon we were over Island Pass and headed down the other side. The outsides of my rain clothes were wet from the rain, and my clothes underneath were sticky with sweat from the trapped body heat. As the hiking became easier, I actually began shivering. All I could think about was getting warm and dry.

Through the gathering fog Sarah and I could see Thousand Island Lake with its abundant, tiny land masses scattered across the surface. There was supposed to be a beautiful view of Banner Peak, but it was far too hazy to see. John had caught up to us near Island Pass and told us that he remembered many camping spots near the lake. It took so long to get down to the lake that it seemed like a mirage.

Approaching the lake we could see a few pops of color from tents scattered around the rocks on the far right side, but the trail curved to the left. We didn't want to get too far off course, so we stopped at the first flat spot we reached. Technically, to prevent contamination, you're supposed to camp at least 200 feet from a water source, but there was an established campsite near the water. Throwing an apology up to the trail gods, Sarah and I dropped our packs. John claimed a spot just across the trail from us.

As soon as my pack was off my back and the wind could reach my sweaty skin, my shivering became uncontrollable. I dug in my pack for my clothing stuff sack while my teeth chattered in my head like a typewriter.

I was much too cold for modesty. "I'm getting naked. If you don't want to see, turn around."

"What if I do want to see?" John asked with a teasing grin.

"Turn around anyway."

I pulled off my wet clothes and scattered them on the nearby rocks and bushes, hoping the wind might help them start to dry before I had to bring them in the tent. I put on every piece of dry clothing I had and then added my still-damp hat and gloves for good measure.

Sarah and I erected the tent as quickly as possible and threw our soggy belongings inside. We hoped the rain was over for the night but didn't want to risk leaving our gear lying around in case another storm popped up unexpectedly. When all our camp chores were done, we set up a kitchen at the edge of the lake.

John's food selection had gotten meager, so Sarah tossed him a PayDay candy bar.

"What's this?"

"It's liked a naked Snickers," she explained.

John ate it in about two bites. "Usually I'm a fan of naked. But in this case, I think I need the chocolate—the 'clothing,' if you will. It's good, but I like Snickers better."

I leaned back against a rock and sipped hot chocolate. Packing a hot drink for each night on the JMT had been one of my best decisions. I was able to warm up while my dinner cooked in my Brownie Bag nearby. It was completely dark already, and I stared up at the sky as I cupped the hot mug in my icy hands and let the steam waft over my face.

John saw me looking up. "Normally the stars are amazing here. Some people spend days camped right on Thousand Island Lake."

"I don't see a single star tonight," I lamented, "though I'm not surprised after the weather today." I took another sip. "I can't believe we got hailed on. In California. In August. In a drought!"

"Three times," Sarah hastened to add, holding up her fingers for emphasis.

"This isn't normal. I'm telling you. It's my third time hiking this trail and I've never seen weather like this." John stroked his curly beard. "I'm completely unprepared. My sleeping bag isn't warm enough, my bivy sack isn't actually waterproof—which, it turns out, is an important detail, and I don't even have rain gear with me. I'm miserable. I either have to quit or get different gear."

I swallowed the last sip of my hot chocolate. "What are you going to do?"

"Tomorrow I'm going to take a side trail to Red's Meadow so I can catch the bus to town and get a tent and some rain gear, at a minimum. It sucks because I have all this gear at home. I just never expected to need it here. It's so unusual." He pulled on his beard and stared off at the water. "You guys should come with me," he proposed. "You can get into town early and dry out."

Sarah let him know that we had agreed to stick to the official JMT whenever possible.

"Well, I'll be at Red's when you guys get there. I've seriously got to figure out what I'm going to do. I can't finish like this."

"Are you considering quitting?" I asked him while I stirred my food.

"Honestly, I probably would if I could. This has been pretty miserable. I don't know what I was thinking. I didn't bring the right gear, and I'm in terrible shape." He jiggled his belly for emphasis. "But I sublet my apartment, and I don't have anywhere to go. I don't think I can finish with the gear I have if it keeps raining like this. But I don't want to spend the money to buy gear I have sitting in a closet at home."

"You're in a pickle."

"Tell me about it."

I grinned at him. "Is it Kosher?"

John grimaced. "Are you seriously making Jewish jokes right now?"

While I ate my black beans and rice, I pulled out my next letter. I scanned to the end and saw Erin's name. Erin was one of my partners on the ambulance, and she always kept me laughing, so I was interested to see what her letter would say.

Michelle,

This is what I imagine you will write in your trail journal:

Trail Log Day 1:

>*Arrived safely. Pumped and ready to go! High fives all around. Well, high five to my hiking partner since it's just the two of us for the next twenty-two days. Twenty-two days of up and down the mountain. Up and down. Just the two of us. Maybe that burrito was not such a good idea.*

Trail Log Day 5:

>*Made it five days without pushing my hiking partner off the side of the mountain. It's a good day. Nature is good. Glad I packed chocolate. I like chocolate.*

Trail Log Day 10:

>*Who thought this was a good idea?! There are bugs and birds. And strange animal sounds. Probably strange animals having coitus. Like Marmots. Marmots that have coitus and then come steal your food. Damn Nature. Talking about food is making me hungry. Man, I could really go for a non-dehydrated CHEESEBURGER.*

Trail Log Day 18:

>*"Ain't no mountain high enough, Ain't no valley low enough." "She'll be comin' round the mountain when she comes." There are a lot of songs about mountains. There are probably more, but I can't think of any right now. I wonder if the man at the hotel where we left our luggage*

is sprawled out on my bed in my underwear? Wow, I might not sleep in that bed.

Hope you are having a good time. I hope we don't have to use the "black box" your mom and dad gave you to find you.

Happy trails (Get it? Cuz you're on a trail...),
Erin

I laughed to myself at Erin's sarcastic and offbeat sense of humor. Her ability to make me laugh had transferred seamlessly to her trail letter. *I'm sure going to miss working with Erin when I go back and start a new job. I wonder if any of my new coworkers will make me laugh as hard?*

John cooking dinner
Photo credit: Sarah Jones Decker

16

HIKING WITH MERMAIDS

August 7, 2014

Slept: Red's backpackers' campground
Miles: 17
Weather: sunny/warm
Dinner: grilled cheese and chocolate milkshake at the diner
Mood: content, proud
Letter: none
Dad's quote of the day:

> IT ISN'T WHAT YOU HAVE, OR WHO YOU ARE, OR WHERE YOU ARE,
> OR WHAT YOU ARE DOING THAT MAKES YOU HAPPY OR UNHAPPY.
> IT IS WHAT YOU THINK ABOUT. —DALE CARNEGIE

As we hiked the next morning, Sarah told me about a conversation she'd had on Island Pass the day before.

"I was talking to this guy from California. He told me that he had considered hiking the AT but didn't bother because he knew it would be easy since all the mountains on the East Coast are small. What the f—? Oh, side note: he's never even been east of Ohio," Sarah told me.

"There seems to be a lot of negativity out here about the AT."

"I know. It's bullshit."

"I wonder why?" I mused. "I don't remember people on the AT talking negatively about the PCT. Do you?"

"No. But I swear out here people see our AT patches and think we're incompetent idiots."

"I know," I agreed. "I haven't particularly found the JMT to be harder than the AT, but I don't even know why the two trails have to be compared all the time. They're just different."

It had been slow going initially that morning. When we woke up, all our gear and clothes had still been damp from the previous day's storm. Striving to remain upbeat, I started making up hiking-related lyrics to pop songs.

"Are you singing?" Sarah had asked me incredulously.

"Yep."

Despite my forced cheer, our wet gear was heavy and our backs were feeling the added strain. It was also the seventh day since my last shower at the hotel in Mammoth Lakes. I was getting pretty ripe, and smelling myself was not lifting my spirits. I did still note some positives: since the High Sierras aren't very humid, my hair actually felt remarkably normal considering how long it had gone unwashed. Also, my skin is sensitive, and on hikes with long stretches between showers I tend to get itchy and occasionally develop painful rashes under my arms and where my pack straps rub. My skin didn't hurt or itch despite my stench.

Sarah's blisters had gotten pretty serious, and she was hurting a lot. The second toe on her left foot was also enormously swollen. We'd taken to affectionately calling it Franken-toe. She was doing a great job of keeping the blisters clean, medicated, and dry, but some degree of friction is inevitable during a hike. We walked together most of the day and I tried to keep the conversation going to distract us both. We didn't typically talk a lot during the hiking hours, so this was a pleasant change.

It is interesting how hiking can be so different with different partners. Dad and I normally hiked near each other, though we alternated times of conversation and companionable silence. Sarah and I tended to start and finish days together, with long periods of walking separately in between. Usually she went ahead on uphill stretches and I led on long downhills. I had decided ahead of time that I was just going to move comfortably at my own pace without feeling rushed. It seemed to be working, because I was enjoying the balance of companionship and solitude.

We stopped for lunch beside a beautiful lake and saw a handful of other hikers skinny-dipping in the pristine water. Although I don't normally love to swim, the water was so pretty that I was tempted to jump in. Sarah didn't want to get her blister bandages wet, though, because she was out of spares, and I felt guilty swimming when she couldn't. Instead I settled for stretching out on a big rock and feeling the gentle breeze dance across my face.

The bluish-green lake water was so intense it was surreal. I could identify shades of jade, kelly green, peacock, sage, and teal as I scanned Rosalie Lake. The surface sparkled like a gem, and the ethereal pool appeared to be bottomless. Sunlight filtered through the tree limbs above and glittered on the unmarred surface. It looked more like a painting than a real-life view. Although I've never been one for fairy tales and make believe, even as a small child, at this moment it seemed rational that this must be where mermaids lived. I half-expected one to swim up to me. The absurdity of this thought—its incongruity with my normal way of thinking—would stay with me for months to come.

Sometime in the early afternoon Sarah and I debated stopping to top off our CamelBaks. But when we looked at the map, it appeared that there were multiple water sources coming up. Since we both had some water left, and since water is heavy, we decided to wait.

According to the thermometer keychain on my pack, the temperature was near a hundred degrees. The air was so thick that I felt like I was breathing in particles. And our rapid pace was forcing me to breathe through my mouth, which was drying it out. I regularly took small sips from my bite valve to combat the dryness. As sweat trickled down the sides of my face, it was hard to believe I had recently been bundled in a down jacket and fleece hat during a hailstorm. Not thirty minutes after the "should-we-get-water-now" debate, I sucked on my straw only to find it despairingly empty.

I figured we would cross water soon, so I just kept steadily trekking. Every few minutes I would forget the straw was empty and stick it in my parched mouth for a sip. *We'll cross water soon. Just breathe through your nose.* I had been out of water for about four miles when I said something to Sarah. She was just about out too, but generously shared one of her last sips with me. We kept thinking there had to be water soon, but none was to be seen.

By late afternoon we were getting worn out. Sarah's feet hurt from the blisters and from her shoes rubbing against Franken-toe on the relentless downhill. I was exhausted, and the inside of my mouth felt like sandpaper. We needed a water source. The paucity of water on this stretch of the JMT was unprecedented. We knew that the turnoff for Red's Meadow Resort and Pack Station was up ahead, but that was further than we had initially intended to hike. Once it was mentioned as a possibility, though, I couldn't stop thinking about a cheeseburger and a shower—after drinking an ocean of water. Getting to that cheeseburger would mean tackling a total of seventeen miles.

We consulted our guidebook and I checked the time. "I think the restaurant closes at seven o'clock. If we push it, we can make it an hour before the restaurant closes," I announced.

"Let's move," Sarah responded without hesitation.

With the decision made, we hiked at a swift and steady clip. I knew that with our increased speed Sarah's feet had to be bothering her tremendously, especially Franken-toe. My thoughts were almost exclusively about water—drinking it and showering in it. Any time I felt my pace begin to slow, I reminded myself that our reward for pushing extra mileage would be the treat of a "nero" day the following day.

"I can smell myself," I told Sarah as we hurried downhill, kicking up plumes of dust from the dry dirt.

"Me too."

"You can smell *me,* or *you?*" I asked.

"Probably both," she told me honestly.

"Probably. I can't decide if I'm more excited about a shower or a cheeseburger." Talking was drying my mouth out, but it was distracting us both from the mileage.

"I hope we make it in time for dinner," she said.

I resisted the urge to look at the time again. "Stay positive."

We pushed on until we saw a wooden sign reading "Devils Postpile National Monument." There were multiple trails that split near the sign. Not surprisingly, the signs were unclear. We knew there were multiple routes to Devils Postpile and Red's Meadow, but we didn't know if we had found the one we wanted. After reading our guidebooks and reviewing the map, we decided to veer slightly off the JMT to take a somewhat longer route that would allow us to see Devils Postpile without backtracking.

"Technically, we're going to miss about half a mile of the JMT by going this way," Sarah said.

"True. If the map is right. But, really, this trail is so poorly marked that we might have already missed other sections," I pointed out. "Hell, we aren't even sure we started at the actual beginning!"

"Yep." She tossed her braid over her shoulder and shook her head.

"Besides, we're actually taking a longer route, so we're adding mileage, not taking a shortcut."

"You don't have to justify it to me. I'm afraid that if we wait for the second trail to Red's, we might never find it. Then we would have to backtrack."

I fiddled with my empty CamelBak straw. *I'm so thirsty.* "That would be just our luck. Still, I can't believe we're out of water on the longest day of our trip, and we're *adding* mileage."

We turned down the trail and about a half mile later we entered a well-cleared path with fences, benches, and signage for Devils Postpile. There were clean-looking tourists wandering around reading plaques. We hadn't seen many people in days, and it was disconcerting to hear so many conversations at once. With our huge packs and dirty appearances we got some funny looks. As much as I wanted to skip down the path towards a cheeseburger, I made myself stop and read the signs. I would likely never see this national monument again.

According to the informational signs, the arrangement of columnar basalt was created from volcanic lava flow around 100,000 years ago. I took a handful of photos and then stretched put face-down on a giant log while Sarah continued to snap pictures. I imagined I looked like a beached whale with my pack still on and my cheek pressed against the rock. I stayed in that position until I saw Sarah's feet appear beside me.

"Do you want to walk the loop?" she asked. There was a mile-long trail that offered additional views of the columns.

Is she serious? "No." *I want to drink a swimming pool and eat a cheeseburger.*

"Good. Me neither."

We followed the (yet again) poorly marked trail to Red's Meadow. I was beginning to wonder if we would ever be certain we were traveling on the right trail. My pack was growing heavier by the step. The next thing we knew, without warning, the trail spit us out on a road—a real, paved road.

Sarah whirled around and stared at me. "This wasn't on our map, right?"

I didn't even respond. I just leaned forward on my poles so that she could get the map out of my top hat.

"It's not on the map," she confirmed a minute later.

"They're never going to make this easy, are they?" I asked, and then groaned in frustration. "I feel like we've spent more time not knowing where we are on this trail than I have on any other trip."

"F—ing ridiculous is what this is."

I puffed out a giant sigh. "What do we do now? Turn around? Road walk? We know Red's is accessible by bus. That's how John was getting there from that side trail."

"Let's go right."

I looked up the road in both directions. *Why did she pick right instead of left?* I could have asked her, but I was just too tired and thirsty to have the conversation. I had no reason to disagree, so we started down the narrow shoulder of the road. My feet were killing me, and my poles made an annoying clicking noise on the asphalt. I looked up and down the road but saw no cars. *Please let us be going in the right direction.*

Behind us we heard a low rumble as a bus came into view. We both started waving wildly, and the driver slowed down and stopped beside us.

"Is this the way to Red's Meadow?" Sarah asked him, pointing up the road.

"Yep. Do you guys want a ride?"

We glanced at each other.

"Yes!" we said in unison.

Sarah and I stood at the front of the bus, trying to make ourselves as small as possible. Everyone else on the bus looked clean and was pack-free. I hoped they weren't too offended by our hard-earned smell. Within a minute a massive sign reading "Red's Meadow Resort" stretched across the road.

We were dropped off in a clearing that contained a few buildings and a lot of people. In the middle of the buildings was a collection of picnic tables, benches, and log seats. We saw John, Yogi, and some other hikers we had met surrounded by partially exploded packs. Most of them were in their camp shoes, and they were all drinking beer.

"Michelle! Sarah!" John yelled from his bench. "You took the bus too." He laughed good-naturedly. "*Everyone* took the bus."

"I think we lost the trail," I told him. "We ended up on a road. We were road-walking, and when the bus came along they offered us a ride."

"That's what everyone did. There was a reroute because of erosion or something," he explained.

"The markings were piss-poor," another hiker interjected. "But you made it!" He held his hand up for a high five. "Have a beer."

Sarah accepted an offered beer. I don't like beer on the best of days, and I couldn't even fathom drinking alcohol as thirsty as I was.

I turned back to John. "I thought you would still be in town."

"I never made it. I got here and the guys were drinking beer, and, well, here I am."

"What are you going to do about gear?"

He shrugged. "Supposedly, the weather's going to improve."

They filled us in on the details of Red's. Beer, snacks, and trinkets were for sale in the camp store. There were no camping cabins available, and the only place to sleep was the backpackers' campground which had a fee but allowed six people per site. Sleeping was not currently my top priority. My eyes wandered to the restaurant.

"It's open," John told me. "I recommend the chocolate milkshake."

Milkshakes! I resisted the urge to moan.

"Showers?" I asked.

He pointed across the way. "They're seven dollars. You pay inside. They close early, though—something about generators, I think—so you probably don't have time to eat and shower tonight."

"What do you think?" Sarah asked me.

I glanced down at my hands, stained a strange swirly brown from dirt and sweat. "I never thought I'd say this after a week of sweating profusely in the same clothes—but I'd rather eat than shower."

"Good." She held up her waist-length braid. "This would never dry before bed, and I don't want to sleep with it wet."

We went inside the store and I drank a container of strawberry milk in about two sips, followed by a sweet tea. After talking with the cashier about the shower situation and camping, Sarah and I hurried into the restaurant.

It was already completely dark when we finished eating. I was so tired that I wanted to sleep right there on the picnic table outside of the diner.

Instead, I tied my hiking shoes onto my pack and picked it up one more time. The trail to the backpackers' campground was, of course, hard to find. Thankfully, some of the others had located it earlier in the day, and they led the way. Four-tenths of a mile later, we crossed a small stream and were in the campground. Someone picked a spot, and I gladly dropped my gear. Once again I marveled that these people—some of whom I'd known for hours, and others for days—were instantly friends and would soon be campsite mates. We erected our wet-dog-smelling tent, and then I pulled out my finicky Sawyer Mini water purifier. I had collected water on the way to the campsite because I knew that even after drinking milk, a sweet tea, a milkshake, and three glasses of ice water, I was still dehydrated. The Sawyer had been giving us trouble, though, and I was hoping to sort out why.

Hans, another hiker staying in the same campsite, showed me how to back-flush the filter and get it to flow again. He said he'd been having trouble with his filter too, and he speculated that maybe the altitude was affecting the gravity pull on the hoses. While that explanation vaguely made sense (in the same way most complex, science-y ideas make sense to me), it didn't encourage me that the contraption would cooperate any better on the remainder of the trip.

I talked with John and Yogi at a picnic table for a few minutes, but I was so tired after the long day that I soon collapsed into our tent. Crowded campgrounds are usually noisy, and this one was no exception. I was once again thankful I had had the foresight to pack Advil PM. My body desperately needed sleep, but my overly sensitive ears and overactive brain never would have allowed me to sleep without help. Two blue tablets and two pink earplugs later, I was blissfully unaware of the ruckus that continued around me.

Devils Postpile

Resting at Devils Postpile
Photo Credit: Sarah Jones Decker

17

LIFE AT TWENTY-TWO

August 8, 2014

Slept: Deer Creek
Miles: 5.9 (JMT) + 0.3 (Red's access trail) = 6.2
Weather: sunny/brief raindrops in the afternoon
Dinner: spaghetti
Mood: strong, inspired
Letter: Lark
Dad's quote of the day:

LOSERS LIVE IN THE PAST. WINNERS LEARN FROM THE PAST WHILE THEY ARE
WORKING IN THE PRESENT TOWARD THE FUTURE.
—DENIS WAITLEY

We were awake surprisingly early. With both food and showers in our future on this "nero" day, Sarah and I were in phenomenal moods. Before leaving the campsite, we packed up our gear to take with us. I didn't want to have to waste time or mileage going back to get gear on a day of relaxation.

I ate a hearty breakfast at the restaurant while we began the time-consuming chore of charging our electronics. Sarah and I both had to charge camera batteries, cell phones, and backup phone chargers. Since outlets are in short supply at a backcountry resupply station, they are hard to claim and should be used efficiently. We snagged one during breakfast and rotated items out as soon as they were charged.

From the store we collected our resupply package and opened it immediately. As soon as we had unearthed our shower supplies, we shoved the rest of the pile aside. After changing into our rain gear and putting our filthy clothes into the washing machine, we hurried to the bath house for much-anticipated showers. The facilities were impressively clean, especially considering that they were used regularly by grubby hikers. Each person had a private shower with a glass door, a changing stall with hooks for clothes, and a bench. I bathed, shampooed twice, and shaved my legs. Ten minutes later I felt like a new person.

When I went over to switch out the laundry, I encountered a strange sight. A group of four people were seated at a plastic table outside the laundry area. I probably wouldn't have taken a second look except that a rather hairy-chested older man was wearing a clear raincoat with nothing underneath on his top half except for red suspenders. The other three—a man, a woman, and a child—had on typical nylon hiking raincoats. However, all four of them were wearing what looked like sleeping bags with leg holes on their lower halves. I was hot in my raingear, so I knew they had to be sweltering. *Why in the world are they dressed like that?*

Forcing myself not to gawk, I wandered back to the picnic table with my gear. I wanted to stretch out in a spot of sun and write postcards, but there were so many chores to do on a "town" day. I knew I'd enjoy the relaxation more if I tackled all the necessities first. Still feeling dehydrated from the day before, I bought another sweet tea and settled down at a vacant picnic table.

First I dumped our five-gallon resupply bucket onto the picnic table and separated my items from Sarah's. I put hers back into the bucket and set it aside. Then I pushed my resupply to the end of the table and completely emptied my backpack, spreading all my gear out in front of me. I unzipped each compartment of my pack and shook out debris and dirt. I started repairing gear, replacing used items, and repacking them methodically, one item at a time.

I inspected the tips of my trekking poles and wrapped new pink duct tape around each pole for easy access. Then I tackled each stuff sack systematically. The pink clothing sack was empty since I was washing all my clothes, so I shook it out and set it aside. I patched a hole in the rain pants

I was wearing with a piece of clear Tenacious Tape from my repair kit. That took care of my clothing.

I grabbed the blue technology sack and replaced Deadweight's batteries. Since my phone was charged and the camera battery was charging, there was nothing else I could do with that bag. The orange stuff sack with my kitchen gear was next. I replaced my fuel canister and small scrubbie, washed my spoon, water bottle, CamelBak, and pot at a dishwashing station, and shook my Bic lighter to make sure it still had fluid. I placed the stove and pot holder back inside the pot with the other items. Cooking gear was finished.

My dark green personal hygiene kit was the last stuff sack. I replaced the Ibuprofen and Advil PM, swapped out the toothpaste, and added new wet wipes and toilet paper. I replaced the worn Ziploc holding my journal and maps with a fresh one and took out the letters I had already read. They went in an envelope with the pages of the map and guidebook that we had finished, which I would mail home. It seems silly, but these were things I wanted to keep, and every ounce I could get off my back made a difference. The sleeping bag and tent probably could have used a good shaking-out to remove trail dirt, but they had to stay as they were because I didn't want to spread them out in a public area.

When I was content that my gear was sorted, I set the hated bear canister on the bench next to me. This was a small resupply, so fitting all the food in with my other smell-ables wasn't difficult. *I can't believe we only have two more resupplies left.* Before going to retrieve our laundry, I set my reloaded pack on the ground and carried my extra supplies to the hiker box. With my clean clothes on, I shoved the extra layers into the stuff sack and stuffed my rain gear back into an outside pocket of my pack. *If only putting away laundry was this quick at home.*

In the shower I had noticed an insignificant clear blister on my left foot at the base of my second toe. It wasn't painful, but I knew I needed to keep an eye on it. I cleaned my foot with an alcohol wipe and popped the blister with a borrowed safety pin that I had sterilized with a lighter. It remained painless after being popped, and I only hoped it would dry out before I put my hiking shoes back on.

Pleased that all my chores were accomplished, I settled in an Adirondack chair and addressed postcards to family and friends, wrote in my journal, and ate an ice cream sandwich. All around me was a pleasant flurry of activity. Other long-distance hikers were arranging gear, eating snacks, and drinking beer, while tourists were preparing for horseback rides, bus trips to town, and sightseeing.

Neither Sarah nor I seemed to be in any hurry. At half past three we decided to work our way toward the JMT again. By that point we should have expected that the trail would never be clearly labeled, but for some reason we thought there would be an obviously marked way to get back to it. Instead, a bunch of people pointed us in vague directions. We wandered past the bathhouse, the restaurant, and the store, across a dirt road, past a horse stable and campers, and finally toward an unmarked dirt trail.

"How does anyone else find this?" Sarah asked.

"Maybe this isn't even the JMT."

She cussed.

I stabbed my pole in the dusty dirt. "I'm so tired of this."

"You need to call your book about this hike *Unmarked*. Because that's what this whole damn trail is. There aren't signs anywhere.

I kicked at the dirt in frustration and watched my freshly washed gaiters turn a hazy, brownish hue. "Should we bother looking at the map?"

"I guess."

I leaned over so that she could get it out of my top hat.

"At least my armpits smell better all up in your face now that I've showered," Sarah said, reaching her arms above my head to rummage through my pack.

Predictably, the map offered no information about how to get back to the JMT from Red's Meadow. Since we had arrived on a bus from a road—which we knew was not the actual trail—we were pretty clueless. I approached a man and woman sitting in lawn chairs outside a horse fence.

"Do you know if we're going the right way to get back to the John Muir Trail?"

"Yup," a lady in a plaid flannel shirt said, taking a huge sip from an insulated plastic cup.

"So we just keep going this way?" I pointed.

Her eyes didn't move beneath her black cowgirl hat. "Can't miss it."

We thanked them and drifted further down the trail, hearing them laugh behind us.

"They must get a kick out of getting backpackers lost in the woods," Sarah grumbled. "They probably keep a tally or something."

I squinted and peered as far as I could see into the distance. No signs. No blazes. Not even any other people. "We could end up in another state before even knowing we're on the wrong trail."

The ground around us was scorched, and all of the foliage was burned. Large trees were blackened and their trunks ended jaggedly and abruptly about fifteen feet in the air, like a giant had reached down and popped the tops off. I felt like I was walking through the "Elephant Graveyard" scene from *The Lion King*. We both stopped and stared.

I poked at a desecrated tree with my pole. "It looks like there was a forest fire," I said, stating the obvious.

Sarah spun in a complete circle, looking around. "I think it might have been a controlled burn."

Below the scorched trees, the ground was a combination of blackened, charred earth and vibrantly colored wildflowers. We took photos of as many different flowers as we could, and also of a bright red berry with spikes.

Eventually we worked our way further up the hill on what we hoped was the trail. We saw a sign telling us to go one direction for Red's Meadow, one for Devils Postpile, and another for the PCT. We had to check our map again. Was the sign pointing toward the first entrance to Devils Postpile, where we had already hiked? Or to the second entrance that we hadn't yet reached? *Will navigating this trail ever be easy? John Muir and the adventurers can't have had it much harder than this before an official trail was established. At least back then they weren't looking for someone else's path; they were blazing their own way. That might have been less frustrating.*

Once we knew we were back on the JMT, we moved with enthusiasm and made good time. The extra rest and extra calories at Red's had rejuvenated us. We talked nonstop as we continued climbing further and further uphill. The conversation almost completely kept my mind off the exertion, but still I was aware of my increasing stamina.

I was pleased to realize that our pace had been consistently faster than most estimates. Guidebooks usually calculate that it takes a hiker thirty minutes per mile plus an additional thirty minutes per 1,000 feet of elevation gain. While I knew I moved more slowly going uphill, it had rarely taken me more than forty minutes to go a mile so far. Sarah had remained pretty close to a thirty-minute mile, even on ascents, and I had consistently hiked thirty-minute miles or faster on downhill sections. *What kind of person is considered*

average in these estimates? A person in good shape? Someone who hikes these trails on a
regular basis? A novice hiker? Who do "they" choose as average?

We completed the six-mile climb quickly. That night we camped with Kyle and Tom, two cousins in their early twenties from New England, along with a handful of others. There was also David, a man in his late forties who soon would have completed all of California and Oregon on the PCT. Then there was Paul, a slightly younger man who had previously run the Boston Marathon and had seven-year-old twins. And lastly Jim, a grandfather and avid trail runner who had written a book called *50 Trail Runs in Southern California*. We built a campfire and everyone sat around it preparing dinner and talking.

Kyle's twenty-second birthday was the following week, so we took turns around the circle telling where we had lived and what we had been doing at that age. I was surprised to realize that age twenty-two had been a decade ago for me. When my turn came around, I told everyone, "The year I was twenty-two, I graduated college and started hiking the AT."

As I listened to the others reflect on life at twenty-two, I pictured myself on the AT and realized how much had happened since then. I had lived in six states—Vermont, Massachusetts, New Jersey, Connecticut, Washington, and South Carolina. I had worked even more jobs—administrative assistant, one-year-old teacher, Girl Scout membership specialist, outdoor program coordinator, primitive camp director, preschool teacher, nanny, and EMT. Somehow this amalgam of experiences had brought me to the present: sitting with this group of people on this mountain on the JMT.

Next we took turns imagining where we would be in ten years. I got so lost in trying to imagine my own future that I hardly heard anyone else's answer. I felt myself pulling away from the conversation and letting my thoughts spiral uncontrolled through my mind. *At age forty-two will I have a family? Will I be on another trail? How many more jobs will I have had? How many more states will I have lived in? Do I know what I want my life to look like in ten years?*

I spent the entire evening ruminating. My mind drifted from thought to thought, making me remember a high school writing assignment where we had to record our stream of consciousness for a set amount of time. That English teacher had been my nemesis. He was simultaneously the teacher I hated most and the teacher who pushed me the hardest to succeed. I worked diligently on papers for his class and held my breath when he handed back graded work. He once tore a paper I had labored over intensely in half—in front of the entire class—and told me not to waste his time again. He demoralized me. He also made me into a stronger writer. Because of the skills I learned in his class, I was able to succeed as a writer at Furman, a university where professors are notoriously harsh on written assignments.

Why am I thinking about this? With a shake of my head, I brought my mind back to the present. During my pre-bed body and gear assessment, I noted that the blister on my toe had not gotten any worse. Also, I still hadn't gotten any hip or shoulder bruises from my pack, and my skin was rash-free. My body seemed to agree with hiking on the west side of the country. Since I had just inventoried and repaired my gear that morning, I made only one adjustment: using my pocketknife, I cut the tag out of the back of my skirt. The seam had been rubbing roughly against my sweaty skin underneath my pack.

Stretching out on my Therm-a-Rest, I turned Deadweight on and saw that I had a message, but my phone wouldn't retrieve it. I tried to send my parents a message to explain that Deadweight was being temperamental, but I couldn't tell if it transmitted. Frustrated at having to fuss with technology in the woods, I turned it off and stuffed it in my pack.

In my journal I flipped to the back and made a list of gear additions for my next hike. I included a safety pin, Dr. Bronner's soap, dry shampoo, a sewing needle, and thread. Thankfully these weren't items I had needed often, but I had learned their value.

My exhaustion was settling in quickly, and I couldn't wait to zip myself into my sleeping bag and fall asleep. I was surprised at how well I had been sleeping on this trip. Normally I notice every noise from the outdoors and wake up multiple times each night to use the bathroom. There had been all of the normal outdoor noises of sticks cracking, animals scurrying, and the wind howling, not to mention other hikers zipping and unzipping tents and sleeping bags and tossing and turning on Therm-a-Rests. And Sarah had snored every night. Still, somehow I had been sleeping soundly.

Hoping I could turn off my mind for the night and fall asleep quickly, I pulled out my Ziploc and read Lark's letter.

Dear Michelle,

As you set off for your next awesome hiking adventure (AHA), I've been thinking about how much our lives have changed since your first AHA (haha) on the AT. We've survived our twenties mostly unscathed (although there were certainly a few moments that seemed like the end of the world), lived far apart in different cities (you in several more than me—and you ended up back in SC!), and established successful careers (what a big word) thanks to a shared desire to make the world a better place. I think we should take a moment to pat ourselves on the back, really. These are no small feats. And you're about to add another one to your list!

And all this time, although we haven't been lucky enough to be roommates again, we've remained best friends—sharing laughter and tears over the craziness of life, family, work, boys, and everything in between.

So, while I won't be hiking the John Muir Trail with you, I'll be there in spirit cheering you on as you navigate your next AHA. Take all the pictures and I can't wait to hear all about it when you get back! Stay safe, and happy trails!

Love, Lark

It seemed appropriate that on a night when I had spent so much time reflecting on my life a decade ago, I would read a letter from my college roommate. Lark and I had had a long friendship. Together we'd gone from awkward college freshmen to awkward thirty-somethings, trying to figure out this "adulting" business.

At various points we had lived on the same hall, in the same room, and across the country from one another. Our friendship has remained steady over the years, but our conversations have changed. Where we used to discuss roommate issues, research paper struggles, and what to do after college, we now discuss coworker challenges, doctor's appointments, and the parts of being a grown-up that no one tells you about.

Lark and I share a love of words and reading, though we often appreciate different types of books. We're both older sisters, and we've always shared the joys and hurdles of those relationships with each other. We both enjoy and try to protect nature, dabble at playing the guitar, and love food—eating it, planning to eat it, and cooking it.

We've shared road trips, new adventures (spelunking), and trips out of the country (Jamaica). She attended my wedding (and supported me through my subsequent divorce), and I attended her sister's wedding and her father's funeral. *What will we add to this list in fourteen more years?*

Although I felt sleepy, I couldn't turn off my mind. I tossed and turned on my inflatable pillow, tugging at my purple sleeping bag with each turn so that my face would stay lined up with the opening.

My mind felt so wide awake that I was confident I could write an entire book right that moment if I had a computer. *This must be what mania feels like.* I zipped myself further into my sleeping bag. *Go to sleep. You'll be miserable tomorrow. You can think while you hike.* I kicked my socks off inside my sleeping bag and consciously relaxed my body. *When I get home I need to fix up my studio so that I can focus on writing comfortably. I want the walls to be covered with things that inspire me. Should I repaint? I need a comfortable chair for that new desk.*

I tightened and relaxed my muscles and focused on breathing deeply, but my mind kept spinning. *Why do I have a constant tug between wanting to minimize my belongings and wanting to buy things that better fit me? Is there a balance? Do I need to buy the right things first in order to get rid of the others? Or do I purge first and then invest in replacements? Why do I worry about this so much? I don't have that many belongings to begin with.*

I should figure out what I want to do with my life before I worry about what I own. Ten years ago I thought I would be settled by now. I thought I would have a husband, a family, a job I loved. Why can't I figure out what career I want? I'm so jealous of people who are born knowing they want to be a teacher or an astronaut or a farmer. I've never known. I can tell you things I love, but that doesn't always translate into what I would love to do. I love kids, but I didn't love being a teacher. Do I want to write? Think? Create? Right now I want to sleep. Why can't I sleep? Did I jinx myself by noticing how well I've slept on this trail up until tonight?

I remembered the many sleepless nights when I had worked a twenty-four-hours-on/forty-eight-hours-off schedule in EMS. I had struggled with falling and staying asleep the whole time on that schedule. The lack of sleep made me emotional and cranky. *Which is why you need to sleep right now,* I reprimanded myself. *But the EMS job wasn't all bad. I loved it. It's the happiest I've ever been in a job. Each day I got to make a difference. There was excitement. I got to problem solve and use my brain. But I felt compelled to leave. Other than a bigger paycheck, what do*

I want? I want opportunity for advancement. I want to use my education. I want to continue making a difference in the lives of other people. What am I doing to accomplish these things?...

Burned area near Red's Meadow

18

LOST INSIDE MY HEAD

August 9, 2014

Slept: Fish Creek
Miles: 13.1
Weather: sunny / rain+storm+sleet / sunny
Dinner: chili mac
Mood: pensive
Letter: Carrie
Dad's quote of the day:

WHAT THE HELL WAS I THINKING?!? —DAD

Eventually the Advil PM won the battle against my mind, but I woke in the morning with it running rampant again. I was caught up in a haze of my own thoughts. So many words were swirling around me that I found it almost impossible to carry on a conversation or interact with other people. I just wanted to retreat inside my head and let my brain spin.

As I packed my gear I heard Tom and Kyle talking about dreams and how vivid theirs had been on the trail. Sarah agreed and they all shared stories. I listened through a fog and realized that I hadn't had a single dream on the JMT that I could recall.

I packed up my gear, excited to hit the trail and let the movement of my feet align with the movement of my thoughts. Some of my best thinking happens outside, as if the breadth of the views and the air around me give my mind more room to expand.

As the morning passed by, my brain refocused and I came out of my haze. We reached Purple Lake and had a long, relaxing lunch with our shoes off. My naked toes enjoyed wiggling in the breeze and being free from the constraints of sweaty hiking shoes. Yogi and the cousins caught up and joined us. After lunch we ambled by Virginia Lake, which was equally gorgeous. The colors along the JMT had all seemed so magnified compared with those in my everyday life. I wasn't sure if it was the reduced air pollution, the proximity to the sun, or the euphoria of the experience that was altering my perception.

Just beyond Virginia Lake, we noticed the sky getting darker. Sarah and I each kept one eye on the clouds and one on the ground as we edged closer to McGee Pass. Yogi had rocketed ahead of us. His quick pace always amazed me since he had a bum knee and only one eye. Kyle and Tom had dropped behind after lunch, but just past Virginia Lake they caught up. We all hopped over little inlets to the lake and yelled over the wind about the incoming weather. We were about to start the climb up to McGee Pass, but the sky looked ominous and we'd all been cautioned against being on top of an exposed pass in the Sierras during inclement weather.

The temperature, which had been pleasant enough for normal hiking clothes at the start of the day, began plummeting rapidly. Sarah and I briefly debated setting up camp, but it was much earlier than any of us wanted to stop for the day. Plus, although shelter would be nice during the storm, it would also mean getting our tents wet. And if we set up for the night, we wouldn't be able to warm back up by hiking once the storm abated. We stopped just long enough to shrug into our rain gear, then decided to keep our eyes on the sky and keep moving. Although Sarah and I didn't know these guys well, the adage about safety in numbers seemed to apply.

The four of us continued slowly up the trail. I hunched my shoulders against the wind and cold and tried to remind myself not to tighten up my back muscles. *Why do I have to be so cold-natured?* As a chill rippled down my spine, I wondered whether I should stop and put on more layers. I didn't want to risk getting all my clothes wet, though, because that would put me at risk for hypothermia later. The rain grew colder and harder and then turned to sleet. The wind was ferociously pelting the icy mess into our faces and making it hard to keep our eyes open. I started to feel ice collecting on my eyelashes, and I put on my sunglasses to protect my eyes despite the increasingly darkening sky.

It became too miserable to keep walking. We ducked into a small spattering of trees and huddled together. I took off my raincoat long enough to add my puffy jacket, winter hat, and gloves underneath. Kyle and Tom pulled out a bong while I clenched and unclenched my hands inside my gloves to keep my blood circulating. *It's hard to believe it's August in California.* It was also hard to believe how often I had been surrounded by marijuana. I tried not to care.

The sleet turned into hail, and fervent wind whipped it around us. The four of us huddled in a circle to keep warm and protect our faces from the onslaught. We took turns telling stories to distract ourselves from how cold we were. At some point it started lightning. I'd never seen hail and lightning at the same time before—this was not weather I wanted to mess with.

"Where do you think Yogi is?" I wondered aloud over the squall.

"Oh, man. He was in front of us, right?" Kyle asked.

I stomped my feet. "Yeah. I hope he's OK."

"He might already be over the pass. If not, he probably set up his tent," Sarah said, shoving her hands in her pockets.

"Probably," I agreed. "But I hope he made it over because he just has a tarp, not a tent."

"Oh crap, that's right. Well, he's one tough mother."

The tempest surged around us as the lightning became more and more frequent. When a bolt hit nearby, I began counting the seconds before the next thunderclap. *One one-thousand, two one-thousand, three one-thousand...* I noticed Sarah's head bobbing slightly to the same count. We glanced at each other.

"Four seconds," I announced, tucking my chin into my down jacket. Sound travels about a mile every five seconds, so this meant the storm was directly on top of us.

Sarah regarded the ground below our feet. "We aren't in the safest place. These trees are the tallest thing around and we're standing right on the f—ing roots."

"Yeah." I bounced back and forth from foot to foot, trying to generate some body heat. "I just don't see anywhere safer."

"Should we scatter and get into lightning position?" Sarah asked.

I waffled my head back and forth in indecision. *Am I more concerned about hypothermia, or lightning?*

"Lightning position?" Kyle echoed with a nervous laugh.

"I'm not joking," Sarah told him.

"What is lightning position?" Tom asked as he tightened the hood of his raincoat around his face. "I've never even heard of that."

"You don't know lightning position?" Sarah raised her voice over the sound of hail hitting our rain gear. She turned to me. "You know lightning position, right?"

"Yeah." I tucked my chin further inside my coat, trying to warm the inside of my jacket with my exhalations. I curled and uncurled my toes, noticing how icy they felt against the bottom of my shoes. Normally I don't mind being a cold-natured person, especially on those hundred-degree days in South Carolina when other hikers are miserable. This day, though, I minded. I wished the blood flowing through me was hot instead of freezing.

"Lightning position is when you squat down with your legs close together. You stay on the balls of your feet and curl into a tiny ball with your hands off the ground." Sarah demonstrated.

"Do we take our packs with us?" Kyle questioned as he rubbed at his rain-speckled stubbly beard.

"No." I clamped my teeth together to keep them from chattering. "The frames are metal. We leave everything here but ourselves and try to find spots where we aren't standing directly on rock or near each other."

"I'm not gonna lie. This is sick," Kyle marveled, looking up at the sky with wide eyes as lightning struck again.

One one-thousand, two one-thousand, three one-thousand, four one-thousand. five one-thousand. Thunder. We all exhaled.

I darted my eyes to Sarah. "It hasn't gotten any closer. Maybe it's moving away from us now."

We continued to huddle under the trees until the thunder and lightning receded. It was still raining—a frigid and miserable rain. We saw intermittent blips of blue as the sun and storm clouds feuded above the pass for reign of the sky.

"I either need to set up camp or start hiking," I told the group, rubbing my gloved hands together. "I'm getting really cold."

After some discussion and shared hope about the growing patch of bluish sky ahead, we agreed that we should keep going because there wasn't a desirable place to camp. We decided to start up the pass in hopes that the worst of the storm was behind us. We agreed to turn around, despite the lost mileage, if things got worse or felt dangerous.

Trying to encourage my metabolism to warm my body, I ate a snack. My feet felt like blocks of ice, and my fingers were stiff. I shouldered my pack and couldn't help but tighten up as the weight settled on my wet raincoat and pressed the cold, soaked material against my back. Although I knew I might regret it later, I kept all my layers on when I started hiking. I was too cold to even consider undressing.

Thankfully, our gamble worked in our favor. The rain continued for about half an hour, but the lightning and thunder never returned and we didn't see any more hail. By the time we reached the top of McGee Pass the rain was reduced to a chilly mist. It stopped completely by the time we started descending. Although it had been intimidating climbing in unpredictable weather, I was glad we had pushed on and completed more miles.

We ended up going a mile past our original destination and sharing a campsite with the cousins. As was becoming routine, they pulled out a bong after dinner. It was tiresome how often I felt like the outsider, because I didn't smoke marijuana. As I sat with them, feeling isolated despite being in a group, they talked about weed: where they buy it, how much they pay, and how they store it. I kept my eyes focused on the steaming chili mac inside my Brownie Bag. *Why do I so often feel like the odd one out? Trips like this are supposed to be the time I feel like part of the crowd—like I fit in. Am I just not meant to feel that way?*

When I crawled into our tent, my body ached from being cold all day, and my heart was heavy from feeling like I didn't belong. Dejectedly, I started my nightly gear and body review. My rain gear was losing its waterproofness. I would need to replace my rain pants and re-waterproof or replace my jacket before my next hike. I was in love with my Dirty Girl gaiters, which were so much more breathable than my last pair. I didn't like wearing my breathable hat, but I'd never had a hat I liked. My issue wasn't with the hat itself, it was with hats in general.

I tucked my loved and not-so-loved wet gear against the side of the tent and reached into the vestibule for my CamelBak, so that I could have a sip of water before settling in to read. My body relaxed as soon as I slid into the comfort and warmth of my sleeping bag.

That night's letter was from Carrie. Carrie is a friend who never makes me feel bad for being myself. She accepts me exactly as I am in every situation. We met in a women's hiking group a few years ago and quickly became friends. We share a love of the outdoors and a background in outdoor education jobs. We both play the piano and enjoy different types of art (she paints and does photography, while I quilt and write). Our friendship was easy and comfortable, like slipping on a favorite old sweatshirt.

Since we had so much in common and lived in the same town, it shouldn't have been a surprise when Carrie and I realized we had been on dates with more than one of the same guys. Carrie had ultimately found Mr. Right, and I was looking forward to attending her wedding a month after finishing the JMT.

Dear Michelle,

I would think that naturally it would be appropriate to start off this letter with a John Muir quote, but I'm not going to do that. I will start off with my favorite "Man's Search for Meaning" quote (by Viktor Frankl): "Everything can be taken from a man but one thing: the last of the human freedoms—to choose one's attitude in any given set of circumstances, to choose one's own way." I think it's my favorite because I've tried really hard to take it to heart while in the field—and should perhaps try harder to take it to heart in real life. Things don't always go the way we plan them, our bodies don't always act the way we want them to, our friends sometimes don't feel like friends at all, and we—well I—often feel alone. BUT, the only thing that is within our control is the attitude, the smile, and the positive thoughts we choose to have that day, or not.

ABOVE all, my advice, if you are seeking it—and advice I wish someone had given me years ago—is to remember to have FUN, to remember that suffering is temporary (Frankl's whole premise), to truly live in the moment, to absorb the peace and serenity around you, to not take anything for granted, to know you are not alone, even when you are, and again, to have FUN! I'm so excited for you; to me each adventure I've taken is like a new chapter in life. I'm sure you feel the same way—and perhaps this is especially true for you due to your change in careers. We never discussed it, but I wonder, in regards to this trip, what you want to metaphorically "leave behind" and what you want to "take away." Maybe you haven't even thought about it? But I think you probably have, or at least you will now. I love backpacking because it's like reading the most exciting, deep, philosophical book ever, yet also the most boring, slow, and monotonous book ever—kind of like reading Annie Dillard. (Side note, during the summer of 2012 I read in the hammock all day; it was the best summer of my life. That summer I also read Wild in one day—and I can't wait to read whatever you come up with next, regardless if it's about this hike or not!) Backpacking has always been so serious for me, due to the nature of my work, and I'm excited for it to be something simple, refreshing, and fun—so I really hope it feels that way for you! Every day is a gift!

I'm proud of you for chasing your dreams and getting on the trail again! I can't wait to hear all your stories!!

Carrie

One of the things I love about my friendship with Carrie is that she has never been afraid to challenge me. She encourages me to question why I make certain decisions or hold certain beliefs. Carrie pushes me to discover the innermost, most uncomfortable parts of myself. But she manages to do it without ever judging what I find when I search.

Her letter was a challenge to figure out what this trip was meant to unleash for me. Since Carrie had spent so much time on backcountry trips herself, her advice clearly came from a place of experience. I did want to return from my hike a stronger and more confident person. I took her letter to heart and once again revisited what I was hoping to gain from my experience, aside from the obvious bucket list checkmark.

I was feeling better after reading the encouraging letter from Carrie. I zipped the letter and my journal into their Ziploc and reached over to stash it beside me. My hand landed in a puddle of water.

"Shit!" I blurted out. *The tent is leaking!* Still encased in my sleeping bag, I scrambled into a kneeling position on top of my Therm-a-Rest and fumbled to turn on my headlamp.

"What's wrong?" Sarah glanced over her shoulder at me.

"There's water in the tent. I don't know where it's coming from." I poked at my gear. Everything I touched was wet. My Therm-a-Rest seemed to be an island surrounded by a lake of water. "Shit, shit, shit." I tucked my sleeping bag under me, trying to keep it away from the water. "Crap. What are we going to do?"

She sat up. "Let's figure out where the f— it's coming from."

I lifted the dripping Ziploc bags and dry-sacks stashed by my head. *Oh, no.* "I found it." I held up my suspiciously light CamelBak. The bite valve was in the open position and the bladder had been sitting on top of the valve, holding it open.

Sarah turned her headlamp onto my CamelBak. "How much water was in there?"

"I'm missing at least half a liter." *Which means not only did I soak the inside of the tent, I also have to filter water in the morning.*

"Shit."

"Yeah."

"Well, let's clean up what we can and we'll deal with it in the morning." Sarah was remarkably understanding considering that I had just soaked a tent we had carefully kept dry through a torrential storm.

We pulled out our bandanas and Sarah's small pack towel and sopped up what we could. Mostly we just smeared the water around. My already somber mood was not improved. I'd been wet all day. I didn't want to be wet while sleeping too. Everything on my side of the tent was wet: my already damp rain gear, my pack, and even a bit of my sleeping bag.

"I don't think we're going to get any more cleaned up," Sarah said.

"Me neither. This sucks."

We tossed the soggy rags into the vestibule and clicked off our headlamps.

After I heard the scrape of her sleeping bag zipper in the dark, I said, "I'm really sorry."

"Obviously, you didn't do it on purpose."

"No. But I'm still sorry. This is a shitty way to end a relatively shitty day." As an afterthought I added, "Tomorrow's a new day."

Purple Lake

19

THE UNMARKED VAN

August 10, 2014

Slept: VVR camping
Miles: 9.7+2.2=11.9
Weather: sunny
Dinner: VVR brisket and veggie meal
Mood: strong / disheartened / relieved
Letter: none (town day)
Dad's quote of the day:

THINGS DON'T GO WRONG AND BREAK YOUR HEART SO YOU CAN BECOME
BITTER AND GIVE UP. THEY HAPPEN TO BREAK YOU DOWN AND BUILD YOU UP
SO YOU CAN BE ALL YOU WERE INTENDED TO BE.
—CHARLIE JONES

Perhaps due to Carrie's challenge, and perhaps simply as a coincidence, I spent most of the following morning pleasantly adrift inside my head. I intentionally hiked alone, giving my mind space to wander freely. First I focused on my eclectic past. I reflected on my relationships—the men I've dated, my marriage and divorce, my close friendships, and my family. I reviewed each job I've held, each bucket list item I've accomplished, and some of the big-impact decisions I've made—which college to attend, what subject to major in, and whether to buy a house alone.

I thought about my hobbies, my food choices, my sleep habits, my exercise habits, and which of these I was practicing in ways that made me feel whole and happy. I remembered a book I had started reading by Sara Avant Stover called *The Way of the Happy Woman* that focused on similar topics. The book strives to help women learn to live in harmony with nature. *I need to finish that book when I get home.*

I barely noticed my legs tick-tocking steadily up the mountain as I thought about what changes I needed to make in my life to continue my own journey toward self-satisfaction. I wanted to practice more yoga, to worry even less about what others thought of me, to write regularly, and to freely spend time on the things I enjoyed without multi-tasking to assuage my guilt over not having been constantly productive. I have a tendency to feel obliged to make every second of my time industrious. So, for example, if I take the time to watch a show on Netflix I will simultaneously do a load of laundry, prepare lunch for the next day, or empty the dishwasher. Learning to embrace activities like playing guitar, reading a book, going for a long walk, and taking a nap as worthwhile activities in their own right is important to me. Taking care of myself *is* productive.

With surprise I saw that the summit of Silver Pass was approaching quickly. The realization actually made me feel a bit melancholy. While I would be glad to have the physical challenge of the ascent behind me, I wasn't ready to leave this deeply reflective place in my head. I knew that as soon as I reached the peak and joined the others, my reverie would be broken.

At the highest point of Silver Pass (10,754 feet), I found ten other people: Sarah and nine men. The view was unbelievable. Giant granite peaks surrounded us and we had expansive views of towering mountains, pristine tarns, and alpine vegetation. The sun glinted off the slick rocks and tranquil lakes and made me incredibly thankful for my lightweight, wrap-around sunglasses. I marveled again at how different these peaks looked from the East Coast's predominantly tree-covered ones, which more often than not have no view.

Sarah and I shared a bag of trail mix as we watched one man hop from rock to rock with his arm and head at unnatural angles while yelling into his satellite phone. After a few minutes of unabashedly watching his antics, I pulled my eyes away and tried to sync my phone to Deadweight to see if I could retrieve my messages. I fiddled with it for five minutes, but once again I had no luck. As I tucked my technology away, Satellite Man was still hopping around and waving his arms above his head.

"Do you think he'd order us a pizza?" I asked, cramming a final handful of trail mix into my mouth.

Sarah moaned. "Don't talk about pizza."

"Can you imagine the delivery charge?" I joked.

The brisk wind swirling through the gap in the mountains was quickly causing my body temperature to drop. I suggested packing up and taking a longer break in a place where there was less wind. Sarah and I started the descent with the cousins we'd hiked with the day before and quickly scrambled down rocks until we reached a creek crossing.

The rocks beside the creek were in direct sunlight, and their warmth was welcome after the chilly wind on the pass. We decided that this was the perfect spot to stretch out in the sun and enjoy lunch while our gear dried on the hot, sunbaked boulders. Within minutes it looked like an REI store had exploded beside the creek. We anchored our belongings with rocks and stretched out to warm ourselves like lizards.

After a lazy rest we checked the time and decided we'd better hike on. All of us were planning to make it to Vermillion Valley Resort (VVR) that night. VVR is a backcountry resupply station and primitive wilderness resort located just off the JMT on Lake Edison.

Under normal circumstances, VVR could be accessed by a water taxi at a ramp not far off the trail, but the drought had drastically lowered Lake Edison and the pickup point had to be moved due to inaccessibility. Rumors from other hikers indicated that it would be a long walk and that at times the taxi boat—which typically followed a regular schedule—wasn't running at all. Since we didn't know exactly what we had coming up, we decided it would be best to keep moving.

After lunch the four of us hiked more or less as a group. Since I love to stretch my legs and gain speed on downhill jaunts, and since Sarah's knees struggle with going down extended steep grades, I sometimes got ahead of the others and then waited. I loved the long, seemingly endless 3,000-foot descent and raced downhill with the nearby stream. The tantalizing possibility of a cheeseburger at the end of the day only fueled my speed. We had left the alpine environment behind for a bit and were in a dense green forest with giant trees towering over us.

We knew we were moving quickly, but I think we were all surprised when we reached a small, flat clearing and saw a laminated sign attached to a tree. The sign indicated that we had to take a 1.4-mile-long side trail to the VVR water taxi, which only ran once a day at nine in the morning.

"That's total crap," Kyle observed, glaring at the sign.

I took my pack off and propped it against the tree under the offending sign. "You'd think they would post that information at other places on the trail. It would've been nice to see a sign about this at Red's or Tuolumne. They have to know that's where a lot of us are coming from." *Then again, it's not like we've seen useful signage at any other point on this hike.*

"We don't have any idea how old this sign is," Sarah pointed out as she tightened the elastic on her braid. "It might not even be current."

A quick debate ensued about whether or not we could trust the information. Although technically we could access VVR by walking, we unanimously agreed that we were not walking all the way around Lake Edison. We would either catch a ferry that night or camp and catch a ferry in the morning.

"If we're hoping for a shuttle at five, we'd better start moving," I told them. "It's already four fifteen and the sign says 1.4 miles."

We took off down the trail as a group. In under thirty minutes we made it the 1.4 miles and found another sign telling us the launch had been moved further down the trail because of the drought. We grumbled but kept going. Finally we reached a camping area with yet another sign. This sign again stated that shuttles left at nine in the morning, but it also provided a phone number for VVR that could be called to schedule a shuttle. The sign indicated that only phones with AT&T service had reception there.

Sarah and I both had Verizon service, but Tom had AT&T. While he called, I sat on a boulder and took off my shoes. After checking for blisters and hot spots (there were none), I wiggled my sweaty toes in the breeze. As always, my feet were glad to be released from their wet and rigid prison.

"We have a reservation for nine tomorrow morning," Tom announced.

I flopped onto my back and covered my eyes with my arm. *I was really looking forward to sleeping in a camping cabin tonight.* Setting up camp seemed a gargantuan and impossible task when I had been imagining a bunk all day.

"It couldn't hurt to ask if they would add a shuttle tonight, would it?" I mused aloud, as improbable as it seemed that the decision would change.

"Do you think they would do that?" Kyle asked.

"Since there are four of us and that means four shuttle fees and four hot meals purchased tonight, they might be willing," Sarah suggested hopefully.

"Call them back, Tom," I requested, propping myself up on my elbows.

We crossed our fingers and toes, and with a bit of encouragement he called back. When VVR found out there were four people in our group, they agreed to send a shuttle boat and said to be at the launch in thirty minutes. In what seemed like a bizarre scavenger hunt, we were told to follow the fluorescent flags stuck in the sand on the dried lake bottom for about a quarter mile until we reached an American flag.

I started to stuff a hot, swollen foot back into my shoe, but decided I just couldn't. Instead I tied my shoelaces together, attached them to my pack, and slipped on my Crocs.

"You know, we've added well over two miles today just trying to get to this boat."

Sarah nodded. "Seems like we should get a discount on the water taxi since they aren't taking us as far."

"They'd better be serving dinner when we get there," Kyle said matter-of-factly as he led the way toward the land that used to be a lake.

We navigated a lumpy area of semi-hard ground with grasses growing out of it. Then the ground became softer and sandier, reminding me of dunes at the beach. It was hard to get traction or take normal steps, so I slogged my way along the flagged route. Petrified stumps stuck out from the sand. The receded waters of Lake Edison were visible far in front of us, but they didn't seem to be getting any closer as we followed the fluorescent flags stuck in the ground.

"This is a lot more than a quarter mile," I complained as I stopped to shake sand out of my Crocs for the fifteenth time.

"Maybe they said three quarters of a mile," Tom recollected.

"If I'd known that," I muttered in frustration, "I probably would have put my shoes back on."

We heard a low rumble behind us and turned around in surprise. Ominous dark grey clouds had rolled in over the mountain range. Lightning sliced through the sky.

"That f—ing boat better show up," Sarah said without amusement.

It had easily been thirty minutes since Tom's second phone call by the time we dumped our packs under the flag. I was shocked to realize it was a full-sized American flag. From a distance it had appeared to be a garden flag. The sky was becoming more menacing and the lightning more frequent. *What are we going to do if the boat doesn't show up?*

While we waited, Tom paced with his arms crossed and Kyle sat rubbing the back of his neck. Sarah undid her braid and raked her fingers like a brush through her waist-length hair. I tugged my raincoat on and kicked at the sand.

Soon I heard the distant chugging of a motor, and a speck appeared on the horizon. In a few minutes we could make out a faded, wooden dinghy. *Not exactly what I pictured when reading about the ferry.* A shirtless and barefoot man with corduroy pants rolled up to his knees was standing in the back of the boat smoking a cigarette. His curly, chin-length brown hair whipped in the wind of the approaching storm. The man introduced himself as Carter. Using as few words as possible, he loaded our packs into the bow of the boat and motioned for us to get in.

The boat chugged laboriously across the choppy water toward an unseen destination. Water sprayed up into the boat, and I shivered in the mist. Behind us the sky was getting increasingly darker. I was glad I'd be able to sleep indoors.

When we reached the shore, Carter pointed to an unmarked white van. "Put your stuff in there."

We schlepped our gear up the small hill to the van, and Kyle opened the back doors. When we peered inside we discovered that there were no seats—in fact, the inside was all but gutted. The fabric that would normally cover the ceiling of a vehicle was missing, and molded foam insulation was visible in the places where it was still intact. The carpet was missing entirely. Plastic milk crates scattered around the floor functioned as unsecured stools, and ropes tied across the ceiling served as handholds. Sarah, the cousins, and I exchanged incredulous glances.

"This is the part where we get kidnapped," Sarah mumbled.

Kyle swiveled from the van to Carter and back again. "This is sick. Maybe we should have walked the 4.8 miles."

"The extra mileage might have been worth it," Tom agreed. "Do you think this is safe?" he whispered, hovering with his pack halfway into the van.

"Definitely not," Sarah confirmed. "But we seem to be out of options."

"Safety in numbers, right?" I reminded them. "There are four of us and one of him." I discreetly made sure Deadweight was still tracking our location as I tried to hide my nervousness at the absurdity of the situation. Every horror film I'd ever watched flashed before my eyes.

Carter climbed into the driver's seat without a word. Not seeing any other options, we all piled in the back. He accelerated and skidded through the sand as though he were competing in a NASCAR race. In the back we gripped the ropes with white knuckles and leaned against each other in an effort to avoid toppling over.

As the van came to an abrupt halt, my head slammed into the unpadded wall. "Store's to the left. First drink is free," Carter announced, practically doubling the number of words he had spoken since we met him.

We unfolded ourselves from the van and collected our gear. Taking a quick peek around outside VVR, we scurried into the store. The man at the cash register reiterated that our first drink was free, including beer. He also told us that tent camping was free for thru-hikers, but that there were no other lodging options available that night. *So much for that elusive bunk.* I grabbed a bottle of chocolate milk and drank it in one giant chug. I'm not much of a milk drinker at home, but on the trail it always tastes so good.

Soon we found ourselves settled into a wooden booth on the back porch looking at the dinner menu. The food was expensive and fancier than my hiker appetite desired. In a different setting, beef brisket with steamed vegetables or baked rosemary-infused chicken with mashed potatoes and greens are meals I would love, but on the trail I just wanted a greasy cheeseburger and fries. Sarah and I shared a meal, and while it was fine, it wasn't what I had been craving.

We set up our tent in the free camping area across from the store. Despite my lack of desire to sleep in a tent, I tried to at least be grateful that it was dry after our lunchtime session in the sun. The temperature had dropped steadily, so I decided to wait until morning to shower since I was already chilled without wet hair.

Many hikers were enjoying beer and drinks on the back deck and around a campfire behind the building. Some were playing card or board games, and a few were watching a TV mounted in the corner. Sarah joined a group playing a game at a picnic table. I wanted some solitude, so I burrowed into my puffy coat and hat and settled with my journal at a back booth. It was astonishing how luxurious a seat with a back felt after sitting on the ground for days. The endless walk across the dried-out lake and the life-threatening ride in the sketchy van seemed like distant and worthwhile ventures now that I was comfortable, full, and warm.

Sarah crossing Lake Edison

The white van

Me beside a giant tree
Photo credit: Sarah Jones Decker

20

THE HAMMOCK BOYS

August 11, 2014

Slept: VVR camping
Miles: 0
Weather: sunny+cool/POURING
Dinner: none (late lunch)
Mood: relaxed, out-of-place
Letter: none
Dad's quote of the day:

IT DOESN'T MATTER WHAT YOU DID OR WHERE YOU WERE.
IT MATTERS WHERE YOU ARE AND WHAT YOU'RE DOING.
GET OUT THERE! SING THE SONG IN YOUR HEART AND NEVER LET ANYONE
SHUT YOU UP! —STEVE MARABOLI

I woke in the middle of the night to the sounds of frenzied hollering, angrily tap-dancing raindrops, and the distant rustling of camping gear. When I opened my eyes it was still darker than the inside of my walk-in closet during a power outage. I overheard snippets of the yelling and ascertained that other campers had been awakened by a river of water running through their campsites and were scurrying to relocate. When I woke again at dawn, our tent was so wet that beads of water splattered on me when I reached up to touch the saturated fabric. Everything in the tent was damp and sticky. I ran my hands across my face disconsolately. *So much for sleeping in. So much for drying our gear.*

The day proceeded as a typical zero day (the hiker term for a day with zero mileage). In between chores I enjoyed a long, hot shower, ate warm meals, journaled, and rested. I even managed to make a quick call to my parents' house—but at the ghastly cost of three dollars per minute, we didn't talk for long. I let them know that Deadweight was no longer receiving or sending messages so that they wouldn't activate the National Guard. They relayed that they were still able to see my location pings and would track me that way.

In the afternoon I wandered down to the dried-out lake and sat contentedly for quite some time eating peanut M&Ms with my back against a tree. As I stared out into the distance and listened to the mellifluous lapping of waves on the sand—the only sound I could hear—I reflected on the fact that I wasn't as interested in the social aspect of hiking on the JMT as I had been on the AT. I was much more interested in having time for introspection and reflection: *What will I take away from this hike? How would it be different if I were with Dad? How will I be different when I get home?*

Late in the afternoon Sarah and I retrieved our mail drop and packed our bear canisters. I found that despite my meticulous planning and sorting I was somehow short a number of dinners for the next section. I figured the mix-up had happened when I repacked after we changed our final resupply destination. My mistake annoyed me, but thankfully I was able to supplement my resupply from the hiker box and quickly finish my packing. I was disappointed that I wouldn't be able to eat exclusively meals that I had dehydrated, though.

I watched with amusement as other hikers tried unsuccessfully to fit massive resupplies into their bear canisters. Then I saw two young guys who had a total of four massive peanut butter jars and twenty-eight ounces of Nutella between them. Their only other food was homemade energy bars and rice. They revealed that they had no mileage plan and no tent (only hammocks, which can't be used at high elevation where there are no trees). Plus, they hadn't planned on showers or other resort amenities costing anything, so they didn't have enough money.

Sarah and I discreetly exchanged baffled glances as we watched them trying to repack. We dubbed them the Hammock Boys. Making a mistake on a mail drop I could understand. Miscalculating mileage I could understand. But doing no research shelter needs, making no resupply plan, and having no itinerary at all—that shocked me. Hiking reinforces my natural inclination toward order and preparedness, and I had spent a great deal of time researching details for the JMT. It was jarring to encounter people who seemed to take on a long-distance trail with no more thought than they might put into an afternoon trip to Walmart. Still, I realized that they would likely finish the trail—perhaps even before we would. I knew that my obsessive organization wasn't the only reason my trips had been successful, but it sure helped me maintain my sanity.

When all my chores were completed and I was showered and dressed in clean clothes, I settled at the outdoor patio for a hot meal. Someone had the corner TV on, and when I glanced up from my plate, I saw a news clip saying that Robin Williams had committed suicide. Any type of news on the trail is surprising, but bad news is especially shocking. I pictured Robin Williams' laughing face in *Mrs. Doubtfire* and *Patch Adams*. It was hard to wrap my head around the fact that behind those seemingly genuine smiles and contagious laughs lay the kind of despair that led him to choose suicide.

I turned away from the TV screen and pulled out my journal. I'd had as much news and "reality" as I could handle for the day. Sometimes the isolation and protection afforded by a lack of technology and media was welcome. The rest of the world's news would still be there and waiting after Whitney. I would rejoin society then.

21

TIME WARP

August 12, 2014

Slept: Bear Creek
Miles: 13.1
Weather: sunny+hot
Dinner: stroganoff (good!)
Mood: determined
Letter: Barbara (Old Paint)

Breakfast cuisine and Mexican food are two of my guilty pleasures. I often enjoy a homemade breakfast burrito with a big mug of coffee on quiet mornings at home. When I stumbled into the diner bundled in my down coat and hat, I was excited to see a breakfast burrito on the menu. Yet even as I ate one of my favorite foods and sipped from a steaming mug of perfectly sweetened coffee, my detached mood didn't lift. I alternated between writing in my journal and aimlessly swirling my spoon around in my mug.

I wasn't unhappy, exactly. I was just deep inside my head in a place of uncomfortable and yet familiar self-recognition. *I don't quite fit in here. But have I ever felt like I fit in anywhere? I felt less intelligent than every other student at*

Furman, I often couldn't relate to my coworkers at my jobs, and I felt a little outside the cliques on the AT. I pushed home fries around on my plate. Then it struck me. *There's one place where I always fit in—at camp. I always felt comfortable being completely myself at summer camp.* Even when I first worked as a camp counselor at the age of seventeen, I knew that I had the skills to facilitate a ropes course, lead teambuilding, teach songs, build a campfire, and teach survival skills. *How do I carry that confidence into the rest of my life?*

I was abruptly pulled from my thoughts when Yogi slid into the booth across from me. I offered him the rest of my toast and home fries. In true Yogi form, he pulled the plate toward him and slathered it with ketchup. It was gone in about six giant bites. After settling my substantial bill with VVR, I finished packing my gear. Soon Sarah and I were loaded into an SUV for a ride to the trailhead. VVR had been a pleasant break during our hike, but it was not the most conveniently located stopping point.

From the trailhead we had to hike 2.5 miles to Bear Creek Trail. Then it was 7.5 miles uphill to rejoin the JMT. The trail was only moderately difficult despite the relentless upward angle. Still, miles that "don't count" feel interminable, and I was positive I was moving more slowly than a line at the DMV. It didn't help that my pack was full of resupply and my belly full of an ever-expanding burrito. Sarah must have felt the "town drag" too because I was keeping pace with her for once.

We passed a few enchanting swimming spots and the weather was just about perfect enough to entice us to stop for a dip, but we were too focused on getting back to the JMT. We took just short break to get more water. We stripped off our shirts to dry them on a rock and enjoyed a few minutes of the warm sun on our sweaty skin.

"How far do you figure we have left until we're back on the JMT?" Sarah asked as we hung the water bladder to filter.

I quickly consulted my internal odometer. "I'm thinking two miles or so."

"Me too. That would mean we've made good time."

We stretched out on the rocks, letting our bare skin soak up the heat. Once the water finished filtering, we begrudgingly put our shirts back on and re-shouldered our packs to continue hiking. Within minutes I twisted my left ankle and fell to my hands and knees. I didn't have so much as a scrape on my limbs, but my ankle was tender and the enormous rock steps became challenging as I kept walking. I pinched my salty lips together, leaned harder on my poles, and kept trekking. Just as it was beginning to seem too arduous to continue and I was about to declare that I wanted a break, I saw a hiker coming down the trail toward us.

"The JMT is right up there," he called out as we stepped aside to let him pass.

I wiped sweat from my forehead as I blinked at him. "No way."

"Seriously. It's about a hundred feet up."

Sure enough, we encountered a wooden sign after a few dozen more steps.

As I shook two Vitamin-I tablets into my hand, I observed, "There's something just plain wrong about the fact that we've hiked ten miles and none of them officially count."

Sarah shook her head. "Don't remind me."

We wanted some of our mileage for the day to be official, so we kept on hiking. The next two miles were uphill, but somehow it was more tolerable since these miles were on the JMT. The final mile—uphill, of course—lasted an eternity. I didn't think we would ever reach a campsite. We ended up setting up camp with the Hammock Boys. We had spent a lot of time so far in the company of men in their early twenties. This was interesting since there were certainly hikers in other age brackets on the trail—though admittedly most were men.

In the tent that night, Sarah and I talked about how astounding it had been to hear about some hikers' lack of preparations. "I'm glad I did the AT before this," she remarked. "The AT was like training wheels. Now we know how to handle rain and wet gear. We know what to eat, how to treat blisters, when our bodies need breaks, and how much water to drink." We had both completed 2,200 miles on the AT without previous long-distance hiking experience, though, and likely most of these people would make it 210 miles on the JMT. Nevertheless, my experience and preparation had given me more confidence in my abilities and decisions.

When our conversation faded, I picked up an envelope with the words "STUMBLE ONWARD JOYFULLY" written on the outside. As I opened the envelope, I glanced past the letter with pictures and quotes to the signature at the bottom. This letter was from Old Paint, whose real name is Barbara. She's seventy-seven years old and lives thousands of miles from me. We became email pen pals after she read my book and sent me a snail-mail Christmas card with accolades and lingering questions. Our weekly email exchanges bring me a lot of joy. In her messages she often refers to me as Brownie, and we decided to give her an honorary trail name too. She now goes by Old Paint—because she's an old artist who specializes in oil paintings of nature scenes.

Despite an age difference of fifty-three years, Old Paint and I have a good deal in common. We both love to play guitar, read (especially books about the outdoors), and create—she with her painting, and me with my quilting. We are both strongly opinionated. We send each other articles from magazines and newspapers, quotes we relate to, and photos of our lives. Our emails discuss recent adventures, health, books, music, and family. We talk about our excitements and fears, and Old Paint generously passes on her wisdom without ever seeming judgmental. Each time her email address shows up in my inbox, I can't help but smile. With that same familiar feeling of anticipation, I turned my attention to her letter.

> *Dear Brownie,*
>
> *You are on a trail which is higher and steeper than most all the AT. This is presenting new challenges! Ah, but look back to your book, and remember that you have met every challenge with creativity, strength, knowledge, and determination. Now, go. Do the same thing on the JMT. You have all you need in your amazing can-do spirit.*
>
> *Today is a gift from the mountains, from the trail, from the rocks, from the sky.*
>
> *You bring your light to the mountain to applaud nature's creation which is there for you.*
>
> *All the best,*
> *Old Paint*

I reflected on the variety of people who had sent letters for my excursion: family members, college friends, co-workers, local friends, and even a long-distance pen pal. I recognized that although I might not always feel like I belonged in group settings, I have a lot of wonderful one-on-one relationships with people of all ages and backgrounds from around the country. So many strong, loving, insightful people have impacted the woman I was still in the process of becoming.

22

I AM STRONG

August 13, 2014

Slept: camp at Piute Pass Trail
Miles: 12.8
Weather: sunny+hot
Dinner: mac and cheese
Mood: annoyed
Letter: Aunt Barbie
Dad's quote of the day:

> FOR MOST PEOPLE, THE FEAR OF LOSS IS GREATER THAN
> THE HOPE OF GAIN. DARE TO BE DIFFERENT!
> —UNKNOWN

We were up early and on the trail before eight o'clock. *Maybe those five-in-the-morning EMS shifts have been good for something after all.* As we strolled between giant mountains, we passed Marie Lake. It was full of the most unbelievably blue water that complemented the cloudless blue sky above. I felt like I had stepped into an oil painting. Before my breakfast had digested, I had already seen hundreds of postcard-worthy views. I could hardly believe that so much beauty was concentrated in this one area of the country.

The day was sunny and warm, and it was easily the best weather we had encountered so far on the JMT. Hiking up toward Selden Pass I was once again aware of my increased endurance. Despite an unremitting incline I wasn't out of breath, my legs felt strong, and my pack weight wasn't bothering me at all. The sun beckoned me toward the top of the pass, and I was so full of fervent energy that I barely stopped to rest during the climb. I peaked at 10,898 feet by eleven thirty.

On top of Selden Pass a group of hikers—including the Hammock Boys, a mid-twenties couple, and four guys who had just finished high school—pulled out a bong. I couldn't stand the idea of sitting around watching people smoke yet again, so barely stopping for a picture, I started the descent.

I was probably hurrying a bit in my frustration, and twice I stepped wrong on my left ankle, which was still sore from falling the day before. The ankle was visibly swollen but bore my weight normally and didn't hurt as much as it looked like it should. I leaned on my poles and rolled my ankle in circles, wincing slightly at the pain. Stubbornly, I kept plodding along.

The sprawling descent continued for approximately nine miles. I enjoyed moving quickly and stretching my hip flexors with long, unrestrained strides. About three miles from our destination I ran out of water. The map showed plentiful water crossings, but in real life there were none to be found. I was glad to be moving downhill so that I wasn't as out of breath and didn't feel as compelled to drink from my empty CamelBak every few steps.

A mile later I stopped to eat a snack and wait for Sarah to catch up. Although I enjoyed our independence in hiking separately at times, it made sense to wait for each other occasionally to check in and make sure we were both doing well. Sarah came smiling down the trail not too long afterwards, and we continued on together.

The snack had bolstered my energy, but I was ready for some water. Finally, we rounded a bend in the trail and saw a wooden bridge over a flowing stream. Underneath the bridge was a naked woman lying on a rock, reading a book. Completely unfazed by our arrival, she glanced up without so much as a wave and then returned to her reading. Sarah and I crossed the bridge and saw a sign indicating the start of the Piute Pass Trail. This let us know where we were in our guidebook, and we decided it was a good stopping point for the night.

Our new friends Gabi and David were set up at the camping area beyond the bridge. We dropped our packs near their tent and began settling in for the night. My first mission was to filter water and have a long drink. Then we began setting up the tent. As we unpacked the four of us shared stories and discussed our respective plans for the next day.

Sarah and I had spent an increasing amount of time with Gabi and David over the past few days, and I had enjoyed their company. This was their first long-distance trail, but they were experienced hikers and climbers. Although Gabi is originally from the Czech Republic and David is from Canada, they met through a hiking club in Seattle, Washington, where they both live now. I'd enjoyed conversations with them about other trail experiences, trail food ideas, and life in general. It was nice to spend time with people who were older than college age and weren't smokers. Watching their dynamics as a couple made me yearn for my own romantic companion with whom to share these experiences.

We established a group kitchen area beside some large fallen trees and cooked and ate dinner together. While preparing my meal I noted that the auto-ignite feature on my Snow Peak GigaPower stove wasn't working. This was the fourth day in a row. Thankfully, the stove would still light using a lighter. *Will the manufacturer replace it?* For dinner I had macaroni and cheese that I had pilfered from the hiker box at VVR. I had to cook traditionally since it wasn't a dehydrated meal, so I paid close attention to the boiling water, wanting to use as little fuel as possible.

While my dinner cooked I thought about other gear that needed replacing or rethinking. My long-sleeved sun protectant shirt was working well, but I hated the way it looked in pictures. I would need to find a more flattering option for future high-altitude hiking. While I knew protecting my skin was a higher priority, I did want photos from such a beautiful, once-in-a-lifetime experience to be ones where I felt confident.

The macaroni and cheese had a dusty, chalky texture and was almost completely flavorless. I was disappointed to be eating a pre-packaged, processed product instead of one of my own meals that I had spent months dehydrating and packaging. I washed the sludge down with a hot chocolate, a chai tea, and about sixty ounces of water. I wanted to make sure I wasn't dehydrated after running out of water during the afternoon.

Before I went to sleep I wandered away from the group and settled against a rock with my journal and a letter. This was becoming one of my most treasured times of day. I loved the opportunity to reflect and to connect with people in my life from afar. This letter was from my Aunt Barbie, who had been at my parents' house the night before I flew to California.

Michelle,

I saw two quotes today and thought of you. One: "The mountains are calling and I must go." --John Muir. And two: "Today is your day, your mountain is waiting, so get on your way." --Dr. Seuss. May those mountains be all you've dreamed of and more. May each step lead you to another amazing view of God's creation. Wishing you an awesome adventure!

Love, Aunt Barbie

23

TOPLESS LUNCH

August 14, 2014

Slept: North Evolution Lake
Miles: 12.6
Weather: sunny and hot with a nice breeze
Dinner: burritos in a bag!
Mood: happy, proud, content
Letter: none
Dad's quote of the day:

FEAR LESS, HOPE MORE, EAT LESS, CHEW MORE, WHINE LESS, BREATHE MORE,
TALK LESS, SAY MORE, HATE LESS, LOVE MORE.
AND GOOD THINGS WILL BE YOURS. —SWEDISH PROVERB

A long wooden fence running parallel to our path added confusion to our morning. Out in the middle of nowhere in the High Sierras was the last place we expected to be traversing along a fence line. "Do you think this is the trail?" I asked Sarah, staring in bewilderment at the fence that extended as far as I could see.

We stopped and turned in a circle, considering our options.

"These are boot prints," Sarah confirmed, gesturing at the dusty ground beneath us.

"Yeah. But why would there be a fence on the JMT?"

"Could it be to contain grazing animals?" she asked.

I shrugged. "Possibly. Or maybe it's a property line."

We checked the time and agreed we would continue no more than thirty minutes further if it didn't become apparent that we were on the trail. Clouds of dust plumed around our feet as we plodded down the dry path following the fence. Every step can feel utterly exhausting when it might be in the wrong direction. Eventually we came to a gate that cut straight across the trail we'd been following.

Sarah threw her hands up in exasperation. "Would it f—ing kill them to put a sign here?" She flung her braid over her shoulder. "I've got words for these trail maintainers."

I squinted into the distance. "I'm feeling more and more love for the frequent blazes on the AT. I think I love blazes."

Sarah gave a sarcastic smile. "The AT. That's a trail out East, right? It can't be too difficult to begin with. It probably doesn't even need markings."

I smirked back at her and felt grateful we were still finding humor in the challenging parts of our trip. I was also thankful I wasn't alone. At least if we got lost, we were lost together. It helped to share the burden of decision-making.

We looked at the time. Only fifteen minutes had passed, so we decided to go through the gate and stick with our thirty-minute plan. Working together, Sarah and I lifted a stout wooden post out of a wire catch and dragged the gate so we could get through. When we had reattached the post, we stood sizing up our surroundings.

"Well, this looks just like the unmarked trail on the other side of the fence. Which looks largely like the rest of the unmarked JMT," I observed wryly.

Sarah scowled. "When I get home I'm writing a letter to whatever organization is responsible for the signage on this trail," she told me. "And it won't be nice."

A short time later we came to a trail intersection and met a large group of teenage boys accompanied by a couple of men. A number of the boys had on hot pink knee-high socks. A quick conversation with the adults reassured us that we were in fact on the JMT. As Sarah and I pulled out snacks, I watched with amusement as the boys interacted.

"Boy Scouts?" I asked one of the adults.

"Yes. Our group does hikes every summer."

I explained my previous involvement with the Girl Scouts and expressed admiration and appreciation for the fact that the leaders were sacrificing their time to give the boys this experience. In all my hiking I've run into numerous Boy Scout troops, but never a Girl Scout troop. I knew there were troops that hiked—after all, backpacking with the Girl Scouts was what had led to my desire to tackle the AT—but I wished it happened more frequently.

Not long after our snack we came to a river crossing without a bridge. The water was too high to allow us to rock-hop. We scanned above and below the trail crossing, hoping for a fallen tree or other crossable route, but saw no viable options. I removed my pack and started untying my boots. Sarah became visibly irritated, flinging her poles on the ground and spewing curses. I later realized that her reaction was so strong because her blisters were taped very carefully and she worried that if she got her feet wet, she wouldn't have enough supplies to treat them until our upcoming resupply.

As soon as we crossed, we plopped down on the soggy ground and ate lunch while our feet dried. The eventful morning had worn me out, and I was glad to sit for a bit. I fanned my sweat-soaked shirt away from my stomach while I ate, trying to dry the material. Sarah lay against a rock eating lunch in her sports bra. She'd hung her shirt on a nearby branch to dry. I glanced around and considered the fact that we were alone in the middle of nowhere. *Why not?* Swallowing my self-consciousness with a bite of my tortilla, I took my shirt off and enjoyed the sun's warmth on my sweaty skin.

When we started hiking again, we found ourselves in another JMT vortex. It felt like we were moving at a good clip, but McClure Meadow, which according to our guidebook was only 2.8 miles beyond our lunch spot, seemed unattainable. We had astounding views of a distant mountain called The Hermit that we practically circled on our route.

"That mountain is great, but I didn't need to see every single freaking side of it," Sarah observed.

It did seem like the trail was going around the mountain. Finally, we reached the elusive McClure Meadow. Colby Meadow, a mere half mile further, was our original destination for the night, so we pressed on. We didn't see any appealing spot to camp when we got there, though, so we continued on again after consulting our map and seeing a marked campsite a mile further.

At the campsite we flopped onto the ground and propped our feet up on a giant log. While we rested our legs and let the sweat on our clothes dry, we laughed and talked. It was impressive that we were both in good moods after such a frustrating morning.

"There's still a lot of daylight left," I observed, peering up at the sky from my horizontal position on the ground.

Sarah flopped her head to the side to look at me. "Do you want to keep hiking?"

"Well, it's early. If we kept going we could cut down tomorrow's mileage. Gabi said the camping at North Evolution Lake is supposed to be amazing. That's where they were headed tonight."

"How much farther is it?"

"I'm not sure. In a minute I'll work up the motivation to go over to my pack for the map."

We confirmed on the map that we would have another 2.6 miles and a thousand-foot elevation gain to get to North Evolution Lake.

"I'm in," Sarah said. She peeked at the time. "Let's rest for thirty more minutes."

"Deal. And resupply water too."

There were endless switchbacks on the challenging climb, but in the fading daylight the views were incredible. I focused on the repetitive sound of gravel crunching underfoot. Sarah got marginally in front of me, but I maintained a thirty-minute-mile pace despite the grade and the exertion my body had already experienced that day. I saw numerous pikas scurrying beside the trail and had a mini photo shoot with one. Summoning all the moxie I had left, I hiked without stopping.

When I had muscled to the top Sarah was standing on a boulder, staring back down the trail into the setting sun. As soon as she saw me she began cheering and calling my name.

"I'm killing it out here," she said, grinning triumphantly and pumping her fist in the air.

I leaned heavily on my poles and beamed back at her. I was sweaty, tired, and perfectly content.

We walked just a little further and found ourselves in a sculpted bowl between giant towering mountains. In the center of the bowl was glittering North Evolution Lake. The setting sun caused the mountains to reflect into the water. I watched as two deer gracefully approached the lake and scanned the area around them before leaning in to sip from the crystalline surface. *This is why I love backpacking. So many people choose not to, and they'll never see a sight like this firsthand.*

In reverent silence we set up our kitchen area with Gabi and David. It seemed as though our voices might pollute the tranquility of our environment. I rewarded myself for the strong unexpected climb with my favorite dinner of burritos in a bag. Still sipping my hot chocolate, I wandered away from the group and stretched out on a giant rock in the last remnants of sunlight to write in my journal.

The temperature dropped quickly, and the cold from the rock beneath me seeped through my puffy jacket and thin leggings. Soon it became hard to grip my pen, so I retreated to the tent. Since there were no letters left to read until my final mail drop, I re-read each of the quotes my dad had supplied. Dad's handwriting—precise, predictable, confident, and solid—is a perfect reflection of his personality. Each letter is so uniform in everything he writes that I used to think his signature was a stamp. I was curious whether his sense of self was as precise as his handwriting. And if so, at what point in life had that confidence developed?

Sarah and I left the fly off our tent because Gabi had told us that a meteor shower was supposed to start around nine thirty. We hoped to be able to watch while snuggled into our down bags. Since that timeframe far surpassed our typical camp bedtime, we studied the map and told stories to keep ourselves awake. Sarah had been working on a rhyming alphabet book for children that contained photos she had taken on her farm. We played with the wording and photo ideas. Not far away we could hear the muted voices of Gabi and David in their tent.

I heard David unzipping their tent and knew it had to be about time for the meteor shower. We killed our headlamps and stared through the mesh into the sky. With a complete lack of light pollution, the stars were magnificent. Every time I blinked, more and more became visible.

As I stared at the blanket of stars that extended indefinitely, I felt my insignificance and importance in this world in equal measure. I'm so microscopic in comparison to the number of stars in the sky or people on the earth. Yet here I was, having an immeasurably intimate experience with nature that so few people will ever have. I may be only a tiny portion of Creation, but I'm lucky for my spot in existence.

While Sarah and I watched the sky, we both became quiet. For the millionth time I felt gratitude for having been exposed to backpacking and for having the physical ability, financial means, and gumption to get out and do trails like this one. I saw only three meteors, but the dazzling diorama was enough for a lifetime of remembering.

24

MEETING DOT

August 15, 2014

Slept: Big Pete Meadow
Miles: 12.8
Weather: sunny
Dinner: Lipton alfredo
Mood: determined
Letter: none
Dad's quote of the day:

THE ART OF BEING WISE IS KNOWING WHAT TO OVERLOOK.
—WILLIAM JAMES

Even though I had gotten less sleep than normal, I woke up with a smile. After the meteor shower we had been giddily tired and still thinking in rhymes for Sarah's book, so in our delirium we had worked together to make up a JMT alphabet poem:

A is for Altitude—the heights that we reach
It's also for Armpits—and boy do ours stink!
B is for Blazes, of which there are none

(or is it for Belly, like belly-be-gone?)
C is for Chocolate—the best hiking treat
*   And also for Calluses covering our feet.*
…

P is for Passes (and pack mules, too)
Q is for Quiet, long overdue
…

S is for Sleep, which we've done a bunch
T is for Topless—the best kind of lunch
…

Despite our late night, we rose earlier than normal and walked around North and South Evolution Lake before the sun completely crested the towering mountains. Next we skirted Sapphire Lake, which was truly the color of its namesake. The way the sun bounced and shimmered off of the surface, it appeared to have the texture of a jewel. More stunning scenery and sparkling waters awaited us as we approached Wanda Lake and Lake McDermand.

Just past Lake McDermand we passed a woman who was moving rapidly. "You're almost on top of Muir Pass," she told us.

"Really?"

"Yes. It's right up ahead and it's the perfect spot for a break. You'll love it."

I scrutinized the sky beyond her, and the mountain didn't appear to go much higher. My hopes soared in anticipation of a rest. I felt an extra pep in my step as I continued upward. Over an hour later, I paused to lean forward on my poles, staring grimly at the deceptive trail that meandered ever upward in front of me. *Never believe distance or timing assertions from other hikers—especially those going in the opposite direction.* I sucked in a deep breath, puffed out my cheeks, and forced my foot forward on the scree-covered, sun-infused, never-ending ascent. It took conscious effort to regulate my breathing. Blood pulsed in my ears.

I began to see colorful blips above me. Although I wanted to stop, the bubbles of color compelled me to continue my snail's pace. A few switchbacks later, the colorful blobs sprouted arms and legs. When I could hear laughter and conversation drifting down to me, I knew I was close to the top. Sarah's smiling face appeared above the rocks over my head.

"Come on, girl! You're almost here."

I found a hidden reserve of energy and astonished myself by picking up my pace. Quickly I tackled two final switchbacks and reached the top of Muir Pass. A circular stone shelter called Muir Hut dominated the pass. It was built by the Sierra Club in 1930 as a temporary shelter for hikers in this extremely exposed area. I took a few seconds to ogle the iconic structure before slipping off my pack and exchanging greetings with Sarah, Gabi, and David. We decided to eat lunch on top of the pass and watched with amusement as a mischievous marmot inched closer to our lunch rock.

Right there, at 11,991 feet, I experienced one of my most inspiring moments of the John Muir Trail. I was sprawled across a sun-warmed rock eating hummus on a tortilla when I noticed a beaming, grey-haired woman in a flowing, knee-length strappy sundress standing on the steps to Muir Hut. Her deeply wrinkled and sun-weathered skin glowed and her eyes sparkled as she posed for a photo. She bickered good-naturedly with a man half her age about when they would get to eat lunch.

I would soon learn that the woman was Dot. At that moment, Dot Fisher-Smith was eighty-six years old. She was on a two-week backpacking trip with her son, daughter-in-law, and two granddaughters.

I wandered over and introduced myself to Dot. As we talked about each of our trips, Dot touched the pack at her feet and told me, "This is my new pack. I'd been using my old external frame since I started backpacking in the sixties." I noticed her hands as she carefully picked up the pack— thick purple veins standing at attention, with swollen knuckles knotted like the limbs of an ancient tree. *How much life does one have to live to earn battered, world-weary hands like these?* She bounced on her toes to settle the unblemished pack on her bony, hunched shoulders. I noticed that she had wrapped hand towels around the straps for extra padding. As she fussed with the chest strap, she conspiratorially told me, "I'm not sure I actually like this new one."

"Why did you get a new one?" I asked.

"My son and his wife"—she gestured at the nearby couple—"didn't think my old one had enough support." She waved her hand dismissively said wistfully, "This is the first time I'm not carrying all of my own gear. My granddaughter has my sleeping bag and they aren't letting me carry any food."

"I'm just amazed you're out here," I told her honestly.

"Well, that was the deal. I want to backpack and my son said this was the only way they would bring me along." She flashed an award-winning smile and joy radiated from her. "Soon I won't be able to do this anymore. I've been hiking in these mountains since my twenties. I like to connect with nature. That's why I sleep outside right under the stars. I never use a tent unless it rains." She flashed that captivating smile again and her eyes twinkled as she added, "That drives my son nuts. But I like to be right there in nature. I don't need a tent between me and the earth."

I could've stayed and talked with Dot all day, but I could tell her family was waiting for her. Reluctantly I said, "I know you have to start hiking soon, but can I ask you something first?"

She nodded encouragingly.

"You have so much experience. If you were to give one piece of advice to a new hiker, what would it be?"

"That's simple," she answered with a confident nod. "Go slow. That's my advice for all things in life."

"Mother, you don't believe that at all," her son chimed in.

She waved her hand in his direction and winked at me. "He doesn't know everything about me like he thinks he does." Many months later, Dot would teach me the one song she had written—*Go Slow.*

In our ten-minute conversation I was captivated by Dot's vitality. She must have enjoyed me too, because she asked for my email address. Later, following months of email exchanges, I Googled Dot's name and learned that she was even more extraordinary than I had initially realized. She was featured in a documentary called *An Ordinary Life,* made by Slow Moving Pictures. The film's website raves, "Dot Fisher-Smith is a mystical, masterful artist, a war resister, an environmental activist, a community presence, a jailbird." This is vividly accurate, but touches only minimally on her accomplishments and vibrant personality.

Dot would become one of those trail people who were forever part of my life. We became regular email pen pals, and she generously invited me on a number of women's travel trips that she led around the world. On the day we met, I couldn't have imagined that I would attend one of her women's rejuvenation retreats with Lark in Oregon in 2016.

With a wave and a wink, Dot followed the trail down Muir Pass with her sundress floating around her. I turned to take photos with Sarah, Gabi, and David, but my thoughts stayed on Dot. *What will I be doing in my mid-eighties? I hope it'll be something that makes me that happy.*

Eventually it was time to begin our decent from Muir Pass. At Helen Lake Sarah and I stopped to filter water and found that our filter was clogged yet again. I was becoming increasingly disenchanted with my Sawyer Mini. I still maintained that I was not interested in a pump, with its many parts and arm-tiring function, but the Sawyer Mini wasn't winning my favor either.

"Does it have to be so hard to drink water safely?" I asked Sarah.

She shook her head and sighed in agreement, then took her shirt off and flopped down on a rock.

In frustration, I hung the uncooperative filter and gravity bag on a rock ledge and hoped for the best. I pulled my shirt off also and stretched out on a sun-splashed rock for a break. With my eyes closed, I forced my irritation with the water filter to dissipate and remembered how lucky I was to have clean drinking water most days of my life and to be here at all.

Briefly my mind wandered to the changes I would experience upon returning home. Knowing I was going to start a new job when I got back was intimidating. Although I looked forward to a new opportunity and a clean slate, the unknown was scary. Feeling myself start to deflate after speculating for only a couple of minutes about the changes to come, I forced the thoughts out of my head until closer to the end of the trip.

When we started hiking again, we cruised down, down, down. My short legs were happy to pump more quickly and enjoyed the ability to lengthen and stretch. The trail followed a rushing river that had pounded so forcefully against the rocks that it had beaten a deep fissure into the dip between mountains. At times during this section we had to rock-hop over small tributaries, and following the trail through the gorge became tricky. We had to stop a few times and backtrack to make sure we hadn't gotten off course. *Why, oh why, does this trail have no blazes?*

Miles into the unclear stretch we encountered an older man who was carefully and slowly picking his way down some large rocks. He had no pack and looked rather out of place. Sarah and I exchanged concerned glances and stopped when we reached him.

"Hey! How's your hike going?" I asked him.

He stopped and shuffled back and forth on his feet. "It's, uh, good." His eyes darted around uncomfortably.

"Are you hiking far today?" Sarah asked.

He picked at some mud on his shirt with a shaky hand.

When he didn't answer for a while, I tried another approach. "I have a hard time keeping track of mileage myself. Where did you start this morning?" As he turned his head to look around the area, I noticed dried blood on his mouth. I caught Sarah's eye and inclined my head toward him as I touched my mouth.

He never made eye contact. "Umm, it was… Left at…"

I wondered if he had fallen and might have a head injury. I decided to try and find out if he was alert and oriented. "Hey, I just realized how rude I'm being. I didn't even get your name. I'm Michelle. What's your name?"

He mumbled something I wasn't able to catch.

Sarah raised her eyebrows to show that she didn't understand either. "It seems like we've been out here forever. What day did you start your trip?" Sarah asked him.

Unsurprisingly, there was no intelligible answer.

"Are you hiking alone?" I asked.

Just about that time a figure appeared, moving toward us. As it got closer we could tell the figure was an older woman. She was also without a pack. We engaged her in conversation and she haltingly explained that she had carried each of their packs down the precarious stretch separately and was coming back to help him because he was unsteady on his feet with water crossings. Sarah and I tried to express concern for him, but the woman hushed us and made motions to hurry us off. Not sure what else to do, we said worried goodbyes.

As we continued descending the steep, poorly marked chasm, we passed a number of people headed in the opposite direction. It was getting later in the day and I couldn't figure out where they would camp without climbing many, many miles back to flat ground. We had been going downhill since our early lunch.

Maybe three miles further down the trail we ran into another older couple. As soon as we got within earshot they asked, "Did you happen to see another couple about our age?"

We were relieved to realize that the first couple wasn't alone on the trail. As respectfully as possible, we expressed our concern about the gentleman. They agreed that he was struggling and probably shouldn't be on the trail.

We learned that the two couples had started the trail together another year, but health problems had forced the man off the trail. Finishing the trail was on his bucket list, and he was back this year to make it a reality. They said he had been impossibly slow and that they had hardly made any mileage—in fact, they'd been waiting in this location since lunchtime and it was now approaching dinnertime. Additionally, they were worried about his stability. They were hoping to convince him that the trip was becoming unsafe and suggest getting off the trail at the upcoming trail split.

We offered what encouragement and support we could.

"There's room for a couple more tents here with ours, if you'd like to stay here tonight," they offered kindly.

We were still feeling energetic, though, so we pushed on. We passed a pile of rocks someone had arranged to resemble a giant face. Then we reached Pete's Meadow—putting us 2.2 miles past our original destination. In a flat area just off the trail, we set up for the night. The spot would have been perfect if it weren't for an unidentifiable bad smell. Despite a thorough and repeated search, we never found its source.

When our chores were done and our dinner eaten, we had a relaxed yoga session. Stretching my abused muscles in a series of unhurried asanas felt so refreshing. After about the third sun salutation, I began to hope that they might one day return to their normal level of flexibility.

I bent forward, keeping my legs straight and letting my back curve until my palms flattened on the ground in a forward fold position. This stretched my taut lower back and hamstrings that had been strained by my pack. I savored the discomfort in hopes that the temporary pain would bring relief the next day. When I reached my hands overhead and arched into a slight backbend, even more tension was released from my battered muscles. I saved my favorite pose, pigeon, for last. The hip stretch felt incredible. I'd been practicing yoga at a local studio for a couple of years, and bringing it to the trail was a beautiful joining of two distinct parts of myself.

With Dot on Muir Pass

David, Gabi, me, and Sarah in front of Muir Hut

25

THE GOLDEN STAIRCASE

August 16, 2014

Slept: Lower Palisade Lake
Miles: 12.7
Weather: sunny and blisteringly hot
Dinner: spaghetti
Mood: happy, content
Letter: none
Dad's quote of the day:

DANCE LIKE NOBODY'S WATCHING. SING LIKE NOBODY'S LISTENING.
LOVE LIKE YOU'VE NEVER BEEN HURT. AND LIVE LIKE IT'S HEAVEN ON EARTH.
—WILLIAM W. PURKEY

We left our inexplicably stinky campsite at eight thirty the next morning. The relief from the assault on our noses must have empowered us because by eleven o'clock we had reached the Middle Fork Trail, which meant we had already traversed five and a half miles. We plopped down beside the trail sign for a break. As we ate lunch, a mama deer and her two fawns approached. We watched in quiet reverence as the babies nursed and the mama snuggled and bathed them. It was a beautiful reminder that we were merely visitors in their home.

After they wandered off, Sarah and I studied the map and discussed whether or not we should search for water. A figure in a familiar fluorescent-orange shirt appeared on the trail.

"John!" we both called in unison.

He grinned. "Well, look who it is."

John joined us on the ground, sitting with one foot propped on the opposite knee in his monk-like style. "I was hoping I would catch up to you ladies today. How far are you planning on going?" He unzipped his pack.

"Deer Meadow was our original plan," Sarah told him. "But I don't think that's very far from here. What about you?"

"I think I'm going to push up the Golden Staircase tonight," he said. "That climb is a bitch, and I don't want to have to do it first thing tomorrow. I'm dreading it and just want it over with. You should hike it with me. Then you can have a relaxing day tomorrow." He opened his bear canister. "Well, not *with* me, because I'm slower than a turtle in quicksand, but you know what I mean."

Sarah raised her eyebrows at me hopefully.

"Maaaybe," I hedged. Even though I knew I could tackle higher mileage, I didn't like to commit myself to it.

John dumped chocolate protein powder into his water bottle and shook it. He held up the bottle as if toasting us and took a noisy slurp. "Mmmm. Belly-be-gone!"

"That's so gross," I told him. "I would be miserable if I only ate protein shakes while hiking. It isn't even eating. It's drinking."

"Belly-be-gooone!" he roared, jiggling his belly through his dirty orange shirt. He took another gulp and stroked his chocolate-tinged beard. "Seriously, though. Am I smaller since you met me?" He put his hand on his hip and turned from side to side. "Do you think I've lost weight?"

"I think so," Sarah told him, nodding.

"Me too. Definitely," I agreed. "But you still have to eat."

The three of us continued on. It seemed to get hotter by the minute. Sweat was running in rivulets down the side of my face, soaking my back underneath my pack, and making my hands so slick that it was hard to keep a grip on my poles. I sipped from my CamelBak straw every few steps, keeping my pace rapid so that I would reach our destination sooner. Sarah and I pulled ahead of John.

I swiped the sweat out of my eyes for the second time in under a minute. "It's hard to believe we were in a hail storm just a couple of days ago."

"No kidding." Sarah agreed.

"I can't believe how much I'm drinking today."

"For real. If you could have anything to drink right now, what would it be?"

I didn't hesitate. "Sweet tea."

"Let's say you're stranded on a desert island and you can only have five drinks for the rest of your life. What would they be?" she asked.

"Sweet tea, coffee…does water count?"

"No."

"You know, I really don't drink many things other than coffee, tea, and water. I guess since I have five I'd stock Propel, too. And pineapple-orange juice and strawberry milk. What are your five?"

"Chocolate milk, OJ, coffee, V8, and beer."

"I don't think I've ever had V8."

"You're missing out. OK, what are the top five books you've read that made an impact on your life?"

We continued sharing our lists for at least an hour: the top five meals we wanted to eat when we got home, the top five items always in our kitchens, the top five outdoor adventures we wanted to take. The conversation distracted us from the heat and kept our bodies moving.

Around three o'clock we reached Deer Meadow. I propped my pack against a tree. "I can't believe this is where we were supposed to camp tonight."

Sarah held up her hand for a high five. "It's because we're bad-ass, girl." She leaned her pack on a log. "What do you think about going up the staircase tonight? Once the sun drops some and it cools off, obviously."

"I'm not thrilled about it," I responded honestly. My enthusiasm about tackling one of the most-discussed climbs of the trip at such a late point in a sweltering day was lackluster at best. "The heat has really worn me out. But I'll do it. I have to climb it sometime, so it might as well be today."

"Let's rest. I'm going to prop my legs up on this log to drain some of the lymph," Sarah told me. "Want to join?"

We hunted fruitlessly for a bit of shade, then pulled our sweat-soaked shoes and socks off and settled in the dusty dirt in front of a giant log. We yanked our shirts up to expose our sweaty stomachs to any potential breeze and propped our legs up on the massive log.

"It if weren't a million f—ing degrees, this would be perfect," Sarah said.

I closed my eyes and tried not to think about the hydration that was leaking out of my pores like a sieve. We lay motionless in silence. The heat had zapped any desire for conversation or movement. Eventually I tired of lying on the ground, so I stuffed my swollen feet into my Crocs and located the water purifier. Down at the stream I soaked my feet in the arctic current. I dunked my hat and poured the freezing water over my head again and again. The air almost instantly warmed the water against my skin and left me feeling sticky instead of refreshed though, so I filled the gravity bag and wandered back up to the dusty clearing.

I settled with my back against a tree just before John arrived.

"Pull up some shade, man," Sarah invited him, "if you can find any."

We all concentrated on moving as little as possible. The sweltering air bred somnolence. I was so hot that I felt like I was melting into the ground underneath me. I was too overheated to participate in conversation, so I listened to Sarah and John talk about comedians and old movies while I inventoried my body. My shins were badly sunburned and the skin felt tight and raw. I'd been using sunscreen religiously on my arms, neck, chest, and face but had skipped my legs the previous day because I was worried about running out. While I gave myself a pep talk for the upcoming climb, I poked at the tender, red skin.

I scratched an itch on my chest just above the last button I had fastened on my shirt. I felt a bump under my fingertip. When I moved my finger, I felt another bump. John looked up.

"Oh, wow. You have sun blisters."

I moved my fingers around the small "v" of exposed skin at the top of my shirt, feeling a handful of pencil-eraser sized bumps. "Is that what those are?"

"Yeah. Oh, man. That's bad. Have you been wearing sunscreen?"

"Religiously."

"She has; she puts it on all the time," Sarah backed me up.

"I'm just so pale. I burn easily even in normal conditions."

"Well, you have blisters," John told me. "Hang on, I have some burn cream. You need to put something on those."

While he dug in his extensive medical kit, I went back to the stream and soaked my bandana. Carefully, I wiped my burned shins and then rewet the bandana. I dabbed gently at my chest, afraid of popping the blisters and risking infection. When I returned to the shade spot I grabbed my camera and took a "selfie" of my chest so I that could see the burns for myself. They weren't pretty, but I thought I would be able to avoid infection or scarring. I stuck the medicine from John in my pack and said I would wait to use it later so that I wouldn't sweat if off going up the staircase and waste it.

 By mutual agreement we got our shoes back on and our bags packed by four thirty. The sun had just begun to drop and we hoped the timing would allow us to make the 3.8-mile push up to the campsite at Lower Palisade Lake before it was completely dark. Still, I knew I had to protect my skin even more than normal. I slathered on sunscreen and then buttoned all but the top button on my sun-protectant shirt, popped the collar, rolled the sleeves down, tied my bandana around my neck, and put on my hat. I even contemplated wearing my long underwear or rain pants but decided I would die of heatstroke. By the time we set off I was sticky and miserably hot, but my delicate pale skin was as covered as possible.

Almost as soon as we started, Sarah surged ahead. I hiked with John for a bit, but before long he had dropped behind me. As I ascended determinedly on my own, I felt the need for a mantra. Lark had given me one for tough days on the AT, but I couldn't quite remember her wording. A quote from the book *The Help* had stuck with me: "You is kind. You is smart. You is important." Editing slightly, I repeated this mantra as I placed one foot in front of the other and pushed my way up the interminable mountain. *I am strong. I am smart. I am important.*

Although every step was definitively uphill, the grade was not nearly as steep as I had feared. I had been picturing three miles of steps made for giants that would require me to take frequent breaks to rest my quivering legs. Instead, stepping over and around rocks kept me distracted and my body felt strong. I glanced over my shoulder often to watch the view as the sun dipped and vibrant color spread across the sky. Thankfully, the disappearing sun carried away some of the hellacious temperature. As the air cooled ever so slightly and my body continued cooperating by moving forward, my mood soared. *I am strong. I am smart. I am important.*

During the ascent I repeatedly glanced up, trying to follow the trajectory of the trail with my eyes. A number of times I thought I was at the top because I couldn't see any more mountains above me. More than once I reached a turn and was incredulous to find more climbing ahead. In other situations this would have been discouraging, but on the Golden Staircase it became a marker for my strength. The mountain kept going up, and I kept ascending with an urgency I didn't understand. I marveled at my strength. *I am strong. I am smart. I am important.*

For the whole climb I was alone. I didn't pass another person, and no one else passed me. I thought of all the times I was passed on ascents during my AT hike and felt proud at how far my fitness had progressed. I saw marmots and pikas scampering on the rocks. These up-close, one-on-one encounters with the unfamiliar and mischievous little varmints made me feel like part of their secret world. *I'd like to stick a marmot in my pack and take it home as a pet.*

The trail twisted behind a large rock, and I saw a tent nestled into a small clearing. *They must have been too tired to climb to the top.* I waved at the occupants and kept moving, glancing behind me at the sky full of deep purples, reds, and muted oranges. The sun was almost completely gone and it would be dark in a matter of minutes. I pushed myself to hike faster even though my thighs were beginning to burn and quiver. Just as I was debating pulling out my headlamp, I heard a shout.

"Brownie!"

Sarah was standing about twenty-five yards above me.

"WOOT, WOOT! You made it, girl!" She fist-pumped over her head.

I felt my smile take over my face as I realized I had just climbed the entire Golden Staircase without stopping. *I am strong. I am smart. I am important!*

I smacked Sarah's hand in a high five.

Golden Staircase ascent

Marmot

Pika

26

ROCKSLIDE

August 17, 2014

Slept: 0.3 miles past Taboose Pass Trail
Miles: 11.8
Weather: sunny, cloudless
Dinner: black beans and rice
Mood: tired, annoyed, but ended the day strong
Letter: none
Dad's quote of the day:

> THE THINGS YOU DO FOR YOURSELF ARE GONE WHEN YOU ARE GONE.
> THE THINGS YOU DO FOR OTHERS REMAIN AS YOUR LEGACY.
> —KALU KALU

The clearing on the shore of Lower Palisade Lake had rivaled North Evolution Lake for the most beautiful place I'd ever camped. John, Gabi, and David had stayed there too. While sharing dinner on our "kitchen rock" we had seen two giant bucks grazing across the trail. Along with the mama deer and fawns earlier and all the marmots and pikas, that was officially a larger variety of wildlife than I'd seen in a single day on the AT.

Before bed I had cleaned my sun blisters and slathered on the burn cream from John. The spots were tender but tiny so I hoped they would reabsorb without creating too much of a problem. I resisted the urge to scratch the incredibly itchy blisters because my fingernails were filthy and I was afraid of infection. When we started hiking the following morning, Mather Pass looked deceptively tame. At first all five us of were within sight of one another. Then Gabi and David pushed ahead and disappeared from view. Next, Sarah got ahead by small degrees until she too disappeared from view. I could still see John's ever-present orange shirt winding up the path behind me when I peeked over the edge of the switchbacks.

I hiked without stopping, but my progress felt miniscule as I wound up switchback after switchback. The climb seemed interminable, but I had to admit the grade was modest. I was steadily slugging up another switchback when I heard a deep grumbling noise from the ground. A loud cascade of falling rocks ricocheted and bounced. My heartbeat picked up to triple time. *A rockslide. Is it above me? Below me?* I looked up at the steep climb and strained my ears to pinpoint the location. Tilting my head, I realized that the sound was coming from below me. It stopped as suddenly as it had started.

"John!" I called behind me. "John?" I peered cautiously over the edge looking for glowing orange and hoping not to see a smashed pumpkin.

"Michelle, down here!" John waved his pole at me from a few switchbacks below.

Exhaling in relief, I yelled, "Are you OK?"

"I'm OK. You?"

"I'm good." I gave a thumbs-up.

He threw his arms up in wonder. "A rockslide?!"

"Crazy. Want me to wait on you?" I shouted back.

"No. I'm slow today." He waved me on. "Be careful."

I scooted away from the edge and took a few deep breaths. *That scenario could have ended very differently.* It was a stark reminder that nature was in charge. When my heart rate was back to "hiking normal," I pushed on. I was surprised to finish the 3.8-mile climb at half past eleven, especially considering the 1,500-foot elevation gain.

Lunch felt well earned and I savored my hummus, sundried tomatoes, and cheese on a tortilla. This had become my favorite lunch and I made a note to be sure to pack it for future trips. Despite being well-fed and well-hydrated on the wandering descent, my body felt tired, and I couldn't quite identify why.

Eventually we reached the south fork of the King River, our original destination for the night. Sarah and I forded the river together and then took a long rest with our shoes off. As I reclined on the ground, I inventoried my body. Nothing specific hurt; I just felt weak. Still, without pain and with so much daylight left, there was no reason to stop. We decided to make the 800-foot climb up to the Taboose Pass Trail junction.

Joyously, I got my almost-expected four o'clock energy surge and the climb wasn't bad at all. About a third of a mile past the split we found Gabi and David in a small clearing underneath arching trees. We dropped our packs beside them and hurriedly erected our tent.

Since we still had daylight and warm temperatures to spare, we went down to the lake and spot-washed our clothes and our bodies. It was amazing what a little water and peppermint soap could do to lift my spirits after a challenging day.

That evening we shared stories and laughs with Gabi, David, and John. For the first time we began to discuss the end of the trail. We were all shooting to finish the trail on the same day, but John wasn't planning to hike the Whitney portion since he had already done it. We campaigned for him to change his mind, but in the end he stuck to his guns.

My body check-in was comforting. I had some hamstring tightness but no other complaints—I hadn't even gotten a headache since the altitude sickness had abated. Satisfied that my body was holding up, I prepared to go to sleep. As I was settling in to my sleeping bag, the zipper pull came off in my hand. I was devastated and immediately began to worry about the upcoming high-altitude nights that were bound to be chilly. I tucked the ends of the bag underneath me and hoped for the best.

27

OHMYGAWD, I'M HIKING!

August 18, 2014

Slept: Wood Creek
Miles: 9.5ish
Weather: slight wispy clouds and windy
Dinner: tortilla soup
Mood: pensive and happy
Letter: none
Dad's quote of the day:

THE TROUBLE WITH BEING IN THE RAT RACE IS THAT EVEN IF YOU WIN,
YOU'RE STILL A RAT. —LILY TOMLIN

The John Muir Trail had started its subtle magic of changing me—like all long hikes do—the minute I started planning. From the first step I had felt the pull of the trail whispering knowledge and questions into my heart. After an extended time in the woods, I always return with my awareness of the world expanded and my soul deliciously rejuvenated.

We had woken early and walked by the peacefully beautiful Lake Marjorie. The crisp blue of the water, contrasting the surrounding grey stone and reflecting the puffy white clouds, made me wish we could stop for the day to take in the view longer. Only the knowledge that the views on the trail became better with each step made me excited to keep walking.

I had expected alpine terrain to feel barren and unwelcoming—full of endless expanses of whitish rock. But my actual experience was quite the opposite. The views were vast and extravagant and full of vivid color. *I've never been so glad to be wrong.* The challenge I had been issued pre-hike to find a non-postcard-worthy view was proving impossible. It was like living inside a prized postcard collection, and I never wanted to leave.

Aside from the mental changes, I had also continued growing stronger. I could see my calves becoming more defined and felt the way my skirt sat more loosely on my hips. I wished those changes were permanent, but I knew my more sedentary post-trail life would steal my temporarily chiseled legs and shrunken waist. But on the sixteenth day of the hike, I experienced what would become an enduring physical mark.

We climbed Pinchot Pass and I felt strong until the last dozen switchbacks, where I felt myself pursing my lips and concentrating on my breathing. Deliberately I focused on equalizing the lengths of my inhalations and exhalations. Above me I could see the brightly colored jackets of other hikers resting on top of the pass, and my pride was all that kept me from taking copious breaks as I pushed to join them on the evasive summit.

As always, Sarah had beaten me to the top. I was glad that my typically competitive nature didn't compel me to change that. Hiking at my own pace made me much happier and allowed me to enjoy the scenery and mull over the mysteries of the universe. When I summited, Sarah was with the Carolina Four (two North Carolina couples we had met at VVR) and Gabi and David. They cheered and slapped my palm with high fives as I waited for my breathing to regulate.

I sat on a rock and peered all around at the jagged granite peaks, the sparkling lakes nestled in culls between mountains, and the trail winding through all the beauty. For the hundredth time I felt grateful that I'd been given the opportunity to hike this trail. Any number of things could have prevented my trip from taking place: I could have been unable to get a permit, the forest fire could have spread, my new employer could have refused to delay my start date, or I could have been unable to find a new hiking partner when Dad was no longer able to join me. *Thank you, world.*

A quick snack bolstered my energy reserves and I soon felt ready to tackle the dizzying descent. We had 6.9 downhill miles to our campsite. I hoped to make camp early and have almost twenty-four hours to relax before meeting the cowboy and mules with our resupply the next day.

As always, I picked up my pace on the descent. My legs marched quickly, avoiding awkward steps, pebbles, and obstacles as they scurried in synchronicity with gravity. Sarah and I stopped repeatedly on the incredibly steep incline to marvel at the fact that people ride pack animals up and down such a sheer path. I was slightly nervous on my own two feet and couldn't imagine trusting an animal with me perched on top. The fist-sized, ankle-biter rocks we were stumbling over seemed like an invitation to be tossed off the back of a donkey or horse.

After our lunch break, Sarah started down the trail a minute before I did. I dallied, staring out at the mountains, not quite ready to start hiking. Soon I hefted my pack and was bustling along quickly. Traversing the ankle-biters was like navigating a minefield. All of a sudden, I set my foot down the wrong way on a rock and found myself plummeting headfirst to the ground. In the nick of time, I planted my poles and was able to slow my fall enough to prevent any injuries. I dusted myself off and rolled my ankle clockwise and then counter-clockwise to evaluate. The ankle was sore but seemed fine, so I took a deep, stabilizing breath and kept going at a slightly slower pace.

Only a few minutes later I rolled the same ankle on a very steep, rock-covered section. This time I couldn't brace myself and came hurtling down, skidding many feet before coming to a stop facedown on my stomach with my poles wedged awkwardly underneath me. Sarah, who was only a few steps in front of me, turned at the clamorous noise.

"Are you OK?" She hurried back toward me.

I remained facedown in the dirt and rocks. "No," I groaned. I rotated my right ankle in a circle for the second time in less than five minutes, cringing as pain shot up my leg.

"Do you want help?" She was reaching towards me.

"No. Thanks." I knew from extensive trail-falling experience that it's sometimes easier to get upright on your own when you're awkwardly balancing a pack the size of a minivan on your back.

Sarah backed up a step. "OK," she hesitated. "Just let me know."

What I wanted to do was stay facedown in the pebbles indefinitely, maybe even to cry in exhausted self-pity. Instead, I did a quick inventory of my body: palms stinging, right knee throbbing, right ankle like a cantaloupe, lower left ribs bruised. Forcing out a deep breath I hadn't realized I'd been holding, I took my hands out of the loops on my poles and attempted to lift my lower body off of the ground. With the weight of my pack and my upside-down position on the steep grade, this proved impossible. Shifting to plan B, I rolled over to my right side and awkwardly hauled myself and my uncooperative pack to a standing position, wincing as I put weight on my right ankle.

"Ohhhhh," I heard Sarah say as she watched me move with the grace of a rodeo bull after the red flag is waved.

I grimaced as I looked down. Blood ran in a bright red river from my knee down my dirty shin. I could feel burning in my knee, but there was too much blood to tell exactly where it was coming from. Closer inspection revealed that dozens of pebbles were embedded in my skin and I had a deep, jagged gash about an inch wide.

"Do you want to stop for a bit?" Sarah offered sympathetically.

I shook my head and bit back tears. "No. I just want to keep going."

"I get it. Just let me know. I won't get too far ahead, OK?" She turned and headed down the trail, allowing me a minute to recover my pride.

I tried to squirt water from my CamelBak straw onto my knee, but it wouldn't work. So I took a big sip and spit water onto my knee. I could hear my mother's voice in my head telling me my mouth was full of bacteria. *They're my own germs; they can't hurt me too much.* I watched pink rivers run down my shin and soak into my sock and gaiter. When I'd flushed out most of the dirt, I decided to let the fresh mountain air do some of its healing magic. I pushed the final few miles to camp on a tender ankle with fresh blood still trickling down my leg, making rivulets in the layers of sweat, dirt, and sunscreen that coated my skin.

Sarah was waiting for me at Woods Creek, and together we checked the area to determine where we would meet the pack mule and our cowboy the next morning. There were hitching posts for animals, so we assumed the cowboy would stop nearby. A long, wooden suspension bridge crossed the river, and we suspected there might be prime tenting real estate on the other side. Respecting the somewhat intimidating "one person at a time" sign on the bridge, we crossed and found a perfect campsite by three o'clock.

"I know it's a little cold, but since we have the sun and it's early, should we take hooker baths?" Sarah asked me.

I looked up from picking at my knee. "Hooker baths?"

"You know, pits and tits?"

I laughed so suddenly I snorted. "I've never heard it put like that. I could definitely use a bath, though. We haven't showered in what, six days?"

"Seven, I think."

"It's bad when it's been so long you can't keep track."

She nodded. "I'll help you with your hair if you'll help with mine."

We ambled down to the stream with our bandanas and cleaned up. I stood ankle-deep in the creek, hoping the frigid water would keep my sore ankle from swelling any more. Using a few drops of Dr. Bronner's, we helped each other wash our hair. After changing into dry clothes and brushing out my hair, I felt the cleanest I had in days. While my semi-laundered clothes dried on rocks, I sat down with tweezers and picked gravel from the still-bleeding wound on my knee. *I could probably use some Dermabond. Which I don't have.*

Around dinnertime a group of five guys on a men's weekend arrived. They were a noisy and wild group. Juan, Jose, and Miguel were brothers, and they were with their friends Jesse and Matthew. They yelled back and forth loudly as they set up camp and passed around a plastic water bottle full of whiskey. John arrived too, and soon we had a group set up in the clearing.

We all gathered at the fire circle and cooked our dinners. The five guys were low on food because their trip was taking longer than they had expected. Sarah and I shared some with them since we would receive a resupply in the morning. As we all talked with the distant sounds of other groups echoing in the trees around us, they made mushroom tea and passed around a joint. I leaned against a rock and listened to the goings-on around me. I would never see these people again, and in the real world we would have nothing in common. But for tonight, we were friends.

"If you could eat anything right now, what would it be?" John asked the group as he sat cross-legged and stirred his food.

I stretched out my legs in front of me. "A milkshake. And tacos."

"That's a gross combination," John informed me.

I shrugged.

"Our mom makes the best tacos in the world," Juan told me. "Seriously, she's an amazing cook."

"It's true," Miguel agreed.

"What about you, Sarah? What would you eat?" John asked.

"My husband's cooking. Probably a root bake—onions, garlic, sweet potatoes, beets, carrots and herbs—a garlic burger, and a big old salad with produce from our garden. He's the best cook. He spoils me completely. I can't wait to get back home and eat his amazing cooking."

"John?" I asked.

"Right now, probably a burger. Really juicy. I'm ambivalent about the cheese." He scratched his beard. "No, I'd definitely have the cheese. And onion."

Jesse glanced around the circle at all of us. "How often do you guys have this conversation?"

"Almost every night for the last week or so," John told him.

Just as we were all wrapping up dinner, another hiker arrived in our little area. She was around twenty years old with legs up to the clouds. She wore cheerleading shorts that barely covered her butt cheeks and a white button-down shirt tied in a knot just below her bra.

"Do you know where I could, like, camp?" she asked. "I'm just, like, so excited to be here! You know? It's just, like, ohmygawd, I'm hiiiking!"

I let my eyes roam the gigantic open area with more flat spots for tents than I could count and raised my eyebrows at Sarah across the fire.

One of the guys jumped up to "help" her. She set up camp wearing nothing but her microscopic cheerleader shorts and a sports bra.

"Ohmygawd!" Legs exclaimed, her words all running together, when she plopped down at the fire circle. "I just can't believe I'm hiking! This is, like, amaaazing!" She had added a wool serape on top of the sports bra, but her abdomen—complete with pierced belly button—was still noticeably bare above her impossibly tiny shorts.

I studiously avoided looking at Sarah, and I could feel her avoiding making eye contact too. Legs asked questions about where she could buy more food and where she was supposed to go to the bathroom. I wondered how much food was in her pack. She was headed in the opposite direction, and it had been a week since our last food drop. She interrupted my musings by explaining how she was opting not to treat her water and expressed amazement once again at the fact that she was hiking.

The fire died down, and I bandaged my still-bleeding knee with gauze and Neosporin and prepared to settle in for the night. I was just getting comfortable on my Therm-a-Rest when I heard Sarah mimic in a voice just above a whisper, "Ohmygawd, I'm hiiiking!" We collapsed into giggles until we could barely breathe.

Happy in the Sierras

On Pinchot Pass

28

THE COWBOY

August 19, 2014

Slept: 0.2 past Middle Rae Lake
Miles: 6.4
Weather: partly cloudy with wind
Dinner: burrito in a bag
Mood: determined, content
Letter: Hailey
Dad's quote of the day:

WE CANNOT CHANGE THE CARDS WE ARE DEALT,
JUST HOW WE PLAY THE HAND. —RANDY PAUSCH

An unpleasant cacophony of noises awakened me. First the metallic zing of zippers being undone. Then the whoosh of air being deflated from mattresses, the rustle of nylon stuff sacks being packed, and the crunching and scuffling of feet walking nearby. When I begrudgingly opened my eyes, it was still dark.

"Hey!" It was a loud yell-whisper that sounded like Miguel. "HEY!" The swooshing sound of a tent being rustled preceded more ongoing stage whispers. "Are you up, man? We have to get moving."

"I'm awake," came the muffled reply.

"Shhhh, be QUIET," came an even louder stage whisper.

"OKAY."

"We have to hurry."

"I'm HURRYING."

Their whispers were so loud that I was positive normal voices would have been less disturbing. I tossed onto my other side and rearranged my inflatable pillow under my head. *Be patient.* Sarah flipped over and moved around on her mattress, and I realized the noise had awakened her as well.

"Could the Five Amigos make any more f—ing noise?" she asked in a muted voice.

"I don't think so." I tucked my chilled nose into my sleeping bag. "How many times do you think we told them we were sleeping in today?"

"At least a dozen."

The screaming whispers continued for at least five more minutes. Finally I flopped onto my back in exasperation and called out, "Hey, could you keep it down? Some of us don't have to leave before sunrise today."

The guys mumbled apologies, but the noise level didn't change much before they finally left camp.

"Do you think they'll make it out of the woods today?" I asked Sarah.

"Not before dark." She was quiet for a couple of minutes, then without any segue she said, "Ohmygawd, I'm hiiiking!"

We quit talking, but I don't think either of us went back to sleep that morning. When I finally grew claustrophobic, I crawled out of the tent and was pleased to see the sun. Although it was chilly, I did some laundry in the stream and spread it out on sunny rocks to dry. Then I laid my Therm-a-Rest in a patch of sun and stretched out on top to journal.

I decided to pull out my letter for the day. When I unfolded the paper there was a crayon drawing of two people on top of a mountain. Penned in my sister's precise handwriting was a dictated letter from my niece.

Dear Aunt Shel,

I love you so much. You know you love me. This picture is about me and you hiking. I hope you are having fun hiking.

Love, Hailey

I loved her four-year-old version of encouragement. The previous spring I had taken her on her first hiking trip. Hailey had gone almost three miles and learned to read trail blazes. She'd been so proud of her adventure. I couldn't wait to get home and take her out on a trail again.

I was stretched out on my stomach reading when I felt something sticky underneath my leg. Upon investigation, I found that the cut on my knee had bled through the bandages. Carefully I pried the long-underwear fabric off of my knee. Then I cleaned the wound, pulled out more gravel, and applied antibiotic cream and fresh gauze. *I'll bet I end up with a scar.*

Sarah was over at the metal bear box sorting through her bear canister. "How'd you do for food this time?" she asked me.

"Pretty good. I had a little bit left over, but I gave most of that to the Five Amigos last night."

We dumped our leftovers into a pile. Between us we had one Crystal Light drink mix, some Italian herbs, and dried celery.

Sarah poked at the pile. "That cowboy had better show up."

I paced back and forth to the drawbridge, keeping watch for horses. *What if I had the meeting spot wrong? What if there was a mix-up in dates? We don't even have cell service to call anyone…*

We heard noise and a young family appeared in the clearing. The mom was carrying a small child in a carrier on her back, while the dad wore an enormous pack. As soon as they stopped walking, they set the tiny toddler on the ground and she happily pattered around the campsite. Sarah and I talked with them and learned that the couple had always backpacked together and didn't want to stop when they had a child, so they just started taking Sage with them. They said they had gotten a lot of flak from family and other parents of young children about the safety of bringing a toddler out to the backcountry.

"What would you do in an emergency?" people would ask, and they would respond, "What type of emergency are you imagining?" The way they saw it, being out in the woods with Sage was no more dangerous than being out there on their own. They kept a close watch on her body temperature since she wasn't walking herself, and other than that they just let her enjoy it. It was clear that Sage was ecstatic to be hiking with her parents, and I immediately hoped that if I ever had children I would be a confident enough parent to take my small child on similar endeavors.

After a seemingly interminable amount of time, our cowboy arrived. His name was Brett and he rode a horse named Blue. He didn't look like a movie-star cowboy, with a chiseled chin and tight plaid shirt, but his mules—Pippi Longstocking and Carla—had our resupply and a bag of fruit for us, which made him pretty dreamy. We devoured fresh fruit and emptied our resupply boxes on the ground. I quickly sorted my food into four piles for the remaining four days. There was a ton of extra food. *So this is where my missing food from the VVR resupply went.* I sat down in the middle of the piles and started eating.

By the time I stood up, I had devoured a package of tuna fish, a block of cheese with crackers, a bag of squash and zucchini chips, and a handful of animal crackers. Sarah was enjoying a similar feast nearby. Brett talked with us while we ate like wild animals. He told us about being the third generation in his family to do pack resupply runs. He explained that he trained the horse to come back to him, and then he could just let the horse and mules loose at night because the mules never left the horse. We learned that the fence we had encountered across the trail was to prevent horses from wandering too far. Brett took all of our trash before he left, and also the trash from John, Gabi, and David that we had collected that morning.

I stuffed the remaining food into my bear canister and repacked the rest of my pack. With the generous resupply, my pack was especially heavy when we started the climb that afternoon. My hipbelt was pinching my sciatic nerve and making the side of my foot go numb. I spent the next several miles fiddling with my pack straps to redistribute the unwieldy load.

When I caught up to Sarah a couple of miles in she asked, "You OK?"

I knew I looked as exhausted as I felt. I leaned forward on my poles and tugged at my sweat-soaked bandana. "I feel like I'm hauling a baby elephant up this mountain."

During a snack break I took the gauze off my knee and was dismayed to find the cut yellow and full of pus. I was thankful to have antibiotics with me in case it got worse. I washed the cut out and decided to leave it uncovered to dry in the air. Unzipping my hipbelt, I grabbed two Vitamin-I tablets and swallowed them as an anesthetic for my aching muscles and throbbing knee. Repaired and temporarily satiated with a snack, I was ready to hike on.

When I went to heft Baby Elephant onto my back, I misjudged the arc of my swing due to the newly added weight. I accidentally scraped the pack across my raw knee and spent the next minute cussing and squeezing my eyes shut in pain.

The afternoon hike seemed never ending. My legs, which could normally guess hiked mileage within a tenth of a mile, seemed to need recalibrating. Our 6.4 miles felt like an ultramarathon. John had told us about a gorgeous campsite up ahead and we were planning to meet him there. We found him near Middle Rae Lake. Clouds rolled in as we set up camp, and the temperature dropped steadily.

John leaned his head back and, throwing his arms out wide, turned in a complete circle. "Look at those clouds. We may not make the pass tomorrow morning."

"F—ing sick, man," Sarah said, emulating the cousins from earlier in our hike.

I smirked and kept cooking my dinner while they talked about the dark weather. It was down to almost freezing by the time we finished with dinner. Still, I wanted to enjoy a minute more of the eerie evening before retiring. I made hot chocolate and settled back against a large rock. I thought about how close our hike was to being over and how different my world would be in a week. Although I was ready to have my bed and regular hot showers back, I would miss the minimalism of the trail.

In the "default world," I mused, it is staggering how much time we put into checking emails, making phone calls, mopping floors, cutting grass, scheduling appointments, and all the other chores that rarely get tackled out in the woods. In the woods, all non-hiking work is limited to survival necessities: food, shelter, warmth, and essential hygiene. The small amount of waking time that remains is devoted to pleasure: reading, writing, taking photos, conversing, and daydreaming. *How can I bring this simplicity back home with me?*

Brett the cowboy

Leftover food pre-resupply
Photo credit: Sarah Jones Decker

29

PENULTIMATE PASS

August 20, 2014

Slept: about 1.5 miles past Center Basin Creek
Miles: 11.3
Weather: windy, cool, slightly cloudy
Dinner: chicken and rice with peas
Mood: contemplative and reflective
Letter: Al
Dad's quote of the day:

> LIFE ISN'T ABOUT WAITING FOR THE STORM TO PASS;
> IT'S ABOUT LEARNING TO DANCE IN THE RAIN.
> —VIVIAN PREANE

It was a cold, windy night, and I was glad I had a fifteen-degree bag. My circulation and body heat maintenance are about on par with those of a ninety-year-old anemic. I'd slept cinched into my mummy bag—which David had fixed the zipper on—with my fleece hat snugged over my ears all night long. Thankfully, my bladder had received the memo about the temperature and I hadn't needed to get up.

Despite the cold, we woke early and were hiking by seven thirty in an attempt to make the summit of Glenn Pass ahead of any incoming bad weather. The foreboding clouds had partially cleared, but the cold and wind remained. I kept my long underwear on under my hiking skirt—an even more stylish look than normal thanks to the blood-stained knee from my fall. I also wore two shirts, my puffy jacket, and my fleece hat. For the first mile I hiked with my shoulders hunched and my chin tucked into the collar of my jacket. My sunglasses were protecting my eyes, but my cheeks were exposed and I felt them turning red from the unbuffered wind. Even cold and working hard for a pass, I was gloriously happy. I couldn't think of anywhere else I'd rather be.

After scrambling up the rocky trail for a couple of hours, Sarah disappeared in front of me and I couldn't see any more mountains ahead. Naïvely, I thought this meant I was nearing the summit. My legs quivered and I was ready for a break, but since the end was in sight, I kept pushing upward as I congratulated myself on a strong climb. I was convinced I would push to the top of the next big rock, round the corner, and see hikers high-fiving and letting out whoops of accomplishment.

Instead, I rounded the corner and was aghast to see an endless expanse of rock-covered mountain climbing closer and closer to the sky as far as I could see. *How is it possible that I couldn't see that monstrosity ten seconds ago?* I blinked, hoping it was a mirage. But no; colorful, ant-like hikers were winding their way up until they became too distant to see. Conceding that I wasn't going to make it up Glenn Pass without a break, I leaned against a rock the size of a small house and caught my breath. This climb was tough, and I was glad we weren't taking it on in worse weather. Squinting behind me, I could see John's glow-in-the-dark orange shirt slowly approaching— many, many switchbacks below.

I gave myself a pep talk. *This is the penultimate pass. You've got this. One more pass tomorrow, and then Whitney. That's it.* I bumbled onward, sending occasional glowering glances at the trail above me. Each step was a challenging and deliberate motion as I propelled myself on with calm resolution. By ten o'clock I was shivering on the summit. Gabi and David were there with Sarah when I hauled myself over the final switchback. We all huddled behind rocks to hide from the wind and wait for John. When John's jack-o'-lantern shirt rounded the final turn, we started cheering.

"Yeah, John!"

"WOOT, WOOT!"

"You got this!"

"Just a few more steps!"

Laboriously, he leaned on his poles and dragged himself the final fifteen yards. With a weary smile he collapsed like a rag doll on the rock beside me. "That—was—a—bitch." He sat down to catch his breath. "You guys—didn't have to—wait—on me."

"We wanted to," I told him. "We're in this together."

He leaned his head against my shoulder.

"But I can't wait much longer. I'm frozen." I put my icy fingertips on his arm to emphasize my point.

After everyone had taken photos, I settled Baby Elephant on my back and started the descent. In spite of my love for downhills, this one hurt. Every time I extended my right knee, I felt the still-raw scrape tearing back open. When I glanced down, there was fresh blood leaking through my long underwear.

Since we were making good time, Sarah and I decided to push slightly past our original destination. We actually had enough energy to go further, but the trail was starting to climb again and it was already brutally cold at the current elevation. We picked a flat spot away from other hikers and made sure the area had space for John's tent too. Gabi and David pushed on.

It was so cold that we immediately changed into dry clothes and added all of our outer layers. We raced to set up camp, stopping every couple of minutes to defrost our fingers in our armpits and hop around to keep our toes mobile. I devoured a Snickers bar for fortification while I shivered inside my puffy coat. *How did I make it the whole AT without a puffy?*

At dusk, as we were setting up the kitchen, John arrived.

I welcomed him and told him, "We're about to eat. I need food to warm myself up. Do you want to eat with us?"

"I want to get my stuff set up. You guys go ahead."

"Do you want help?"

"Nah. I'll be over soon."

While I waited for my water to boil, I asked Sarah, "How do you think Yogi manages eating cold, rehydrated food on nights this chilly?"

"I couldn't do it," she responded. "Where do you think that guy even is? He's probably on Whitney tonight."

"That guy's tough. He's tougher than I am." I shivered and held my hands over the steam escaping from my pot. "Can you believe the next two nights we'll be sleeping at even higher elevations?"

"I don't even want to think about it."

I was so cold that I didn't let my dinner rehydrate long enough before starting to eat it. The vegetables in my chicken and rice were still crunchy, but I didn't even care. I ate every single awful, crusty bite and then heated water for hot chocolate. I sat with John as long as I could, but he took forever to cook his food. Finally I surrendered to my sleeping bag at just after seven. *I would never go to bed this early in real life.*

I stuffed myself into my sleeping bag and sent up a word of thanks to David for fixing my snagged zipper the day before. With my gloves on, I opened the letter for that night.

Michelle,

I know the JMT poses different obstacles than the AT did, but due to all the things you had to overcome on the AT, I know you can do it! I also know you stink. ☺ I'm happy for you that you were/are able to complete this life goal. I'm not into hiking (obviously), so I can't say I understand wanting to spend days on end trudging through the woods and nights on end sleeping in a tent, BUT I know how much you enjoy it so I think it's great you have/took this opportunity. And just think of all the exciting things you have waiting for you when you get home! New job, interesting guy...and of course your niece and sister! I know some days on the JMT will be hard and they will suck. But I also know how strong and stubborn you are and that you'll make it through. Hopefully with some entertaining stories to share—so keep on hiking, and then come home, write another book, and start another adventure.

Love you, Allison

I flicked my headlamp off and settled back on my inflatable pillow. I thought about my sister and how interesting it is that we can be so perfectly alike in some ways and so starkly different in others. I'd love to sit and talk with her by a campfire or on a difficult summit, but I know we'll never get the chance. Al would never, ever do something like long-distance hiking. Sleeping sweaty, bug-bitten, and dirty on the ground is not her idea of fun.

Although we differ in our views of backpacking, we share so many other interests. Al and I are both obsessively organized, we both read voraciously (and on the same, sometimes unusual topics), and we both play piano. We love to craft and cook and drink coffee. We are both obsessed with holidays—especially Christmas. We believe family and traditions are important, and we genuinely enjoy our (much too infrequent) time spent together.

But some of our differences are as glaring as the difference in our eyes—mine a deep brown and hers a sparkling, marbled blue. I love shoes, while Al would wear flip-flops every day if it were socially acceptable. I love dangly earrings and swapping out my jewelry, while Al prefers to wear her favorite simple pieces every day. I'm more outspoken; she's more reserved.

I like to tell people we are fifty percent exactly alike and fifty percent completely different—and I wouldn't have it any other way. My little sister is really someone I enjoy and admire. Her amazing, dry, sarcastic—and often unexpected—sense of humor makes me laugh until I cry. She's married to a great guy, Chris, who has become an important part of our family. He works hard as a police officer to provide for them and is a great husband and dad. Their spunky, big-hearted, imaginative daughter, Hailey, has brought so much joy to our family.

It's funny that my sister, who is five years younger, has a life that in some ways is so much more grown up than mine. She has the husband, child, and white picket fence while I'm off playing on mountaintops. Although I love my adventures and hope to have many more, I'd happily put them on pause for my own shot at family life. *Or maybe I can have both?* I drifted off to sleep daydreaming about backpacking trips with my future husband and children.

On Glenn Pass

30

CHANGE

August 21, 2014

Slept: Wallace Creek
Miles: 12.2
Weather: sunny with slight clouds
Dinner: chili (made without the Brownie Bag; didn't rehydrate well)
Mood: content
Letter: none
Dad's quote of the day:

> IF YOU HANG OUT WITH CHICKENS, YOU'RE GOING TO CLUCK;
> AND IF YOU HANG OUT WITH EAGLES, YOU'RE GOING TO FLY.
> —STEVE MARABOLI

We started the morning with a 2,400-foot ascent over three miles. We ended on top of Forester Pass at 13,118 feet, which was our highest elevation yet. I was completely lost in thought for the first two-thirds of the climb, so I barely even noticed I was gaining elevation.

Up until this point in the hike, I had tried to guide my thinking away from anything work related. Having a month between jobs was such a gift that I wanted to enjoy the chance to focus on myself. But with the trip drawing to a close, I allowed my mind to wander briefly to the new job I would be starting in just over a week. *Was taking a new job the right decision? Will I miss EMS?*

Changing jobs has always been a bit stressful for me. My dad has oft cautioned me to make sure my changes are for the right reasons. He has been known to question, "Are you running toward something or away from something?" This time I was confident I wasn't running away from something; I had loved my job in EMS. Every day had been an opportunity to help other people in potentially life-changing ways, to problem-solve, and to learn new skills. My two most frequent partners, Erin and Janice, were people I enjoyed and had shared many laughs with, and my rule-following, authority-respecting, type-A personality had been a good fit for the fast-paced, cutting-edge, slightly militaristic system where I worked. In fact, I had loved my job so much that I hadn't been seriously searching for other opportunities.

A new job has always felt like a clean slate for me—new responsibilities, new coworkers, new skills to master. The upcoming start of this job made me think back through the numerous jobs I had held since college. For being so much of a planner, it still shocks me that I am not one of those people who was born knowing the answer to, "What do you want to be when you grow up?" I know my skills and my shortcomings and I'm pretty versed in what I like and don't like, but I've never known exactly how it all rolls into the perfect job for me.

If you had asked me at any point in my life what I would do for a living, being an EMT on an ambulance would not have been in my top one hundred predictions. Yet that is the job in which I spent the longest amount of time and found the most fulfillment. It seemed fitting that I was following a winding dirt trail up a rocky mountain as my mind wandered the twisted trail of my life.

My multitude of jobs had afforded me the opportunity to live in many different parts of the country. I mentally traced the trail of places I'd lived since college: a tent on the AT, my parents' house in Massachusetts, a water buffalo farm in Vermont, a tent on the AT again, my parents' house in Massachusetts again, a duplex in Salem, Massachusetts. Then there was the basement of a carriage house in Port Murray, New Jersey, a primitive cabin in New Fairfield, Connecticut, and an apartment outside Seattle, Washington. Then my parents' retirement house in South Carolina, the house where I nannied, an apartment in South Carolina, a friend's house in

South Carolina, my parents' house one last time, and finally the house I built in 2013.

I would later reflect back on this journey-through-time moment when I was instructed to fill out a ten-year residence history on my new hire paperwork.

"You need to know every address?" I asked the woman doing my intake processing.

"Just for the last ten years." She said this like it made the task simple.

"What if I don't know all of the addresses?"

"You don't know everywhere you've lived?" She appeared stunned.

"I've lived more than ten places in that timeframe."

She blinked at me behind her gold-rimmed glasses. "In ten years?"

"Yes. In six states."

She regarded me like an unknown animal species. "It's a federal document. I guess just write down what you can remember."

I was surprised to focus back on the present moment and realize I had hiked a long distance without stopping. Turning around to gaze at the undulating trail I'd already hiked, I wiped the droplets of sweat on my forehead back into my hair. In the distance I could see other hikers making the arduous climb behind me. I wondered briefly what they were thinking about.

My mind was still racing, so I decided to push up toward the top of the pass while I was distracted. During some activities being so lost in thought is detrimental to productivity, but while hiking it seemed to distract my brain and fuel my feet. My thoughts moved to the trajectory of my life, and my feet trucked along in complacent harmony with my busy mind. I wondered how my life would have turned out differently if I had made alternative choices.

I don't believe in regret, and I can't change past decisions anyway, but I definitely believe that every decision you make leads you to where you are today. If my mom hadn't put me in Girl Scouts when we moved to Massachusetts to help me make friends, I wouldn't have started going to a primitive Girl Scout camp in the summer. If it hadn't been for camp, I might not have been introduced to backpacking. Falling in love with backpacking had led to hiking the AT. If it hadn't been for the AT, I wouldn't have made the string of life choices that led me to working as a summer camp director at a Girl Scout camp. That job had been what introduced me to EMS, and learning my comfort in emergent situations had led me to EMT school after leaving Seattle. If I hadn't gone to college at Furman, I wouldn't have developed connections to Greenville, South Carolina, and I might not have stayed in Greenville following EMT school.

By the time I finished analyzing I had been hiking for quite a while. I was pleased to look around and see that there wasn't much rock above me. I thought this meant I had distracted myself for the duration of the climb. I was ready to slap myself on the back for a strong hike. My internal cheerleading section was thwarted, however, when I rounded a corner at the edge of a sparkling blue tarn and saw even more trail climbing toward the sky.

In reality, I was only about two-thirds of the way up Forester Pass when I snapped out of my reverie. I heard voices and scanned upward to see tiny dots of color way above me, decorating the ridge like ornaments on a Christmas tree. I recognized the vibrant colors of Gabi's and David's coats. Simultaneously sighing and glaring at the offending mountain, I wiggled Baby Elephant into a more comfortable position and continued the ascent. Despite my best efforts, I couldn't retreat into my mind again. For the last bit of the climb to Forester Pass I remained focused on the ground beneath my feet. The struggle to get oxygen into my lungs seemed indirectly proportionate to the shrinking distance between me and the colorful fabric dots above.

I made a game out of guessing how many switchbacks I had left until the top. Three times I exceeded my guess and started over. Finally I heard a voice above me and discovered Sarah sitting on a giant rock, talking on the phone. *She has cell service?* When I caught up I could tell she was on the phone with Morgan. I threw a wave in her direction and pushed on fifty yards to the official top of the pass. Gabi and David both slapped my hand. After I caught my breath and took in the beautiful views on both sides of the pass, I pulled out my own cell phone.

"Mom!" I practically yelled into the phone when she answered. Although I recognize there is no truth to this, I always feel the need to speak more loudly when I'm on the phone in remote areas.

"Hey! Aren't you on the top of a mountain? I just looked at you on the DeLorme map."

"Yep. I'm on top of Forester Pass. The highest pass so far."

"Wow! And you have cell service?" she asked incredulously.

"Apparently."

I could hear Mom whisper, "Hailey, come here! Pick up the phone."

A little voice piped up, "Hi, Aunt Shel! You're on a mountain. Nana showed me on the 'puter. I couldn't really see *you*, just a dot."

"Hey, Peanut! Yes, I'm on a mountain."

"There aren't phones on mountains," she informed me confidently.

"Well, I—"

"Are you hiking, Aunt Shel?" She saved me from having to explain when she interrupted.

"Yes, I am."

"OK. I went hiking. I love you, bye. Bye, I love you." And just like that, with the signature farewell from our family, she and her four-year-old attention span were gone.

I chatted with my parents a bit more and told them that Sarah and I might be finishing the trail a day early.

"Be careful. I'm tracking you on the computer," Mom told me.

"I'm sure you are. By the hour."

"That might be an understatement," Dad chimed in.

I turned in a circle and took in the view from the top of Forester Pass from every direction. I felt a twinge of pride knowing that hikers who traverse the entire 2,663-mile Pacific Crest Trail never climb higher than I was right at that moment. *Maybe the PCT is in my future after all.* Finally I started down the other side of the intimidating pass. Looking over the initial dropoff, I experienced a moment of vertigo. *What would it be like to do this trail on a pack animal?* Being on my own two feet on a rocky, steep precipice was intimidating enough—I couldn't fathom trusting an animal to carry me. I wasn't afraid of heights, but I couldn't deny being ready to descend.

The top of the pass had marked our entrance into Sequoia National Park. I had been excited to see sequoia trees but was disappointed to realize I didn't even know what I was looking for. *Is that one a sequoia? Is that one?* The trees were all majestic, but I couldn't tell them apart.

During the sprawling descent—our reward for the taxing climb—our surroundings changed completely. We passed many trees with twisted, bicolored trunks that fascinated me. I stopped to photograph one of these unique trees and my camera started acting up. It would turn on, the lens would extend, and the shutters would open, but then it would extend and retract about seven times before an error message showed up on the screen. I could neither take pictures nor review old ones.

I spent a good twenty minutes fiddling with the camera. I removed and replaced the batteries, cleaned the lens, and finally resorted to shaking it. Nothing. My camera was broken on the second-to-last day of a major hike with glorious views. *Dammit!* We were just entering Bighorn Plateau, an eerily beautiful spot that made me think of ancient Indian battlegrounds, and I had no camera.

Halfway through the plateau, I sat down on a rock beside the trail and tinkered with the camera some more. While I randomly pushed buttons, I charged my nearly dead iPhone with the Powerocks charger so that I could use it for pictures. I knew Sarah was taking photos and would share them with me, but it wasn't the same as being behind the lens myself.

During the descent from Forester Pass, Sarah and I talked about our plans for the final stretch of trail. The summit of Mount Whitney—the official terminus of the John Muir Trail—is a 1.9-mile jagged climb from a three-way split called Whitney Junction. Southbound thru-hikers approach the junction from the north and continue south on the JMT to reach the Mount Whitney summit and officially complete the JMT. Then they still have to descend back to the junction and take the third split to go down 8.1 grueling miles on Whitney Portal Trail.

Our initial itinerary had us doing a short day the next day to camp at Guitar Lake. We had planned to summit Mount Whitney the following morning and descend all the way to Whitney Portal the same day. However, as we came down Forester we discussed the option of going all the way up Whitney the next day. We would return to the junction and camp a few tenths of a mile down at Whitney Trail Camp.

The proposed plan had a number of highlights, but the most significant one was that it would put us summiting Whitney on a Friday instead of a Saturday. We hoped this would reduce the number of people with whom we shared our grand finale. In truth, Sarah was probably more in favor of this plan than I was. My biggest incentive was that Gabi and David were planning to summit the same day—and the sentimental side of me wanted to finish as a group. They were planning to camp on the summit, though, which I thought was crazy. Even the base camp Sarah and I were discussing was 2,000 feet higher than any other campsite where we had slept to that point. I had no intention of camping on top of the tallest mountain in the continental United States.

We settled at Wallace Creek and set up our camp kitchen to share a final meal with Gabi, David, and John. I was cold and tired and realized when I settled on the rock that I had forgotten to grab my Brownie Bag. I decided to just put the Ziploc of hot water and food inside my jacket instead. The pouch served as a heating pad for my belly, but the food didn't rehydrate well and some of the liquid leaked out and soaked my pants and jacket. I ended up eating crunchy chili in wet, sticky clothes.

While we ate, more and more backpackers arrived in the clearing. There were easily more hikers than we had seen on a single night the entire trail. *Where did all these people come from? Are they thru-hikers? Are they catching up to us? Did we catch up to them?* I had a hard time finding a private area to use the bathroom because tents were everywhere.

The excitement of the end of the trail was evident. Every clique of hikers was just slightly louder than on a normal trail night. On my way back to the tent I stopped on a big, flat rock and turned off my headlamp. I stared up at the stars above me. *Thank you for this experience.*

I crawled into the tent shortly after dinner and pulled out my journal. I ran my fingers across the John Muir quotes I had written in Sharpie across the front. Just three weeks on this trail had changed me—not in ways I could voice, but in small, subtle ways on the inside. I was confident I'd grown and stretched my beliefs in these few short weeks. I couldn't imagine what a lifetime of traipsing through these woods had done to impact the man John Muir was. *How much would a lifetime in these mountains change you?*

I started to journal about these thoughts and found that my pen wouldn't write. Now I had a dead camera and a dead pen. This trail was clearly coming to an end. I used my awkward, pint-sized back-up pen to write a few stilted paragraphs.

I had run out of letters to read, which disheartened me more than I'd like to admit. As independent as I can be, those letters really encourage me at the end of long hiking days. Since I didn't have a new letter, I opened Dad's spiral notebook and re-read each quote he had written from the beginning. When I got to that day's quote, I read it twice: "If you hang out with chickens, you're going to cluck; and if you hang out with eagles, you're going to fly."

I clicked the headlamp off and tucked myself into my now-familiar and slightly smellier mummy bag. *Am I soaring? Am I surrounded by the right people?* I thought back through all the letters I had read. I had laughed, cried, smiled, remembered, and been encouraged. The letters had served their purpose. There were definitely some eagles in my life. Over the last few years I had become increasingly less social, and I felt I had done a commendable job at sorting the friendships that were virtuous from the ones that were draining me. I'd work at distancing myself from any remaining chickens over the next few months.

With Sarah on top of Forester Pass

Sarah descending Forester Pass

Trail view

Trail view

31

I'M A BEAST

August 22, 2014

Slept: Whitney Trail Camp
Miles: 15.4
Weather: sunny and cool
Dinner: tuna and bites of Sarah's broccoli mac
Mood: triumphant, dreamy
Letter: none
Dad's quote of the day:

> FOR OF ALL SAD WORDS OF TONGUE OR PEN,
> THE SADDEST ARE THESE: "IT MIGHT HAVE BEEN!"
> —JOHN GREENLEAF WHITTIER

I woke up on summit day with a familiar combination of contradicting emotions: excitement and sadness. Sometime later in the day I would stand at the southern terminus of the John Muir Trail. This would mean my thru-hike was complete and I had succeeded in tackling the trail. It would also mean the trip was done and it was time to leave the beauty of the woods for the hectic pace of the "default world" and a new job. I squeezed my eyes shut and breathed in the fresh mountain air until my lungs could hold no more. *How do you balance such opposite emotions?*

Our alarm had been set for five thirty, and by five forty we were already getting out of the tent. Sarah and I didn't talk much, but the anticipation was almost palpable as we hurried to break camp quietly. Gabi and David were moving around beside us in the dark as they too prepared for a long trek. We hadn't been able to convince John to join in on our march to the terminus. Since he had already completed the trail a couple of times, he was skipping the Whitney summit altogether and taking an extra day to complete the final portion of the trail. We would meet up with him in town.

It was a cold morning, so I stomped my feet and tucked my hands in my armpits in between bites of granola bar and swigs of frigid water. It was still dark when Sarah and I whispered goodbyes to Gabi and David and hit the trail.

Sarah pulled in front of me quickly as the dirt path wound up from our campsite toward a forest of giant trees with twisty trunks. I wanted to take so many pictures, but since I could only use my iPhone I was hesitant to drain the battery. I hoped that Sarah was documenting our surroundings up ahead of me. Since we had so much mileage to complete and I knew we had challenging terrain ahead, I was conscious of my pace so that I wouldn't tucker out later in the day. The moderate pace served a dual purpose because I wanted to soak in every single sight and sound as the trip wound to an end.

At a quarter after ten we had made it the 6.4 miles to Guitar Lake. The lake was in a valley between tall mountains, and it was cold and windy with nowhere to hide from the elements. We climbed on top of a gargantuan flat rock to rest for the final climb. Above us we could see towering mountains, and we tried to guess exactly where the summit of Whitney might be. It astounded me that I couldn't pick out the tallest mountain in the lower forty-eight states—but then again, *all* of the mountains around us were huge.

We pulled off our shoes to rest our abused feet and our sweaty shirts to dry them in a sunny spot on the rock. I wanted to enjoy one more topless lunch since this would be our last chance, but the wind in the exposed meadow seemed to be blowing straight through me. I had to put my puffy coat on over my damp bra and lean back against Baby Elephant.

I ate tuna fish from a foil pouch and followed it immediately with a Snickers bar. I wondered where else in my life this situation would seem appropriate—wearing a sports bra and an unzipped down jacket over a skirt while sitting barefoot on a rock, eating a strange combination of foods with filthy hands. I decided that my life would be happier if I spent lunch breaks like this more often.

"How much water do you have?" Sarah asked.

"More than I should," I replied. I hardly drank anything this morning. I need to camel up during this break and fill my water bottle since this is the last water source until tonight. I'll probably drink a lot going up Whitney."

"I'll go fill up the water after we eat."

I nodded. "Thanks."

After eating I tried to stretch out on the rock, but it was too cold. When I gave up and sat up, I saw two hikers appear in the distance and recognized Gabi's mustard-yellow long-sleeved shirt. I pulled my still-damp shirt back on before they got closer. Gabi and David slowly came into focus and joined us on the rock, but they didn't look happy.

From the tidbits of conversation I overheard, Gabi didn't have any energy and was having a tough hiking day. David wanted her to follow his advice to fix the situation. After rummaging around in their still-large food bag, David turned in our direction. "Did you guys eat enough? You need a lot of energy for this climb. A hot meal is a good idea. And you have to stay really hydrated at these elevations."

"We've got this," Sarah told him. Her voice was pleasant, but I suspected she was one piece of unsolicited advice away from letting it be known she could handle herself.

A few minutes of quiet passed, during which I closed my eyes and rested against my pack. I heard the quiet rustle of Sarah arranging her gear. "Brownie?" she asked. "How about we leave in fifteen minutes? It'll be eleven thirty."

I slatted my eyes open. "Sounds good to me."

Although I would have loved a longer break, I was getting cold. I was also ready to make the final push. As much as I didn't want the hike to be over, I did want to summit Whitney. It would be a tough afternoon. We were about to climb 2,000 feet in three miles just to get to Whitney Trail Junction. Then we would climb another 1,100 feet over 1.9 rocky, mostly knife-edge miles to Whitney summit. All at the highest altitude—and therefore the lowest oxygen level—I'd ever experienced.

We said goodbye to Gabi and David. Although they were pushing for the summit that day, too, we had two extra miles of hiking since we were planning to descend to Trail Camp. The trail wound gently up for a bit and I hiked steadily, taking plenty of time to gaze at the mountains around me.

"How are you doing with the altitude?" Sarah asked.

I took a deep breath and thought about how it felt. "I'm good so far. You?"

"I don't even notice it. I spend so much time in the winter in the Uinta Mountains in Utah that my body is used to it."

Shortly afterward she pulled ahead of me, but it wasn't long before she stopped to talk to a man who was seated on a rock beside the trail. He was an older, white-haired hiker with an unruly beard and the trail name Paint Your Wagon. He told us he was on his third attempt at hiking the PCT. Each year he started at the beginning and made it slightly farther before quitting. *Why not just pick up where you left off?*

"I know Whitney isn't technically part of the PCT, but I figured I couldn't be this close without summiting it, so I took a detour," he told us.

"Maybe we we'll see you at the top," I offered.

We said our goodbyes and Sarah soon disappeared. Turning around, I saw Guitar Lake behind us. From this height the reason for the lake's name became obvious. At the proximal point the lake was wide, in almost a fattened figure-eight shape, and then it narrowed like the body and thin neck of a guitar. I snapped photos on my iPhone and once again cursed my camera for breaking during some of the most picturesque moments.

The trail became much steeper and I sang quietly to myself—first out loud, and then in my head as the terrain became more challenging and breathing more difficult. I tromped up switchback after switchback. Below me I could see our lunch spot getting smaller, but looking up I couldn't figure out where the trail was going to go over the crest of the mountains. Sarah had disappeared long ago, and I didn't see any other hikers. For a long time it felt like I had the entire trail to myself. I kept moving deliberately, but my pace slowed noticeably. *I'm so glad there are restrictions on the grade on this trail.*

Eventually I heard voices. The switchbacks were getting shorter, but the dropoff was very steep down the side. I could hear other hikers long before I could see them. Many minutes later, a woman and two men came into view. As I trudged along, placing one foot endlessly in front of the other and relying on the rest-step—a change of gait used by hikers and climbers to rest their muscles on steep ascents—I noticed them stopping more and more frequently. Soon I caught up and passed them after exchanging a few words. *I just passed other hikers on the ascent to Whitney Junction. I'm a beast!*

I continued my slow but steady pace. Soon I passed three more hikers—this time headed down. From our brief conversation it became clear that they had been unable to summit because of altitude sickness. I expressed sympathy and kept pushing on. Soon I heard more voices filtering down from above. I glimpsed Sarah's red jacket in the distance. There was a group of hikers standing in one tiny area. I figured she had caught up to another group and was waiting for me. I kept plodding on, placing each foot carefully on the scree-covered path. My body felt strong, but I was starting to notice that I had to work harder to breathe. I felt the tiniest hint of dizziness creeping into my forehead, so I pursed my lips and concentrated on making my inhalations and exhalations equal and deep, and fully engaging my diaphragm—just like the pranayama breaths we practice in yoga.

I continued watching my feet and eyeing the steep dropoff beside me, so I was surprised when I looked up and Sarah and the other hikers were close enough to see clearly. When they saw me approaching, they started yelling and fist pumping.

"Brownie!"

"Yeah, Michelle!"

"Go, girl!"

I realized with some shock that they were standing at the sign for Whitney Junction. I had completed the first difficult ascent of the afternoon. A huge grin spread across my face as I slapped all of the hands held out to congratulate me.

Sarah pulled me into a hug and pointed. "That sign says Whitney. First, there's a sign—that's shocking enough. Second, it says Whitney. We f—ing did it. We're here. About to go up Whitney."

I threw my hands up over my head in pure joy. This was a moment where words weren't needed.

Climbing to Whitney Junction
Photo credit: Sarah Jones Decker

32

TOPLESS ON TOP

"Pull up a rock!" A middle-aged male hiker I didn't know slapped his hand on a large boulder. We were nestled in an alcove where big rocks blocked us from the wind.

I dropped Baby Elephant and immediately began digging for my clothing bag. "Are you going up?" I asked him. He was bundled in at least four layers of clothing.

"Just came down." He gestured at three other hikers and said, "My son, my daughter, her boyfriend, and I just finished the JMT."

"Congratulations!"

"You'll be done too in a couple of hours."

I nodded determinedly. Although the man and I didn't know each other, we exchanged the proud smiles of hikers at the end of a momentous journey.

The trail passed straight through the alcove. Behind me was the JMT going north back toward Guitar Lake. In front of me was the trail south to Whitney Portal, the trailhead we would take after descending Whitney. And to my left was the trail up to Whitney summit. "One point nine miles to the top of the tallest mountain in the contiguous U.S.," I told anyone who was listening.

Just then we heard voices and three women appeared. The wind made it hard to detect approaching hikers until they were in close range. "Oh, loooook!" one of the ladies called out. "It's the Caroliiina girls." She looked at the others. "Can you believe they made it?"

I gritted my teeth. All three of the women had an unbelievable ability to draw out the word "Carolina" and make it sound all nasally.

"North Caroliiina," another one called out.

Sarah, who was kneeling in front of me taking gear out of her pack, didn't respond.

"North Caroliiina!" she repeated. "North Caroliiina, I'm calling you."

Sarah stood up abruptly and spun around. "I heard you. I didn't respond because my name is *not* North Carolina. As I've told you before, my name is Sarah. Or Harvest. I'll answer to either of those. But until you can respect me enough to call me by my name, I feel no need to answer you."

The woman took a step back and looked wide-eyed at her friends. "Well…I…well…"

I hid my proud smirk inside the collar of my jacket. I had been wanting to say something similar since we had met them on top of a pass a few days before.

"Did you have something you wanted to say to me?" Sarah demanded, her hands on her hips, not backing down.

"I guess not."

The women parked themselves as far away from us as they could get in the niche the size of a closet.

I could feel my cheeks and nose getting stiff with cold. "Should we head up?" I asked Sarah. We had left our non-crucial gear hidden behind a rock at the juncture. This was common practice since there was no point in carrying a full pack up the narrow, steep path to the summit.

We took photos by the sign pointing to Mount Whitney and started climbing. As soon as I was moving again I felt the familiar, vice-like strain on my lungs return. *Slow in, slow out*, I reminded myself. My muscles felt strong, but I kept my pace moderate and steady to aid my breathing. I reminded myself that two out of every three people who attempt to climb Mount Whitney are not successful. I needed to listen to my body if I wanted to be a part of the successful third.

The trail was only about two feet wide in some places. Looking down to my left, the mountain dropped off abruptly. I could still see Guitar Lake below me, and I tried to trace the path I had followed before and after that point. I stared in wonder at the stark, ominous peaks jutting out around Whitney. These were not polished, rounded mountains, but towering, angular monstrosities not to be reckoned with.

I ran into a group of three college-aged guys. One was slumped against a rock holding his head.

"Are you OK?" I asked him, coming to a stop.

"I'm—not sure." He shook his head. "My head—is—killing me." He paused for a rapid breath. "And I can't—seem—to catch—my breath." He was breathing very quickly.

I unstrapped my hipbelt to give my own lungs more room to expand while I rested. "I've been having to focus on my breathing too. This sounds really cheesy, but picture that you're breathing in through a straw, and when you breathe out you're blowing out a candle." I pursed my lips and demonstrated. "Try to breathe in and out for the same lengths of time. Breathe with me for a minute."

He regarded me curiously, but nodded.

"In to three…" I took a long breath in, pursing my lips as though a straw was between them, and held up one finger at a time until I reached three fingers. "Now out." I ticked the fingers back down one at a time.

His friends watched with curious concern.

"Again, OK?" I encouraged. "In…out." We did this a few times and his breathing regulated.

He kept breathing slowly, pursing his lips.

"That's good. Keep doing it. Have you thrown up?"

"Not yet."

I nodded. "I had altitude sickness at the beginning of our trip. It was awful. It took me days to get over it."

"How long have you been hiking?" his buddy asked.

"Three weeks."

"Wow. Are you doing the whole John Muir Trail?"

"Yep. About a mile left I guess."

"That's incredible. We just came to do Whitney. There are some other guys up ahead, and we do a hike together every summer. We all go to different colleges. I guess maybe climbing Whitney in one day was pretty stupid."

"You guys came all the way up and are going back down today?"

"Yeah. That's the plan."

I gave their tiny packs a once-over. "Do you have overnight gear?"

"No."

I did some quick math in my head: 1.9 miles from the summit to the junction, 8.1 from the junction to the portal, and we still had at least a mile to the summit. "Isn't it like ten miles back to Whitney Portal?"

"Yep."

"So you're doing twenty miles, including more than 6,000 feet of elevation gain and loss."

"I think it's twenty-two miles," the guy amended.

I glanced up at the sun and shook my head. "You'd better get going. There are only about four hours of daylight left."

Just before I took off again, I saw Gabi and David behind me and raised my hand in a wave. Steadily, I continued climbing the narrow route of exposed granite. Soon I saw a building way up in the distance. An emergency shelter sits on top of Mount Whitney, and seeing it meant I was getting close. The terrain became increasingly more jagged and rocky, and I was starting to see small patches of snow.

The wind picked up as I made the final push up Whitney. I pulled my fleece hat snugly over my ears and burrowed my chin into my coat collar. I couldn't believe I had seen people coming down in short sleeves. A few hikers passed me coming down the mountain, but no one had passed me going up.

Soon I saw Sarah's red coat up ahead.

"Come on, we're finishing this together," she called.

I grinned in appreciation. Together we stared in awe at the views in every direction. We wound around the boulders and rocks on the barren summit and found ourselves in front of the Smithsonian Institution Shelter. The stone hut had been built in 1909 after a hiker was struck by lightning while eating lunch on the exposed rock after summiting. We looked around inside at the uneven floors and dark interior. I was glad we wouldn't be spending the night there, but I knew if I got caught on the summit in inclement weather I'd be grateful for its existence.

An aged wooden podium was attached to the outside of the building. When we opened the top we found a John Muir Trail thru-hiker register. I proudly signed my name as Michelle "Brownie" Pugh from South Carolina. In the comments section I wrote "AT—check, JMT—check."

A USGS marker imbedded in the rock labeled the summit as 14,494 feet, though I knew the estimates changed regularly due to advancing technology and shifting tectonic plates. The exact measurement didn't matter to me, though. Regardless of the exact altitude, I was on top of Mount Whitney. Sarah and I snapped photos individually and together. The three college-aged boys arrived and joined their friends, who were already on the summit behind the shelter.

"Thanks for the breathing tricks. They really helped."

"No problem. Congrats on summiting!"

We took a group photo of the eight of them, shirtless and wearing stick-on mustaches. Almost immediately they had to head back down. After a full day of excruciating climbing, they had spent less than half an hour on top of Whitney. They were racing the sun. There was no way they could make it to their cars before dark.

As we waved goodbye to the Mustache Men, Gabi and David appeared. We cheered and high-fived and bounced around giddily with them. So much of our hike had been together that it seemed only appropriate to finish with them. I hated that John wasn't with us too, even though I understood his need to finish the trail his own way.

I wandered out to the edge of the granite outcropping and stared down at Owens Valley miles below me. Bits of snow flecked the gaps between the rocks and the sun glinted off of the crystals. I imagined zooming down to the valley on a zip line.

I was euphoric—I had completed the John Muir Trail. But to my surprise, almost as soon as I had recognized the elation it was joined by a contrasting feeling—sadness. Reaching the end of the trail meant the end of the journey and a return to everyday life.

"Michelle!"

I snapped out of my reverie and turned back to look at Sarah.

She was holding her camera.

I threw my arms wide above my head and tilted my face to the sky. You don't have to be told to smile when you're experiencing pure bliss. When I knew she had captured that pose, I pulled myself up straight and lifted one leg onto the other in a yoga tree pose. There's nothing like doing a balance pose two feet from the edge of the tallest mountain on the trail, in the state, and in the continental United States. *This one's for you, Mom.*

We snapped photos in every possible grouping and pose: by the metal placard, on the large rock, sitting, standing, jumping. Then we sent David away and pulled off our shirts and bras. Gabi served as our photographer while Sarah and I individually took topless photos on top of Mount Whitney. *If you're going to be on top of the tallest mountain, you might as well be topless!*

I re-dressed and then on a whim pulled out my cell phone. I was shocked to find I had reception. I dialed my parents. There was no answer, so I left a message. "I'm on top of Mount Whitney. I'm a JMT thru-hiker! Dad, I wish you were here!"

Guitar Lake as seen from the Whitney ascent

Climbing Whitney

With Gabi, David, and Sarah on top of Mount Whitney

With Sarah on top of Mount Whitney

33

DESCENT INTO THE DEFAULT WORLD

August 23, 2014

Dad's quote of the day:

Two days later I found myself once again seated in the back seat of my parents' car. They had picked me up at the airport upon my return from California. We chatted about some of the highlights of my trip, but we all knew the bulk of the story would be shared in bits and pieces over a lifetime. As we got closer to my house, I caught Dad's eye in the rearview mirror.

"Dad?"

"Yeah?"

"I think I've found my trail for next summer."

Mom turned around and lowered her sunglasses to stare at me. "You just got home. I am *not* ready for this conversation."

I winked at Dad. Mom may not have been ready, but I already knew there were more adventures in my future. There were too many trails left to hike. The quote Dad had provided for what turned out to be the day I returned to society perfectly summed up why I needed to begin planning my next hike already.

But it was Dad's final quote—the one he had intended for my summit day—that turned out to be the quote that resonated most perfectly with me:

THE [DAY] YOU WERE BORN MARKS ONLY YOUR ENTRY INTO THE WORLD.
OTHER [DAYS] WHERE YOU PROVE YOUR WORTH,
THEY ARE THE ONES WORTH CELEBRATING. —JAROD KINTZ

I can't remember the last time I had a birthday party. But I have celebrated March 15, my "Springer-iversary," and September 28, my "Katahdin-iversary," every year. These are the days that bring me the most joy. Now I will add August 23—"Whitney Day"—to my celebration list, with the hope that over the course of my life I'll fill my calendar with a multitude of days worth celebrating.

DEHYDRATED DINNERS

I love to eat. I wake up in the morning and before I've had breakfast, I'm already thinking about what I want for dinner. I'm relatively adventurous in my own kitchen and rarely follow a recipe. I try to use fresh, local ingredients when I can, and I love experimenting with food. When I first started backpacking, however, I was young and naïve. I had been eating in a college cafeteria for almost four years, and my diet needed some help.

On my Appalachian Trail hike, I'm not sure I consumed a single vegetable or fruit during the entire six months. Seriously. I ate a lot of macaroni and cheese, more Lipton Noodles than I care to think about, and an embarrassing number of Snickers bars. This worked out fine for my I-just-finished-college-and-don't-know-what-real-food-is body. Now that I'm no longer in my early twenties, though, my body requires actual nutrients to function well.

I tried a few pre-dehydrated meals, thinking they must at least have more nutrition than what I had been eating. Some of them were OK, some were downright awful, and all of them were expensive. My former work partner, Janice, is an extremely active backpacker and dehydrates all of her own food. She provided some tips and encouragement, and even brought me samples of food she had prepared. I hadn't realized that backpacking meals could be both delicious and healthy.

Soon I purchased my very own dehydrator and Janice held my hand through the learning process. I read websites and recipe books but ultimately came up with my own recipes through trial and error. One tip I can offer is that if you don't like something in your own kitchen, you'll probably still dislike it on the trail. I don't care much for potatoes but for some reason decided shepherd's pie would be a great trail meal. While it was well prepared, I didn't care for it any more in the woods than I do at home.

Listed below are the meals I ended up bringing with me on the JMT. All of my dehydrated meals were stored in quart-size freezer bags. To rehydrate, I simply added boiling water to the bag, placed the meal in my Brownie Bag, and waited approximately ten minutes. When I cook at home I very rarely use exact measurements, and I found this worked equally well with backpacking meals as in the kitchen, so I cannot provide exact recipes.

John Muir Trail Dinner Menu (dehydrated)
     Cheesy grits with sausage and vegetables
     Chicken and rice casserole with peas and spinach
     Burritos (3 beef and 3 chicken)
     Beef stroganoff
     Chili with beef and macaroni (3)
     Chili with beef and rice
     Spaghetti
     Shepherd's pie
     Black beans and rice with chicken
     Chicken and stuffing
     Macaroni and cheese with chicken and peas
     Walking hamburger (eaten in a tortilla)

For my lunches I dehydrated fruit (mango, pineapple, banana, apple, and strawberry) and vegetables (zucchini and squash) as sides. The main courses were unimaginative but kept me full and happy. I also packed a small dessert for every lunch (a mini candy bar, a pack of cookies, or a small bag of M&M's).

John Muir Trail Lunch Menu
     Peanut butter and jelly on a tortilla
     Hummus, summer sausage, and cheese on a tortilla
     Chicken salad from Packit Gourmet
     Pimento cheese from Packit Gourmet on a tortilla with a beef jerky
     stick

Tuna packets
Salmon packets

John Muir Trail Breakfast Menu
        Pop-Tarts
        belVita Breakfast Biscuits
        Carnation Breakfast Essentials
        Clif Bars

APPENDIX 2

HELPFUL RESOURCES

The following are resources that I found indispensable while preparing for my hike.

Websites:
    http://jmt.sierra-hikes.com/Training.html
    http://kevinstravelblog.com/
    https://socalhiker.net/itinerary-for-the-john-muir-trail/
    http://johnmuirtrail.org
    http://www.pcta.org/discover-the-trail/john-muir-trail/jmt-resupply/

Books:
    John Muir Trail: The Essential Guide to Hiking America's Most Famous Trail by Elizabeth Wenk with Kathy Morey; Wilderness Press, 2007.

    John Muir Trail Atlas Pocket Edition by Erik the Black; Blackwoods Press, 2010.

Maps:
    John Muir Trail Map-Pack from Tom Harrison Maps

APPENDIX 3

INTENDED ITINERARY

One of the more time-consuming parts of planning a long-distance backpacking trip is the creation of an itinerary. Water sources, elevation changes, camping locations, and resupply points are among the details considered. Although much time is invested in creating an itinerary, it is almost never followed in the field. Unpredictable factors such as weather, energy levels, and the itineraries of trail friends can alter plans on a daily basis. Still, a starting point is necessary in order to plan resupply stops, transportation, and many other logistics. Sarah and I planned our mail drops based on our itinerary, so we listed the necessary food for each day. We packed breakfast, lunch, dinner, and two snacks unless otherwise noted.

Section 1 – Happy Isles to Tuolumne Meadows

Day 1
Route: Happy Isles to Little Yosemite Valley (as per permit)
Sleep at: Little Yosemite Valley campground
Miles today: 0.5 to trail head + 4.5 (to campsite) = 5
Total trip miles: 5

Day 2
Route: Little Yosemite Valley to 1 mile past Merced Lake Junction
Sleep at: campsite

Miles today: 1.5 to Half Dome Junction + 4-mile Half Dome trip + 2.4 to Merced Lake + 1 to camp = 8.9
Total trip miles: 13.9

Day 3
Route: 1 mile past Merced Lake Junction to Lower Cathedral Lake Junction
Sleep at: campsite
Miles today: 9.4
Total trip miles: 23.3

Day 4
Route: Lower Cathedral Lakes Junction to Tuolumne Meadows
Sleep at: Tuolumne Meadows backpackers' campground
- $5 per person or $20 per site (unclear)
- No showers; bear lockers available
- PICK UP RESUPPLY at post office (open 9AM–5PM)
- Phone: 209-372-4475
Miles today: 6.2
Total trip miles: 29.5
Meal exception: dinner at Tuolumne

Section 2 – Tuolumne Meadows to Red's Meadow

Day 5
Route: Tuolumne Meadows to Upper Lyell Canyon
Sleep at: Upper Lyell Canyon
Miles today: 10.3
Total trip miles: 39.8

Day 6
Route: Upper Lyell Canyon campsite to Thousand Island Lake
Sleep at: campsite
Miles today: 9.7
Total trip miles: 49.5

Day 7
Route: Thousand Island Lake to Red's Meadow
Detour: Devils Postpile
Sleep at: Red's Meadow Campground (fee)

- Free bathhouse!
- $35 to pick up package (pre-mailed with permission form)
- Open 7AM–7PM (packages and beer/ice cream)
- Hotel rooms for $85 per night (2 beds)
- Buy FUEL!

Miles today: 13.3
Total trip miles: 62.8
Meal exception: dinner at café

Section 3 – Red's Meadow to VVR

Day 8
Route: Red's Meadow to Deer Creek
Sleep at: Deer Creek
Miles today: 6.5
Total trip miles: 69.3
Meal exception: breakfast at café

Day 9
Route: Deer Creek to Tully Hole
Sleep at: Tully Hole (possibly buggy)
Miles today: 11.1
Total trip miles: 80.4

Day 10
Route: Tully Hole to Vermilion Valley Resort (VVR)
Sleep at: VVR (one night free—showers too!)

- Water Taxi leaves 3–5PM ($19 per person round trip)
- Pick up resupply

- Get fuel if needed
- Telephone and internet
- Showers $6 per person, laundry $6 per load

Miles today: 11.8
Total trip miles: 92.2
Meal exception: dinner at VVR

Day 11
ZERO DAY at VVR!!

Section 4 – VVR to Bishop

Day 12
Route: VVR to Senger Creek
Sleep at: campsite
Miles today: 12
Total trip miles: 104.2 (past the 100-mile mark, woo-hoo!)

Day 13
Route: Senger Creek to McClure Meadow
Sleep at: campsite
Miles today: 13.7
Total trip miles: 117.9

Day 14
Route: McClure Meadow to Small Lake
Sleep at: campsite
Miles today: 12.2
Total trip miles: 130.1

Day 15
Route: Small Lake to Bishop Pass Trail and 6 miles of South Lake Trail via Bishop Pass
Sleep at: campsite
Miles today: 6.4 + 6 = 12.4

Total trip miles: 142.5

<u>Day 16</u>
Route: South Lake Trail to Bishop
Sleep at: Hotel in Bishop
Miles today: 5.6
Total trip miles: 148.1
Meal exception: dinner in town

Section 5 – Bishop to Whitney Portal

<u>Day 17</u>
Route: Bishop to JMT/Bishop Split
Sleep at: campsite
Miles today: 11.6
Total trip miles: 159.7
Special note: Pick up package in AM (the previous day is a Sunday)

<u>Day 18</u>
Route: JMT/ Bishop Split to Upper Palisade Lake (hard day)
Sleep at: campsite
Miles today: 12.1
Total trip miles: 171.8

<u>Day 19</u>
Route: Upper Palisade Lake to Sawmill Pass Trail
Sleep at: campsite
Miles today: 16.8
Total trip miles: 188.6

<u>Day 20</u>
Route: Sawmill Pass Trail to Middle Rae Lake
Sleep at: campsite
Miles today: 9.5

Total trip miles: 198.1

Day 21
Route: Middle Rae Lake to Tyndall Creek
Sleep at: campsite
Miles today: 15.2
Total trip miles: 213.3

Day 22
Route: Tyndall Creek to Guitar Lake
Sleep at: campsite
Miles today: 14.9
Total trip miles: 228.2

Day 23
Route: Guitar Lake to Whitney Portal (start just after midnight for sunrise summit of Mount Whitney!)
Sleep: Sierra Nevada Resort in Mammoth Lakes
Miles today: 16 (10.6 back down to Whitney Portal)
Total trip miles: 244.2
Meal exception: pack extra breakfast (due to starting early); dinner in town
Special notes:
- Descend 6,300 feet in last 10 miles
- Hitchhike back to Mammoth Lakes

APPENDIX 4

RESUPPLY SHIPMENT LOCATIONS

The following are resupply locations we used on our hike. Some locations require the use of five-gallon buckets so that animals cannot get into packages in the storage areas. Since every location will accept buckets, we opted to use them for all resupplies so that we didn't have to keep the requirements straight. Sarah and I were easily able to share a bucket for each resupply location. For spots where we knew we would take a shower, we also included a small Ziploc of travel-sized toiletries to enjoy.

1. Tuolumne Meadows
    "Your Name"
    General Delivery
    c/o Postmaster
    14000 Hwy 120 E
    Tuolumne Meadows
    Yosemite National Park, CA 95389
    (open 9AM–5PM; no pickup fee)

2. Red's Meadow
    Red's Meadow Resort
    "Your Name"
    P.O. Box 395
    Mammoth Lakes, CA 93546

(open 7AM–7PM; $35 pre-paid fee; signed permission form required prior to shipping)

3. Vermilion Valley Resort
    c/o Rancheria Garage
    "Your Name"
    62311 Huntington Lake Road
    Lakeshore, CA 93634
    (limit 25 lbs.; $20 pickup fee)

4. Cedar Grove Pack Station Dunnage Drop
    Cedar Grove
    "Your Name"
    Kings Canyon National Park, CA 93633
    (Author's note: Although this address looks incomplete, it is correct.)

APPENDIX 5

EXPENSES

One of the most common questions I received about my Appalachian Trail hike was, "How much did it cost?" I wasn't able to answer with any real accuracy because I spent the money over a number of years and didn't keep any records. I decided that for my John Muir Trail hike I would keep a detailed account so that I could provide as precise an answer as possible.

To be very clear, this is money that I chose to spend. I could have seriously reduced my expenses if I had wanted or needed to. However, my gear was largely outdated and much of my clothing also needed updating. I viewed this trip as a vacation, so I didn't limit my spending during the trip either—I enjoyed a hotel in town and good food when possible. Certainly the same trip could be completed on a much smaller budget. To the best of my recollection, this is the money I spent both on the hike and in preparations for it. For simplicity, I've rounded all amounts to the nearest dollar.

My expenses are broken down into categories. This expense sheet does not account for everyday items that I would have purchased anyway, such as Ibuprofen, Benadryl, toilet paper, ChapStick, etc. This also does not account for items I already owned that I used on the trip. A complete list of all of the items I carried is provided in Appendix 6.

Brownie's new gear
Sawyer Mini water filter (AO [Appalachian Outfitters]): $22
GravityWorks hose kit (AO): $20
Osprey Xena backpack (AO): $267

BearVault BV500 (REI): $80
Mountain Hardwear Phantasia 15 sleeping bag (AO): $450
Sea to Summit Alpha Light spoon (AO): $8
Princeton Tec Fuel headlamp (AO): $32
Sea to Summit Ultra-Sil dry sack 13L (AO): $18
Sea to Summit Ultra-Sil dry sack 8L (REI): $19
Sea to Summit Ultra-Sil dry sack 2L (REI): $13
Therm-a-Rest NeoAir pack pillow (AO): $27
Nite Ize Inka mobile pen (REI): $12
Zip-O-Gauge thermometer (REI): $7
Powerocks portable USB charger (Verizon): $40
Moleskine extra small ruled notebook (B&N [Barnes & Noble]): $3
ecosystem 100% recycled blank notebook (B&N): $11
Sea to Summit Ultra-Sil pack cover (REI): $42
Gear Aid seam sealer (Cabela's): $7
Gear Aid Tenacious Tape (Cabela's): $5
Coleman Headnet (Walmart): $3
Smith Optics Pivlock V90/S Sunglasses (SierraTradingPost.com): $90
Nesco American Harvest dehydrator (Bed Bath & Beyond): $55
DeLorme inReach Two-Way Satellite Communicator (Cabela's): $229
Subtotal: $1,460

Brownie's new clothing
Cabela's Women's Triune Skort (Cabela's): $50
La Sportiva Gore-Tex Boots (AO): $134
Dirty Girl gaiters (Dirtygirlgaiters.com): $20
Shayna Crocs (Academy Sports): $32
Patagonia Women's Re-Tool beanie (Moosejaw.com): $21
Outdoor Research Radar Pocket cap (Moosejaw.com): $13
Mountain Hardwear Ghost Whisperer down jacket (REI.com): $136
2 pairs FITS wool socks (AO): $30
SmartWool socks (REI): $18
ExOfficio Kizmet camper shirt (REI): $79
Subtotal: $533

Resource expenses
John Muir Trail Map-Pack from Tom Harrison Maps (Amazon.com): $21

John Muir Trail Atlas Pocket Size by Erik the Black (Amazon.com): $30
Subtotal: $51

Travel/lodging expenses
JMT hiking permits: $8 (per person)
Half Dome permit: $8
Sierra Nevada Resort & Spa in Mammoth Lakes, California (2 nights):
approx. $200 (gift from parents)
Yosemite backpackers' campsite: $5
Hotel in Lone Pine (1 night): $132
Round-trip airfare (per person): $550
Subtotal: $903

Mail drop expenses
5 five-gallon buckets (Lowe's): $13
5 five-gallon bucket lids (Lowe's): $6
Shipping UPS to VVR (19 lb 1 oz): $53
VVR mail drop pickup: $20
Shipping USPS to Tuolumne Meadows (12 lb 8 oz): $30
Shipping USPS to Red's Meadow (13 lb 8 oz): $32
Shipping USPS to Cedar Grove Pack Station (20 lb): $39
Red's Meadow pre-holding fee: $35
Cedar Grove Pack Station dunnage drop: $300
Subtotal: $528

GRAND TOTAL: $3,475

THE THINGS BROWNIE CARRIED

The following is an exact list of the gear I took with me on the John Muir Trail. The gear that Sarah and I shared is shown in *italics*. Starred gear (*) is gear that I already owned and is not included in the expenses in Appendix 5. Each compartment in my pack is listed with the contents separated according to the way I packed them. Indented items were packed inside the item listed above them.

<u>Wearing</u>
Cabela's women's Triune skort
FITS medium hiker crew socks
ExOfficio Kizmet camper shirt
*Patagonia sports bra
*Bandana (as headband)
La Sportiva Gore-Tex boots
Dirty Girl gaiters
Smith Optics Pivlock V90/S sunglasses
*Earrings, watch, necklace, ring

<u>Carrying</u>
Osprey Xena backpack
*Leki Makalu trekking poles
        *Duct tape (wrapped around hiking pole)

Attached to pack exterior
*Crocs (by carabiner)
*Unscented hand sanitizer
*Half bandana (for toilet paper purposes)
Nite Ize Inka mobile pen
*REI thermometer keychain
DeLorme inReach 1.5

Left hip compartment
*ChapStick Ultra SPF 30
*Ibuprofen in travel tube
*Pocket knife
*Mini sunscreen tube SPF 30 (1.5 oz)

Right hip compartment
*Sony Cyber-shot camera (in Ziploc)
Moleskine journal (in Ziploc)
*Pen

Right vertical front zippered compartment
*Clear waterproof emergency gear pouch
        *Ziploc of drier lint
        *4 emergency fire starter ropes
        *3 AAA batteries (for headlamp)
        *2 AA lithium batteries (for DeLorme)
        Tenacious Tape
Blue Sea to Summit Ultra-Sil dry sack (2L)
        *USB wall plug
        Powerocks USB charger & cord
        *Sony camera battery charger
        *iPhone 5 and USB charging cord
        *Driver's license/cash/credit card (in Ziploc)
Coleman Headnet
*REI gloves
Patagonia women's Re-Tool beanie

Left vertical front zipper compartment
*North Face Venture Jacket
*REI rain pants
Sea to Summit Ultra-Sil pack cover
*Yellow drawstring nylon bag for cosmetics
     *2 hair elastics
     *Toothbrush (travel size collapsible)
     *Toothpaste (travel size)
     *Body Glide mini tube
     *Unscented wet wipes, cut in half (in small Ziploc)
     *Nail clippers
     *Tweezers
     *4 Benadryl
     *4 Zantac
     *20 Ibuprofen PM
     *20 Cipro
     *10 Diamox
     *1 NuvaRing (birth control)

Mesh front pocket
*Orange Sea to Summit stuff sack
     *Snow Peak GigaPower auto stove
     *GSI Outdoors Halulite Minimalist cookset
     *Half of MSR PackTowl
     Snow Peak isobutane/propane mix (8 oz)
     *Bic lighter
     Sea to Summit Alpha Light spoon
Outdoor Research Radar Pocket cap

Top hat top zipper compartment
Princeton Tec Fuel headlamp
*Garden gloves (for Half Dome cables)

Top hat bottom zipper compartment
Large Ziploc
     *Journal
     *Inspiration letters

Large Ziploc
>   *John Muir Trail Atlas*
>   **Tom Harrison Maps trail map for current and next section*
>   Itinerary

Water bladder slot
*Brownie Bag
*CamelBak hydration reservoir (2L, Dad's)

Left mesh pocket
*Stanley water bottle (24 oz)
*Maroon drawstring bag
>   *Toilet paper (in small Ziploc)
>   *Unscented wet wipes (in small Ziploc)
>   **GSI Outdoors cathole trowel shovel*
>   Empty Ziploc for trash

Right mesh pocket
*Granite Gear green stuff sack
>   *Sawyer Mini water filtration system (with repair kit)*
>   *Platypus GravityWorks water filter system (4L)*

Main compartment
BearVault BV500
>   Food for given segment
>   Gallon-sized Ziploc for trash
*Off-white/yellow Sea to Summit eVac Dry Sack (13L)
>   Mountain Hardwear Phantasia 15 sleeping bag
>   *Therm-A-Rest stuff sack (black)
>   *NeoAir full-length sleeping pad (Dad's)
>   NeoAir pack pillow
Orange Sea to Summit Ultra-Sil dry sack (8L)
>   **The North Face Roadrunner 23 tent/fly*
Pink Sea to Summit Ultra-Sil dry sack (13L)
>   *1 lightweight EMS long underwear top
>   *1 Nike short-sleeved wicking shirt
>   *1 pair SmartWool mid-weight crew socks

*1 pair Cuddl Duds pants
1 pair FITS mid-weight crew socks
*2 pairs Barely There underwear
*1 sports bra
Mountain Hardwear Ghost Whisperer down jacket

Shared gear in Sarah's pack
The North Face Roadrunner 23 tent poles/ stakes/ footprint
Burt's Bees bug spray

ACKNOWLEDGEMENTS

From training to planning to writing, I have been so lucky to have an extensive network of support. I find myself surrounded by a fabulous, encouraging, helpful group of people and because of that not only is my world brighter, but my book is better.

Jonathan, Diana, and Scott at Appalachian Outfitters in Greenville, South Carolina, thank you for helping me become acquainted with current gear choices and holding my hand through much of my preparation.

Janice Kelsay, your help during the training stage was invaluable. Thank you for teaching me about dehydrating so I could make delicious (and nutritious) meals. Your limitless knowledge of local trails also provided most of the route ideas for my practice hikes. Thank you for tolerating endless shifts where I talked nonstop about the John Muir Trail and my preparations. I hope that I can be half the hiker you are when I'm your age. You're a constant inspiration.

Nicole Bernard, you motivate me in so many ways. Going through the writing and editing processes with our books at the same time was a wonderful experience. It was helpful to have someone with whom to share the small triumphs and the frustrating setbacks. Our many middle-of-the-night phone calls helped me maintain my sanity during this process. I can't wait for our next shared writing venture.

Mom (Donna Pugh), thank you for letting me steal Dad during so many training hikes and for listening to us both talk incessantly about our training and planning. Also, thank you for helping me obtain a JMT permit by sending that late-night fax. And lastly, thank you for the perfect inspirational letter. You put the reasons I love to hike into words better than I ever could have. Your unswerving support for my aspirations is undoubtedly a large part of the reason I have the confidence to attempt trips like these.

Sarah Jones Decker, thank you for stepping in at the last minute as my hiking partner. This trail was far from home and having you there with me as an experienced and confident hiker was a gift. Those memories will last a lifetime. And thank you to Morgan Decker who let me borrow Sarah—his wife, business partner, and best friend—for a harvest month.

Greg Ballard, you've been subject to my excitement, my worries, and my stumbling blocks throughout this writing process. Thank you for your patience and unending support for this book and all my other pursuits. I'm excited to share my next big hike with you.

I am lucky to have an amazing and talented group of editors and proofreaders. Allison Byers, Dot Fisher-Smith, Barbara Kenny, and Lark Wells did incredibly thorough jobs as proofreaders, and Anna Ottosen worked magic with her editing.

Al, although you're my "little sister," you'll also always be someone I look up to. I'm so glad we're sisters and even more glad we're friends. Thank you for supporting my goals and interests—even the ones that are so different from yours.

Dot, meeting you was without a doubt one of the highlights of my John Muir Trail hike. I aspire to project the enthusiasm for life that you radiate. Attending your retreat in Oregon was a life-changing experience. Thank you for becoming a joyous presence in my life.

Barbara Kenny, a.k.a. Old Paint, our long-distance friendship is one of the biggest gifts that came out of my first book. Thank you for always encouraging me to have confidence and strength in myself. You push me to own my experiences and emotions without fear or regret. I aspire to become as strong as you.

Lark Wells, thank you for being a constant sounding board in my life. As we've grown from know-it-all college freshmen to so-much-to-learn thirty-somethings, you've been my unwavering sidekick. Our frequent commute chats help me continue to figure out life. I appreciate your support on my books and look forward to reading one of yours someday.

Anna Ottosen: You have an impressive ability to take my rough work and turn it into something presentable. I'm grateful to have had you on my team for both of my books. You edit with an amazing eye for detail and manage to perfectly place humorous feedback amongst the detailed corrections and suggestions. I hope I'll get the honor of working with you on future books.

Thanks to the Girl Scouts for ingraining in me a passion for hiking. If I hadn't joined the Girl Scouts, I might never have developed a love for adventure, sleeping on the ground, building fires, and going without showers. I'm proud to be a lifetime member and hope to pass on the organization's values on to future generations.

One of the unexpected benefits of publishing my first book was the connections it helped me develop with other people. I've greatly enjoyed the speeches, presentations, festivals, and book booths that have followed. I've been lucky to have wonderful conversations, develop lasting friendships, and create strong business relationships. Thank you to all of the readers of my first book who have encouraged me to keep writing. Your reviews and enthusiasm kept me going during days of writers block.

And finally, thanks to Dad (Burv Pugh). Dad, I loved every minute of the nine months we trained together—even the horrible river crossings. It broke my heart when our plans changed, but I'm grateful for each memory and laugh we shared on the trail. I'm confident that the determination and work ethic I learned from you are two of the reasons I succeeded on this hike, and I'm so glad we'll get to share more experiences—on and off the trail—in the future.

Made in the USA
Columbia, SC
27 February 2018